Kubernetes for Developers

Use Kubernetes to develop, test, and deploy your applications
with the help of containers

Joseph Heck

BIRMINGHAM - MUMBAI

Kubernetes for Developers

Commissioning Editor: Gebin George
Acquisition Editor: Rahul Nair
Content Development Editor: Sharon Raj
Technical Editor: Prashant Chaudhari
Copy Editor: Safis Editing
Project Coordinator: Virginia Dias
Proofreader: Safis Editing
Indexer: Priyanka Dhadke
Graphics: Tom Scaria
Production Coordinator: Deepika Naik

First edition: April 2018

Production reference: 1050418

Published by Packt Publishing Ltd.
Livery Place
35 Livery Street
Birmingham
B3 2PB, UK.

ISBN 978-1-78883-475-9

www.packtpub.com

`mapt.io`

Mapt is an online digital library that gives you full access to over 5,000 books and videos, as well as industry leading tools to help you plan your personal development and advance your career. For more information, please visit our website.

Why subscribe?

- Spend less time learning and more time coding with practical eBooks and Videos from over 4,000 industry professionals

- Improve your learning with Skill Plans built especially for you

- Get a free eBook or video every month

- Mapt is fully searchable

- Copy and paste, print, and bookmark content

PacktPub.com

Did you know that Packt offers eBook versions of every book published, with PDF and ePub files available? You can upgrade to the eBook version at `www.PacktPub.com` and as a print book customer, you are entitled to a discount on the eBook copy. Get in touch with us at `service@packtpub.com` for more details.

At `www.PacktPub.com`, you can also read a collection of free technical articles, sign up for a range of free newsletters, and receive exclusive discounts and offers on Packt books and eBooks.

Contributors

About the author

Joseph Heck has broad development and management experience across start-ups and large companies. He has architected, developed, and deployed a wide variety of solutions, ranging from mobile and desktop applications to cloud-based distributed systems.

He builds and directs teams and mentors individuals to improve the way they build, validate, deploy, and run software. He also works extensively with and in open source, collaborating across many projects, including Kubernetes.

About the reviewers

Paul Adamson has worked as an Ops engineer, a developer, a DevOps engineer, and all variations and mixes of these. When not reviewing this book, he keeps busy helping companies embrace the AWS infrastructure. His language of choice is PHP for all the good reasons and even some of the bad ones, but mainly habit. Apart from reviewing this book, he has been working for Healthy Performance Ltd., helping to apply cutting-edge technology to a cutting-edge approach to wellbeing.

Jakub Pavlik is a co-founder, former CTO, and chief architect of tcp cloud who has worked several years on the IaaS cloud platform based on OpenStack-Salt and OpenContrail projects, which were deployed and operated for global large service providers. Currently as the director of product engineering, he collaborates on a new Mirantis Cloud Platform for NFV/SDN, IoT, and big data use cases based on Kubernetes, containerized OpenStack, and OpenContrail. He is a member of the OpenContrail Advisory Board and is also an enthusiast of Linux OS, ice hockey, and films. He loves his wife, Hanulka.

Packt is searching for authors like you

If you're interested in becoming an author for Packt, please visit `authors.packtpub.com` and apply today. We have worked with thousands of developers and tech professionals, just like you, to help them share their insight with the global tech community. You can make a general application, apply for a specific hot topic that we are recruiting an author for, or submit your own idea.

Table of Contents

Preface

It's getting more common to find yourself responsible for running the code you've written as well as developing the features. While many companies still have an operations group (generally retitled to SRE or DevOps) that help with expert knowledge, developers (like you) are often being asked to expand your knowledge and responsibility scope.

There's been a shift to treating infrastructure-like code for some time. Several years ago, I might have described the boundary as Puppet is used by operations folks and Chef is used by developers. All of that changed with the advent and growth first of clouds in general, and more recently with the growth of Docker. Containers provide a level of control and isolation, as well as development flexibility, that is very appealing. When using containers, you quickly move to where you want to use more than one container a time, for isolation of responsibility as well as horizontal scaling.

Kubernetes is a project open sourced from Google, now hosted by the cloud-native computing foundation. It exposes many of the lessons from Google's experience of running software in containers and makes it available to you. It encompasses not only running containers, but grouping them together into services, scaling them horizontally, as well as providing means to control how these containers interact together and how they get exposed to the outside world.

Kubernetes provides a declarative structure backed with an API and command-line tools. Kubernetes can be used on your laptop, or leveraged from one of the many cloud providers. The benefit of using Kubernetes is being able to use the same set of tools with the same expectations, regardless of running it locally, in a small lab at your company, or in any number of larger cloud providers. It's not exactly the write once, run anywhere promise of Java from days gone by; more we'll give you a consistent set of tools, regardless of running on your laptop, your company's datacenter, or a cloud provider such as AWS, Azure, or Google.

This book is your guide to leveraging Kubernetes and its capabilities for developing, validating, and running your code.

This book focuses on examples and samples that take you through how to use Kubernetes and integrate it into your development workflow. Through the examples, we focus on common tasks that you may want to use to take advantage of running your code with Kubernetes.

Who this book is for

If you are a full-stack or backend software developer who's interested in, curious about, or being asked to be responsible for testing and running the code you're developing, you can leverage Kubernetes to make that process simpler and consistent. If you're looking for developer-focused examples in Node.js and Python for how to build, test, deploy, and run your code with Kubernetes, this book is perfect for you.

What this book covers

Chapter 1, *Setting Up Kubernetes for Development*, covers the installation of kubectl, minikube, and Docker, and running kubectl with minikube to validate your installation. This chapter also provides an introduction to the concepts in Kubernetes of Nodes, Pods, Containers, ReplicaSets, and Deployments.

Chapter 2, *Packaging Your Code to Run in Kubernetes*, explains how to package your code within containers in order to use Kubernetes with examples in Python and Node.js.

Chapter 3, *Interacting with Your Code in Kubernetes*, covers how to run containers in Kubernetes, how to access these containers, and introduces the Kubernetes concepts of Services, Labels, and Selectors.

Chapter 4, *Declarative Infrastructure*, covers expressing your application in a declarative structure, and how to extend that to utilize the Kubernetes concepts of ConfigMaps, Annotations, and Secrets.

Chapter 5, *Pod and Container Lifecycles*, looks at the life cycle of containers and Pods within Kubernetes, and how to expose hooks from your application to influence how Kubernetes runs your code, and how to terminate your code gracefully.

Chapter 6, *Background Processing in Kubernetes*, explains the batch processing concepts in Kubernetes of Job and CronJob, and introduces how Kubernetes handles persistence with Persistent Volumes, Persistent Volume Claims, and Stateful Sets.

Chapter 7, *Monitoring and Metrics*, covers monitoring in Kubernetes, and how to utilize Prometheus and Grafana to capture and display metrics and simple dashboards about Kubernetes in general, as well as your applications.

Chapter 8, *Logging and Tracing*, explains how to collect logs with Kubernetes using ElasticSearch, FluentD, and Kibana, and how you can set up and use distributed tracing with Jaeger.

Chapter 9, *Integration Testing*, covers testing strategies that take advantage of Kubernetes, and how to leverage Kubernetes in integration and end-to-end tests.

Chapter 10, *Troubleshooting Common Problems and Next Steps*, reviews a number of common pain points you may encounter when getting started with Kubernetes and explains how to resolve them, and provides an overview of a number of projects within the Kubernetes ecosystem that may be of interest to developers and the development process.

To get the most out of this book

You need to have the following software and hardware requirements:

- Kubernetes 1.8
- Docker Community Edition
- kubectl 1.8 (part of Kubernetes)
- VirtualBox v5.2.6 or higher
- minikube v0.24.1
- MacBook or Linux machine with 4 GB of RAM or more

Download the example code files

You can download the example code files for this book from your account at www.packtpub.com. If you purchased this book elsewhere, you can visit www.packtpub.com/support and register to have the files emailed directly to you.

You can download the code files by following these steps:

1. Log in or register at www.packtpub.com.
2. Select the **SUPPORT** tab.
3. Click on **Code Downloads & Errata**.
4. Enter the name of the book in the **Search** box and follow the onscreen instructions.

Once the file is downloaded, please make sure that you unzip or extract the folder using the latest version of:

- WinRAR/7-Zip for Windows
- Zipeg/iZip/UnRarX for Mac
- 7-Zip/PeaZip for Linux

The code bundle for the book is also hosted on GitHub at following URLs:

- https://github.com/kubernetes-for-developers/kfd-nodejs
- https://github.com/kubernetes-for-developers/kfd-flask
- https://github.com/kubernetes-for-developers/kfd-celery

In case there's an update to the code, it will be updated on the existing GitHub repository.

We also have other code bundles from our rich catalog of books and videos available at https://github.com/PacktPublishing/. Check them out!

Conventions used

There are a number of text conventions used throughout this book.

CodeInText: Indicates code words in text, database table names, folder names, filenames, file extensions, pathnames, dummy URLs, user input, and Twitter handles. Here is an example: "Mount the downloaded WebStorm-10*.dmg disk image file as another disk in your system."

A block of code is set as follows:

```
import signal
import sys
def sigterm_handler(_signo, _stack_frame):
sys.exit(0)
signal.signal(signal.SIGTERM, sigterm_handler)
```

When we wish to draw your attention to a particular part of a code block, the relevant lines or items are set in bold:

```
import signal
import sys
def sigterm_handler(_signo, _stack_frame):
sys.exit(0)
signal.signal(signal.SIGTERM, sigterm_handler)
```

Any command-line input or output is written as follows:

```
kubectl apply -f simplejob.yaml
```

Bold: Indicates a new term, an important word, or words that you see onscreen. For example, words in menus or dialog boxes appear in the text like this. Here is an example: "Select **System info** from the **Administration** panel."

Warnings or important notes appear like this.

 Tips and tricks appear like this.

Get in touch

Feedback from our readers is always welcome.

General feedback: Email feedback@packtpub.com and mention the book title in the subject of your message. If you have questions about any aspect of this book, please email us at questions@packtpub.com.

Errata: Although we have taken every care to ensure the accuracy of our content, mistakes do happen. If you have found a mistake in this book, we would be grateful if you would report this to us. Please visit www.packtpub.com/submit-errata, selecting your book, clicking on the Errata Submission Form link, and entering the details.

Piracy: If you come across any illegal copies of our works in any form on the Internet, we would be grateful if you would provide us with the location address or website name. Please contact us at copyright@packtpub.com with a link to the material.

If you are interested in becoming an author: If there is a topic that you have expertise in and you are interested in either writing or contributing to a book, please visit authors.packtpub.com.

Reviews

Please leave a review. Once you have read and used this book, why not leave a review on the site that you purchased it from? Potential readers can then see and use your unbiased opinion to make purchase decisions, we at Packt can understand what you think about our products, and our authors can see your feedback on their book. Thank you!

For more information about Packt, please visit packtpub.com.

Setting Up Kubernetes for Development

1

Welcome to *Kubernetes for Developers*! This chapter starts off by helping you get the tools installed that will allow you to take advantage of Kubernetes in your development. Once installed, we will interact with those tools a bit to verify that they are functional. Then, we will review some of the basic concepts that you will want to understand to effectively use Kubernetes as a developer. We will cover the following key resources in Kubernetes:

- Container
- Pod
- Node
- Deployment
- ReplicaSet

What you need for development

In addition to your usual editing and programming tools, you will want to install the software to leverage Kubernetes. The focus of this book is to let you do everything on your local development machine, while also allowing you to expand and leverage a remote Kubernetes cluster in the future if you need more resources. One of Kubernetes' benefits is how it treats one or one hundred computers in the same fashion, allowing you to take advantage of the resources you need for your software, and do it consistently, regardless of where they're located.

The examples in this book will use command-line tools in a Terminal on your local machine. The primary one will be `kubectl`, which communicates with a Kubernetes cluster. We will use a tiny Kubernetes cluster of a single machine running on your own development system with Minikube. I recommend installing the community edition of Docker, which makes it easy to build containers for use within Kubernetes:

- `kubectl`: `kubectl` (how to pronounce that is an amusing diversion within the Kubernetes community) is the primary command-line tool that is used to work with a Kubernetes cluster. To install `kubectl`, go to the page `https://kubernetes.io/docs/tasks/tools/install-kubectl/` and follow the instructions relevant to your platform.

- `minikube`: To install Minikube, go to the page `https://github.com/kubernetes/minikube/releases` and follow the instructions for your platform.

- `docker`: To install the community edition of Docker, go to the webpage `https://www.docker.com/community-edition` and follow their instructions for your platform.

Optional tools

In addition to `kubectl`, `minikube`, and `docker`, you may want to take advantage of additional helpful libraries and command-line tools.

`jq` is a command-line JSON processor that makes it easy to parse results in more complex data structures. I would describe it as *grep's cousin that's better at dealing with JSON results*. You can install `jq` by following the instructions at `https://stedolan.github.io/jq/download/`. More details on what `jq` does and how to use it can also be found at `https://stedolan.github.io/jq/manual/`.

Getting a local cluster up and running

Once Minikube and Kubectl are installed, get a cluster up and running. It is worthwhile to know the versions of the tools you're using, as Kubernetes is a fairly fast-moving project, and if you need to get assistance from the community, knowing which versions of these common tools will be important.

The versions of Minikube and `kubectl` I used while writing this are:

- Minikube: version 0.22.3

- `kubectl`: version 1.8.0

You can check the version of your copy with the following commands:

```
minikube version
```

This will output a version:

```
minikube version: v0.22.3
```

If you haven't already done so while following the installation instructions, start a Kubernetes with Minikube. The simplest way is using the following command:

```
minikube start
```

This will download a virtual machine image and start it, and Kubernetes on it, as a single-machine cluster. The output will look something like the following:

```
Downloading Minikube ISO
 106.36 MB / 106.36 MB [====================================================]
100.00% 0s
Getting VM IP address...
Moving files into cluster...
Setting up certs...
Connecting to cluster...
Setting up kubeconfig...
Starting cluster components...
Kubectl is now configured to use the cluster.
```

Minikube will automatically create the files needed for `kubectl` to access the cluster and control it. Once this is complete, you can get information about the cluster to verify it is up and running.

First, you can ask `minikube` about its status directly:

```
minikube status
minikube: Running
cluster: Running
kubectl: Correctly Configured: pointing to minikube-vm at 192.168.64.2
```

And if we ask `kubectl` about its version, it will report both the version of the client and the version of the cluster that it is communicating with:

```
kubectl version
```

The first output is the version of the `kubectl` client:

```
Client Version: version.Info{Major:"1", Minor:"7", GitVersion:"v1.7.5",
GitCommit:"17d7182a7ccbb167074be7a87f0a68bd00d58d97", GitTreeState:"clean",
BuildDate:"2017-08-31T19:32:26Z", GoVersion:"go1.9", Compiler:"gc",
Platform:"darwin/amd64"}
```

Immediately after, it will communicate and report the version of Kubernetes on your cluster:

```
Server Version: version.Info{Major:"1", Minor:"7", GitVersion:"v1.7.5",
GitCommit:"17d7182a7ccbb167074be7a87f0a68bd00d58d97", GitTreeState:"clean",
BuildDate:"2017-09-11T21:52:19Z", GoVersion:"go1.8.3", Compiler:"gc",
Platform:"linux/amd64"}
```

And we can use `kubectl` to ask for information about the cluster as well:

```
kubectl cluster-info
```

And see something akin to the following:

```
Kubernetes master is running at https://192.168.64.2:8443

To further debug and diagnose cluster problems, use 'kubectl cluster-info
dump'.
```

This command primarily lets you know the API server that you're communicating with is up and running. We can ask for the specific status of the key internal components using an additional command:

```
kubectl get componentstatuses
```

NAME	STATUS	MESSAGE	ERROR
scheduler	Healthy	ok	
etcd-0	Healthy	{"health": "true"}	
controller-manager	Healthy	ok	

Kubernetes also reports and stores a number of events that you can request to see. These show what is happening within the cluster:

```
kubectl get events
```

LASTSEEN	FIRSTSEEN	COUNT	NAME	KIND	SUBOBJECT	TYPE

```
REASON                          SOURCE                    MESSAGE
2m          2m          1          minikube   Node                        Normal
Starting                        kubelet, minikube         Starting kubelet.
2m          2m          2          minikube   Node                        Normal
NodeHasSufficientDisk           kubelet, minikube         Node minikube status is
now: NodeHasSufficientDisk
2m          2m          2          minikube   Node                        Normal
NodeHasSufficientMemory         kubelet, minikube         Node minikube status is
now: NodeHasSufficientMemory
2m          2m          2          minikube   Node                        Normal
NodeHasNoDiskPressure           kubelet, minikube         Node minikube status is
now: NodeHasNoDiskPressure
2m          2m          1          minikube   Node                        Normal
NodeAllocatableEnforced         kubelet, minikube         Updated Node Allocatable
limit across pods
2m          2m          1          minikube   Node                        Normal
Starting                        kube-proxy, minikube      Starting kube-proxy.
2m          2m          1          minikube   Node                        Normal
RegisteredNode                  controllermanager         Node minikube event:
Registered Node minikube in NodeController
```

Resetting and restarting your cluster

If you want to wipe out your local Minikube cluster and restart, it is very easy to do so. Issuing a command to delete and then start Minikube will wipe out the environment and reset it to a blank slate:

```
minikube delete
Deleting local Kubernetes cluster...
Machine deleted.

minikube start
Starting local Kubernetes v1.7.5 cluster...
Starting VM...
Getting VM IP address...
Moving files into cluster...
Setting up certs...
Connecting to cluster...
Setting up kubeconfig...
Starting cluster components...
Kubectl is now configured to use the cluster.
```

Looking at what's built-in and included with Minikube

With Minikube, you can bring up a web-based dashboard for the Kubernetes cluster with a single command:

```
minikube dashboard
```

This will open a browser and show you a web interface to the Kubernetes cluster. If you look at the URL address in the browser window, you'll see that it's pointing to the same IP address that was returned from the `kubectl cluster-info` command earlier, running on port `30000`. The dashboard is running inside Kubernetes, and it is not the only thing that is.

Kubernetes is self-hosting, in that supporting pieces for Kubernetes to function such as the dashboard, DNS, and more, are all run within Kubernetes. You can see the state of all these components by asking about the state of all Pods in the cluster:

```
kubectl get pods --all-namespaces
```

NAMESPACE AGE	NAME	READY	STATUS	RESTARTS
kube-system 6m	kube-addon-manager-minikube	1/1	Running	0
kube-system 6m	kube-dns-910330662-6pctd	3/3	Running	0
kube-system 6m	kubernetes-dashboard-91nmv	1/1	Running	0

Notice that we used the `--all-namespaces` option in this command. By default, `kubectl` will only show you Kubernetes resources that are in the default namespace. Since we haven't run anything ourselves, if we invoked `kubectl get pods` we would just get an empty list. Pods aren't the only Kubernetes resources through; you can ask about quite a number of different resources, some of which I'll describe later in this chapter, and more in further chapters.

For the moment, invoke one more command to get the list of services:

```
kubectl get services --all-namespaces
```

This will output all the services:

NAMESPACE AGE	NAME	CLUSTER-IP	EXTERNAL-IP	PORT(S)
default	kubernetes	10.0.0.1	<none>	443/TCP

```
3m
kube-system    kube-dns                  10.0.0.10     <none>
53/UDP,53/TCP     2m
kube-system    kubernetes-dashboard      10.0.0.147    <nodes>
80:30000/TCP      2m
```

Note the service named `kubernetes-dashboard` has a `Cluster-IP` value, and the ports `80:30000`. That port configuration is indicating that within the Pods that are backing the `kubernetes-dashboard` service, it will forward any requests from port `30000` to port `80` within the container. You may have noticed that the IP address for the Cluster IP is very different from the IP address reported for the Kubernetes master that we saw previously in the `kubectl cluster-info` command.

It is important to know that everything within Kubernetes is run on a private, isolated network that is not normally accessible from outside the cluster. We will get into more detail on this in future chapters. For now, just be aware that `minikube` has some additional, special configuration within it to expose the dashboard.

Verifying Docker

Kubernetes supports multiple ways of running containers, Docker being the most common, and the most convenient. In this book, we will use Docker to help us create images that we will run within Kubernetes.

You can see what version of Docker you have installed and verify it is operational by running the following command:

```
docker  version
```

Like `kubectl`, it will report the `docker` client version as well as the server version, and your output may look something like the following:

```
Client:
Version: 17.09.0-ce
API version: 1.32
Go version: go1.8.3
Git commit: afdb6d4
Built: Tue Sep 26 22:40:09 2017
OS/Arch: darwin/amd64

Server:
Version: 17.09.0-ce
API version: 1.32 (minimum version 1.12)
```

```
Go version: go1.8.3
Git commit: afdb6d4
Built: Tue Sep 26 22:45:38 2017
OS/Arch: linux/amd64
Experimental: false
```

By using the `docker images` command, you can see what container images are available locally, and using the `docker pull` command, you can request specific images. In our examples in the next chapter, we will be building upon the alpine container image to host our software, so let's go ahead and pull that image to verify that your environment is working:

```
docker pull alpine

Using default tag: latest
latest: Pulling from library/alpine
Digest:
sha256:f006ecbb824d87947d0b51ab8488634bf69fe4094959d935c0c103f4820a417d
Status: Image is up to date for alpine:latest
```

You can then see the images using the following command:

```
docker images

REPOSITORY TAG IMAGE ID CREATED SIZE
alpine latest 76da55c8019d 3 weeks ago 3.97MB</strong>
```

 If you get an error when trying to pull the alpine image, it may mean that you are required to work through a proxy, or otherwise have constrained access to the internet to pull images as you need. You may need to review Docker's information on how to set up and use a proxy if you are in this situation.

Clearing and cleaning Docker images

Since we will be using Docker to build container images, it will be useful to know how to get rid of images. You have already seen the list of images with the `docker image` command. There are also intermediate images that are maintained by Docker that are hidden in that output. To see all the images that Docker is storing, use the following command:

```
docker images -a
```

If you have only pulled the alpine image as per the preceding text, you likely won't see any additional images, but as you build images in the next chapter, this list will grow.

You can remove images with the `docker rmi` command followed by the name of the image. By default, Docker will attempt to maintain images that containers have used recently or referenced. Because of this, you may need to force the removal to clean up the images.

If you want to reset and remove all the images and start afresh, there is a handy command that will do that. By tying together Docker images and `docker rmi`, we can ask it to force remove all the images it knows about:

```
docker rmi -f $(docker images -a -q)
```

Kubernetes concept – container

Kubernetes (and other technologies in this space) are all about managing and orchestrating containers. A container is really a name wrapped around a set of Linux technologies, the two most prominent being the container image format and the way Linux can isolate processes from one another, leveraging cgroups.

For all practical purposes, when someone is speaking of a container, they are generally implying that there is an image with everything needed to run a single process. In this context, a container is not only the image, but also the information about what to invoke and how to run it. Containers also act like they have their own network access. In reality, it's being shared by the Linux operating system that's running the containers.

When we want to write code to run under Kubernetes, we will always be talking about packaging it up and preparing it to run within a container. The more complex examples later in the book will utilize multiple containers all working together.

 It is quite possible to run more than a single process inside a container, but that's generally frowned upon as a container is ideally suited to represent a single process and how to invoke it, and shouldn't be considered the same thing as a full virtual machine.

If you usually develop in Python, then you are likely familiar with using something like `pip` to download libraries and modules that you need, and you invoke your program with a command akin to `python your_file`. If you're a Node developer, then it is more likely you're familiar with `npm` or `yarn` to install the dependencies you need, and you run your code with `node your_file`.

If you wanted to wrap that all up and run it on another machine, you would likely either redo all the instructions for downloading the libraries and running the code, or perhaps ZIP up the whole directory and move it where you want to run it. A container is a way to collect all the information together into a single image so that it can be easily moved around, installed, and run on a Linux operating system. Originally created by Docker, the specifications are now maintained by the **Open Container Initiative (OCI)** (`https://www.opencontainers.org`).

While a container is the smallest building block of what goes into Kubernetes, the smallest unit that Kubernetes works with is a Pod.

Kubernetes resource – Pod

A Pod is the smallest unit that Kubernetes manages and is the fundamental unit that the rest of the system is built on. The team that created Kubernetes found it worthwhile to let a developer specify what processes should always be run together on the same OS, and that the combination of processes running together should be the unit that's scheduled, run, and managed.

Earlier in this chapter, you saw that a basic instance of Kubernetes has some of its software running in Pods. Much of Kubernetes is run using these same concepts and abstractions, allowing Kubernetes to self-host its own software. Some of the software to run a Kubernetes cluster is managed outside the cluster itself, but more and more leverage the concept of Pods, including the DNS services, dashboard, and controller manager, which coordinate all the control operations through Kubernetes.

A Pod is made up of one or more containers and information associated with those containers. When you ask Kubernetes about a Pod, it will return a data structure that includes a list of one or more containers, along with a variety of metadata that Kubernetes uses to coordinate the Pod with other Pods, and policies of how Kubernetes should act and react if the program fails, is asked to be restarted, and so forth. The metadata can also define things such as *affinity*, which influences where a Pod can be scheduled in a cluster, expectations around how to get the container images, and more. It is important to know that a Pod is not intended to be treated as a durable, long-lived entity.

They are created and destroyed and essentially meant to be ephemeral. This allows separate logic—contained in controllers - to manage responsibilities such as scale and availability. It is this separation of duties that enables Kubernetes to provide a means for self-healing in the event of failures, and provide some auto-scaling capabilities.

A Pod being run by Kubernetes has a few specific guarantees:

- All the containers for a Pod will be run on the same Node
- Any container running within a Pod will share the Node's network with any other containers in the same Pod
- Containers within a Pod can share files through volumes, attached to the containers
- A Pod has an explicit life cycle, and will always remain on the Node in which it was started

For all practical purposes, when you want to know what's running on a Kubernetes cluster, you are generally going to want to know about the Pods running within Kubernetes and their state.

Kubernetes maintains and reports on the Pod's status, as well as the state of each of the containers that make up the Pod. The states for a container are `Running`, `Terminated`, and `Waiting`. The life cycle of a Pod is a bit more complicated, consisting of a strictly defined Phase and a set of PodStatus. Phase is one of `Pending`, `Running`, `Succeeded`, `Failed`, or `Unknown`, and the specific details of what's included in a Phase is documented at `https://kubernetes.io/docs/concepts/workloads/pods/pod-lifecycle/#pod-phase`.

A Pod can also contain Probes, which actively check the container for some status information. Two common probes that are deployed and used by Kubernetes controllers are a `livenessProbe` and a `readinessProbe`. The livenessProbe defines whether the container is up and running. If it isn't, the infrastructure in Kubernetes kills the relevant container and then applies the restart policy defined for the Pod. The `readinessProbe` is meant to indicate whether the container is ready to service requests. The results of the `readinessProbe` are used in conjunction with other Kubernetes mechanisms such as services (which we will detail later) to forward traffic to the relevant container. In general, the probes are set up to allow the software in a container to provide a feedback loop to Kubernetes. You can find more detail on Probes, how to define them, and how they are used at `https://kubernetes.io/docs/concepts/workloads/pods/pod-lifecycle/#container-probes`. We will dig into probes in detail in a future chapter.

Namespaces

Pods are collected into namespaces, which are used to group Pods together for a variety of purposes. You already saw one example of namespaces when we asked for the status of all the Pods in the cluster with the `--all-namespaces` option earlier.

Namespaces can be used to provide quotas and limits around resource usage, have an impact on DNS names that Kubernetes creates internal to the cluster, and in the future may impact access control policies. If no namespace is specified when interacting with Kubernetes through `kubectl`, the command assumes you are working with the default namespace, named `default`.

Writing your code for Pods and Containers

One of the keys to successfully using Kubernetes is to consider how you want your code to operate, and to structure it so that it fits cleanly into a structure of Pods and Containers. By structuring your software solutions to break problems down into components that operate with the constraints and guarantees that Kubernetes provides, you can easily take advantage of parallelism and container orchestration to use many machines as seamlessly as you would use a single machine.

The guarantees and abstractions that Kubernetes provides are reflective of years of experience that Google (and others) have had in running their software and services at a massive scale, reliably, and redundantly, leveraging the pattern of horizontal scaling to tackle massive problems.

Kubernetes resource – Node

A Node is a machine, typically running Linux, that has been added to the Kubernetes cluster. It can be a physical machine or a virtual machine. In the case of `minikube`, it is a single virtual machine that is running all the software for Kubernetes. In larger Kubernetes clusters, you may have one or several machines dedicated to just managing the cluster and separate machines where your workloads run. Kubernetes manages its resources across Nodes by tracking their resource usage, scheduling, starting (and if needed, restarting) Pods, as well as coordinating the other mechanisms that connect Pods together or expose them outside the cluster.

Nodes can (and do) have metadata associated with them so that Kubernetes can be aware of relevant differences, and can account for those differences when scheduling and running Pods. Kubernetes can support a wide variety of machines working together, and run software efficiently across all of them, or limit scheduling Pods to only machines that have the required resources (for example, a GPU).

Networks

We previously mentioned that all the containers in a Pod share the Node's network. In addition, all Nodes in a Kubernetes cluster are expected to be connected to each other and share a private cluster-wide network. When Kubernetes runs containers within a Pod, it does so within this isolated network. Kubernetes is responsible for handling IP addresses, creating DNS entries, and making sure that a Pod can communicate with another Pod in the same Kubernetes cluster.

Another resource, Services, which we will dig into later, is what Kubernetes uses to expose Pods to one another over this private network or handle connections in and out of the cluster. By default, a Pod running in this private, isolated network is not exposed outside of the Kubernetes cluster. Depending on how your Kubernetes cluster was created, there are multiple avenues for opening up access to your software from outside the cluster, which we'll detail later with Services that include LoadBalancer, NodePort, and Ingress.

Controllers

Kubernetes is built with the notion that you tell it what you want, and it knows how to do it. When you interact with Kubernetes, you are asserting you want one or more resources to be in a certain state, with specific versions, and so forth. Controllers are where the brains exist for tracking those resources and attempting to run your software as you described. These descriptions can include how many copies of a container image are running, updating the software version running within a Pod, and handling the case of a Node failure where you unexpectedly lose part of your cluster.

There are a variety of controllers used within Kubernetes, and they are mostly hidden behind two key resources that we will dig into further: Deployments and ReplicaSets.

Kubernetes resource – ReplicaSet

A ReplicaSet wraps Pods, defining how many need to run in parallel. A ReplicaSet is commonly wrapped in turn by a deployment. ReplicaSets are not often used directly, but are critical to represent horizontal scaling—to represent the number of parallel Pods to run.

A ReplicaSet is associated with a Pod and indicates how many instances of that Pod should be running within the cluster. A ReplicaSet also implies that Kubernetes has a controller that watches the ongoing state and knows how many of your Pod to keep running. This is where Kubernetes is really starting to do work for you, if you specified three Pods in a ReplicaSet and one fails, Kubernetes will automatically schedule and run another Pod for you.

Kubernetes resource – Deployment

The most common and recommended way to run code on Kubernetes is with a deployment, which is managed by a deployment controller. We will explore deployments in the next and further chapters, both specifying them directly and creating them implicitly with commands such as `kubectl run`.

A Pod by itself is interesting, but limited, specifically because it is intended to be ephemeral. If a Node were to die (or get powered down), all the Pods on that Node would stop running. ReplicaSets provide self-healing capabilities. The work within the cluster to recognize when a Pod is no longer available and will attempt to schedule another Pod, typically to bring a service back online, or otherwise continue doing work.

The deployment controller wraps around and extends the ReplicaSet controller, and is primarily responsible for rolling out software updates and managing the process of that rollout when you update your deployment resource with new versions of your software. The deployment controller includes metadata settings to know how many Pods to keep running so that you can enable a seamless rolling update of your software by adding new versions of a container, and stopping old versions when you request it.

Representing Kubernetes resources

Kubernetes resources can generally be represented as either a JSON or YAML data structure. Kubernetes is specifically built so that you can save these files, and when you want to run your software, you can use a command such as `kubectl deploy` and provide the definitions you've created previously, and it uses that to run your software. In our next chapter, we will start to show specific examples of these resources and build them up for our use.

As we get into the examples in the next, and future chapters, we will use YAML to describe our resources and request data through `kubectl` back in JSON format. All of these data structures are formally defined for each version of Kubernetes, along with the REST APIs that Kubernetes provides to manipulate them. The formal definitions of all Kubernetes resources are maintained with OpenAPI (also known as **Swagger**) in source code control, and can be viewed at `https://github.com/kubernetes/kubernetes/tree/master/api/swagger-spec`.

Summary

In this chapter, we installed `minikube` and `kubectl`, and used them to start a local Kubernetes cluster and briefly interact with it. We then walked through some of the key concepts that we will be using and exploring more in depth in future chapters, including container, Pod, node, deployment, and ReplicaSet.

In the next chapter, we will dive into what it takes to get your software into a container and tips for how to set that up within your own project. We will walk through an example in Python, and another in Node.js, which you can use as starting points for your own code.

Packaging Your Code to Run in Kubernetes

2

n this chapter, we will dig into the first thing you need to enable to use Kubernetes: getting your software into a container. We will review what containers are, how you store and share images, and how to build a container. The chapter then continues with two examples, one in Python, and another in Node.js, which step you through how to take simple example code from those languages to build containers, and run them within Kubernetes. The sections of this chapter are:

- Container images
- Making your own container
- Python example—making a container image
- Node.js example—making a container image
- Tagging your container images

Container images

The first step for using Kubernetes is getting your software into a container. Docker is the easiest way to create these containers, and it is a fairly simple process. Let's take a moment to look at an existing container image to understand what choices you will need to make when creating your own containers:

```
docker pull docker.io/jocatalin/kubernetes-bootcamp:v1
```

First, you'll see it pulling down a list of files with arcane IDs. You'll see them updating in parallel, as it tries to grab these as they're available:

```
v1: Pulling from jocatalin/kubernetes-bootcamp
5c90d4a2d1a8: Downloading  3.145MB/51.35MB
ab30c63719b1: Downloading  3.931MB/18.55MB
29d0bc1e8c52: Download complete
d4fe0dc68927: Downloading  2.896MB/13.67MB
dfa9e924f957: Waiting
```

And when the downloads are complete, the output will update to say `extracting`, and finally `pull complete`:

```
v1: Pulling from jocatalin/kubernetes-bootcamp
5c90d4a2d1a8: Pull complete
ab30c63719b1: Pull complete
29d0bc1e8c52: Pull complete
d4fe0dc68927: Pull complete
dfa9e924f957: Pull complete
Digest:
sha256:0d6b8ee63bb57c5f5b6156f446b3bc3b3c143d233037f3a2f00e279c8fcc64af
Status: Downloaded newer image for jocatalin/kubernetes-bootcamp:v1
```

What you saw in the Terminal was Docker downloading the layers that go into a container image, pulling them all together, and then verifying the output. Kubernetes does exactly this same process when you ask it to run the software, downloading the images and then running them.

If you now run the following:

```
docker images
```

You will see (perhaps among others) the image listed akin to this:

```
REPOSITORY                                TAG
IMAGE ID         CREATED         SIZE
jocatalin/kubernetes-bootcamp             v1
8fafd8af70e9     13 months ago   211MB
```

The image is `211MB` in size, and you'll notice that when we specified `jocatalin/kubernetes-bootcamp:v1`, we were specifying both a name, `jocatalin/kubernetes-bootcamp`, and a tag, `v1`. In addition, the image has an `IMAGE ID` (`8fafd8af70e9`), which is a unique ID for the whole image. If you were to specify a name for an image without a tag, the default is to assume you want a default tag of `latest`.

Let's take a deeper look at the image we just downloaded, using the `docker history` command:

```
docker history jocatalin/kubernetes-bootcamp:v1
```

```
IMAGE                   CREATED              CREATED BY
SIZE                    COMMENT
8fafd8af70e9            13 months ago        /bin/sh -c #(nop)   CMD ["/bin/sh"
"-c" "no...    0B
<missing>               13 months ago        /bin/sh -c #(nop) COPY
file:de8ef36ebbfd53...    742B
<missing>               13 months ago        /bin/sh -c #(nop)   EXPOSE 8080/tcp
0B
<missing>               13 months ago        /bin/sh -c #(nop)  CMD ["node"]
0B
<missing>               13 months ago        /bin/sh -c buildDeps='xz-utils'
&& set...    41.5MB
<missing>               13 months ago        /bin/sh -c #(nop)  ENV
NODE_VERSION=6.3.1         0B
<missing>               15 months ago        /bin/sh -c #(nop)  ENV
NPM_CONFIG_LOGLEVEL=...    0B
<missing>               15 months ago        /bin/sh -c set -ex    && for key in
955...    80.8kB
<missing>               15 months ago        /bin/sh -c apt-get update && apt-
get insta...    44.7MB
<missing>               15 months ago        /bin/sh -c #(nop)  CMD ["/bin/bash"]
0B
<missing>               15 months ago        /bin/sh -c #(nop) ADD
file:76679eeb94129df...    125MB
```

This is making explicit what we saw earlier when it downloaded the container: that a container image is made up of layers, which build upon the ones below it. The layers of a Docker image are quite simple—each layer is the result of a command being executed and any changes that the command ended up making on the local filesystem. In the previous `docker history` command, you will see a size reported by any commands that changed the size of the underlying filesystem.

The image format was created by Docker and is now formally specified by the **OCI** (**Open Container Initiative**) Image Format project. If you want to dig into that further, you can find the format and all relevant details at https://github.com/opencontainers/image-spec.

Container images, and each of the layers in the images, are typically available on the internet. All the examples I use in this book are publicly available. It is possible to configure your Kubernetes cluster to use a private image repository, and there's documentation at the Kubernetes project for exactly how to do that task, available at https://kubernetes.io/ docs/tasks/configure-pod-container/pull-image-private-registry/. This setup is more private, but at the cost of being more involved and complex to set up, so in this book, we will be sticking with publicly available images.

A container image also includes information on how to run the image, what to run, what environment variables to set, and so forth. We can see all those details using the docker inspect command:

```
docker inspect jocatalin/kubernetes-bootcamp:v1
```

The preceding command produces quite a bit of content, describing the container image in quite a bit of detail and the metadata that goes along with running the code within it:

```
[
    {
        "Id":
"sha256:8fafd8af70e9aa7c3ab40222ca4fd58050cf3e49cb14a4e7c0f460cd4f78e9fe",
        "RepoTags": [
            "jocatalin/kubernetes-bootcamp:v1"
        ],
        "RepoDigests": [
            "jocatalin/kubernetes-
bootcamp@sha256:0d6b8ee63bb57c5f5b6156f446b3bc3b3c143d233037f3a2f00e279c8fc
c64af"
        ],
        "Parent": "",
        "Comment": "",
        "Created": "2016-08-04T16:46:35.471076443Z",
        "Container":
"976a20903b4e8b3d1546e610b3cba8751a5123d76b8f0646f255fe2baf345a41",
        "ContainerConfig": {
            "Hostname": "6250540837a8",
            "Domainname": "",
            "User": "",
            "AttachStdin": false,
            "AttachStdout": false,
            "AttachStderr": false,
            "ExposedPorts": {
                "8080/tcp": {}
            },
            "Tty": false,
            "OpenStdin": false,
```

```
        "StdinOnce": false,
        "Env": [
"PATH=/usr/local/sbin:/usr/local/bin:/usr/sbin:/usr/bin:/sbin:/bin",
            "NPM_CONFIG_LOGLEVEL=info",
            "NODE_VERSION=6.3.1"
        ],
        "Cmd": [
            "/bin/sh",
            "-c",
            "#(nop) ",
            "CMD [\"/bin/sh\" \"-c\" \"node server.js\"]"
        ],
        "ArgsEscaped": true,
        "Image":
"sha256:87ef05c0e8dc9f729b9ff7d5fa6ad43450bdbb72d95c257a6746a1f6ad7922aa",
        "Volumes": null,
        "WorkingDir": "",
        "Entrypoint": null,
        "OnBuild": [],
        "Labels": {}
    },
    "DockerVersion": "1.12.0",
    "Author": "",
    "Architecture": "amd64",
    "Os": "linux",
    "Size": 211336459,
    "VirtualSize": 211336459,
```

In addition to the base configuration, a Docker container image can also contain a runtime configuration, so there is often a duplicate section defining much of what you say under the ContainerConfig key:

```
    "Config": {
        "Hostname": "6250540837a8",
        "Domainname": "",
        "User": "",
        "AttachStdin": false,
        "AttachStdout": false,
        "AttachStderr": false,
        "ExposedPorts": {
            "8080/tcp": {}
        },
        "Tty": false,
        "OpenStdin": false,
        "StdinOnce": false,
        "Env": [
"PATH=/usr/local/sbin:/usr/local/bin:/usr/sbin:/usr/bin:/sbin:/bin",
```

```
                "NPM_CONFIG_LOGLEVEL=info",
                "NODE_VERSION=6.3.1"
            ],
            "Cmd": [
                "/bin/sh",
                "-c",
                "node server.js"
            ],
            "ArgsEscaped": true,
            "Image":
"sha256:87ef05c0e8dc9f729b9ff7d5fa6ad43450bdbb72d95c257a6746a1f6ad7922aa",
            "Volumes": null,
            "WorkingDir": "",
            "Entrypoint": null,
            "OnBuild": [],
            "Labels": {}
        },
```

The last section included is an explicit list of the overlays for filesystems and how they fit together:

```
"GraphDriver": {
        "Data": {
            "LowerDir":
"/var/lib/docker/overlay2/b38e59d31a16f7417c5ec785432ba15b3743df647daed0dc8
00d8e9c0a55e611/diff:/var/lib/docker/overlay2/792ce98aab6337d38a3ec7d567324
f829e73b1b5573bb79349497a9c14f52ce2/diff:/var/lib/docker/overlay2/6c131c8dd
754628a0ad2c2aa7de80e58fa6b3f8021f34af684b78538284cf06a/diff:/var/lib/docke
r/overlay2/160efe1bd137edb08fe180f020054933134395fde3518449ab405af9b1fb6cb0
/diff",
            "MergedDir":
"/var/lib/docker/overlay2/40746dcac4fe98d9982ce4c0a0f6f0634e43c3b67a4bed07b
b97068485cd137a/merged",
            "UpperDir":
"/var/lib/docker/overlay2/40746dcac4fe98d9982ce4c0a0f6f0634e43c3b67a4bed07b
b97068485cd137a/diff",
            "WorkDir":
"/var/lib/docker/overlay2/40746dcac4fe98d9982ce4c0a0f6f0634e43c3b67a4bed07b
b97068485cd137a/work"
        },
        "Name": "overlay2"
    },
    "RootFS": {
        "Type": "layers",
        "Layers": [
"sha256:42755cf4ee95900a105b4e33452e787026ecdefffcc1992f961aa286dc3f7f95",
"sha256:d1c800db26c75f0aa5881a5965bd6b6abf5101dbb626a4be5cb977cc8464de3b",
"sha256:4b0bab9ff599d9feb433b045b84aa6b72a43792588b4c23a2e8a5492d7940e9a",
```

```
"sha256:aaed480d540dcb28252b03e40b477e27564423ba0fe66acbd04b2affd43f2889",
"sha256:4664b95364a615be736bd110406414ec6861f801760dae2149d219ea8209a4d6"
            ]
        }
      }
  ]
```

There's a lot of information in that JSON dump, more than you probably need or care about right now. Most importantly, I want you to know that it specifies a `cmd` under the `config` section in three parts. This is what will be invoked by default if you `run` the container, and it is often called the `Entrypoint`. If you put those pieces together and imagine running them yourself in the container, you would be running the following:

```
/bin/sh -c node server.js
```

The `Entrypoint` defines what binary will get executed, and any arguments to it, and is the key to specify what you want to run and how you want to run it. Kubernetes works with this same `Entrypoint` and can override it, with commands and arguments to run your software, or run diagnostic tools that you have stored in the same container image.

Container registries

In the preceding example, when we invoked the command to pull the container, we referenced `https://www.docker.com/`, which is Docker's container registry. There are two other common registries that you will see frequently when working with Kubernetes or reading documentation about Kubernetes: `gcr.io`, Google's container registry, and `quay.io`, CoreOS's container registry. Other companies offer hosted container registries on the internet, and you can run your own. Currently, Docker and Quay both offer free hosting for public images, so you will see those frequently in documentation and examples. All three registries also offer options for private image repositories, typically for a relatively small subscription.

One of the benefits of publicly available images (and layering on top of those images) is that it makes it very easy to compose your images, sharing underlying layers. This also implies that those layers can be inspected, and common layers searched for security vulnerabilities. There are several open source projects aimed at helping provide this information, and several companies have formed that help in coordinating the information and scanning. If you subscribe to an image repository for your images, they will often include this scanning for vulnerabilities in their product offering.

As a developer, when you use a library in your code, you are responsible for how it will operate. You are already responsible for being familiar with how those libraries work (or not), and handling any issues when they don't work as expected. With the flexibility and control of specifying the whole container, you are equally responsible for everything that gets included in the container in the same fashion.

It is easy to forget about the layers that your software is built upon, and you may not always have the time to track all the potential security vulnerabilities and issues that have arisen with the software that you are building upon. The security scans from projects such as Clair (`https://github.com/coreos/clair`) can provide you with excellent information about potential vulnerabilities. I recommend you consider taking advantage of a service that can provide those details for you.

Making your first container

Making a container is something easily done with the Docker software and the `docker build` command. This command uses a manifest that details how to create the container, called a Dockerfile.

Let's start with the simplest possible container. Create a file called a Dockerfile and add this to it:

```
FROM alpine
CMD ["/bin/sh", "-c", "echo 'hello world'"]
```

And then, invoke `build`:

```
docker build .
```

If you see a response like this:

```
"docker build" requires exactly 1 argument.
See 'docker build --help'.
Usage: docker build [OPTIONS] PATH | URL | -
Build an image from a Dockerfile
```

Then you are either missing the . in the command, or ran the command in a directory different from where you created the Dockerfile. The . is telling `docker` where to find Dockerfile (. meaning] in this current directory).

What you should see is some output akin to the following:

```
Sending build context to Docker daemon   2.048kB
Step 1/2 : FROM alpine
latest: Pulling from library/alpine
88286f41530e: Pull complete
Digest:
sha256:f006ecbb824d87947d0b51ab8488634bf69fe4094959d935c0c103f4820a417d
Status: Downloaded newer image for alpine:latest
 ---> 76da55c8019d
Step 2/2 : CMD /bin/sh -c echo 'hello world'
 ---> Running in 89c04e8c5d87
 ---> f5d273aa2dcb
Removing intermediate container 89c04e8c5d87
Successfully built f5d273aa2dcb
```

This image only has an ID, f5d273aa2dcb, not a name, but this is sufficient for us to see how this works. If you run this sample example locally, you will get a different ID that uniquely identifies the container image. You can run the code in the container image using the docker run f5d273aa2dcb command. This should result in you seeing the following output:

```
hello world
```

Take a moment to run docker history f5d273aa2dcb and docker inspect f5d273aa2dcb on the image you just created.

When you're done, we can delete the Docker image we just made with the following command:

```
docker rmi f5d273aa2dcb
```

If you get an error removing an image, which can happen if you have a stopped container that references the image locally, you can force the removal with the addition of -f. For example, the command that will force the removal of a local image would be:

```
docker rmi -f f5d237aa2dcb
```

Dockerfile commands

Docker has documentation on how to write a Dockerfile at `https://docs.docker.com/engine/reference/builder/`, and a set of best practices that they recommend at `https://docs.docker.com/engine/userguide/eng-image/dockerfile_best-practices/`. We will cover some of the commands that are common and important to know for building your own container images.

The following are some of the important Dockerfile build commands that you should be aware of:

1. FROM (`https://docs.docker.com/engine/reference/builder/#from`): FROM describes the image that you are using as a base to build your container, and is generally the first command in a Dockerfile. Docker best practices encourage the use of Debian as a base Linux distribution. As you saw from my example earlier, I prefer to use Alpine Linux because it is very compact in size. You can also use Ubuntu, Fedora, and CentOS, all of which are larger images and include significantly more software in their base image. If you are already familiar with a distribution of Linux and the tools that are used with it, then I recommend you take advantage of that knowledge for making your first containers. You can also frequently find containers built specifically to support the language you're using, such as Node or Python. At the time of writing (fall 2017), I downloaded a variety of these images to show the relative sizes:

   ```
   REPOSITORY      TAG        IMAGE ID        CREATED          SIZE
   alpine          latest     76da55c8019d    2 days ago       3.97MB
   debian          latest     72ef1cf971d1    2 days ago       100MB
   fedora          latest     ee17cf9e0828    2 days ago       231MB
   centos          latest     196e0ce0c9fb    27 hours ago     197MB
   ubuntu          latest     8b72bba4485f    2 days ago       120MB
   ubuntu          16.10      7d3f705d307c    8 weeks ago      107MB
   python          latest     26acbad26a2c    2 days ago       690MB
   node            latest     de1099630c13    24 hours ago     673MB
   java            latest     d23bdf5b1b1b    8 months ago     643MB
   ```

As you can see, the images vary considerably in size.

You can explore these (and a wide variety of other base images) at `https://hub.docker.com/explore/`.

2. RUN (`https://docs.docker.com/engine/reference/builder/#run`): RUN describes commands that you run within the container image that you're building, most frequently used for adding in dependencies or other libraries. If you look at Dockerfiles created by others, you'll often see the RUN command used to install libraries using commands such as `apt-get install ...` or `rpm -ivh ....` The commands that are used are specific to the choice of base image; `apt-get`, for example, is available on Debian and Ubuntu base images, but not on Alpine or Fedora. If you put in a RUN command that's not available (or just has a typo), then when you're running the `docker build` command you'll see an error. As an example, when building the Dockerfile:

```
FROM alpine
RUN apt-get install nodejs
Results in the following output:
Sending build context to Docker daemon  2.048kB
Step 1/2 : FROM alpine
 ---> 76da55c8019d
Step 2/2 : RUN apt-get install nodejs
 ---> Running in 58200129772d
/bin/sh: apt-get: not found
```

The `/bin/sh -c apt-get install nodejs` command returned a non-zero code: `127`.

3. ENV (`https://docs.docker.com/engine/reference/builder/#env`): ENV defines environment variables that will persist and be set prior to invoking your software in the container image. These are also set while creating the container image, which may cause surprising effects. If you need an environment variable set for a specific RUN command, for example, it is probably better to define it with a single RUN command rather than using the ENV command. For example, using ENV DEBIAN_FRONTEND non-interactive may confuse using a later RUN `apt-get install ...` command on a Debian-based image. In the case where you want to enable that for a specific RUN command, you can do so by temporarily adding the environment variable in front of the single RUN command. For example:

```
RUN DEBIAN_FRONTEND=noninteractive apt-get install -y ...
```

4. COPY (https://docs.docker.com/engine/reference/builder/#copy): COPY (or the ADD command) is how you add your own local files into the container. This is often the most effective way to copy your code into the container image to run. You can copy an entire directory, or a single file. Along with the RUN command, this is likely going to be how you do most of the work of creating a container image with your code.

5. WORKDIR (https://docs.docker.com/engine/reference/builder/#workdir): WORKDIR makes a local directory and then makes that directory the base for all further commands (RUN, COPY, and so on). It can be extraordinarily convenient for RUN commands that expect to be run from a local or relative directory, such as installation tools such as Node.js npm.

6. LABEL (https://docs.docker.com/engine/reference/builder/#label): LABEL adds values that are visible to docker inspect and are generally used as references for who is responsible or what is within a container. The MAINTAINER command was very common earlier, but it has been replaced with the LABEL command. Labels are built on base images and are additive, so any labels you add will be included with labels from a base image you're using.

7. CMD (https://docs.docker.com/engine/reference/builder/#cmd) and ENTRYPOINT (https://docs.docker.com/engine/reference/builder/#entrypoint): CMD (and the ENTRYPOINT command) is how you specify what to run when someone runs your container. The most common format is a JSON array, where the first element is the command to be invoked, and the second and later elements are arguments to that command. CMD and ENTRYPOINT were made to be used either individually, in which case you use either CMD or ENTRYPOINT to specify the executable to run and all arguments, or together, in which case ENTRYPOINT should be just the executable and CMD should be the arguments for that executable.

Example – Python/Flask container image

To walk through the details of how to use Kubernetes, I have created two sample applications that you can download, or replicate to follow along and try out these commands. The first of these is a very simple Python application using the Flask library. The sample application is directly from the Flask documentation (http://flask.pocoo.org/docs/0.12/).

You can download a copy of this code from GitHub at `https://github.com/kubernetes-for-developers/kfd-flask/tree/first_container`. Since we will evolve these files, the code referenced here is available at the `first_container` tag. If you want to use Git to get these files, you can run the following commands:

```
git clone https://github.com/kubernetes-for-developers/kfd-flask
```

Then, go into the repository and check out the tag:

```
cd kfd-flask
git checkout tags/first_container
```

Let's start with looking at the contents of a Dockerfile, which define what gets built into a container and how that happens.

The goals we have for creating this Dockerfile are:

- Get and install any security patches for the underlying operating system
- Install the language or runtime that we need to use to run our code
- Install any dependencies for our code that are not included directly in our source control
- Copy our code into the container
- Define how and what to run

```
FROM alpine
# load any public updates from Alpine packages
RUN apk update
# upgrade any existing packages that have been updated
RUN apk upgrade
# add/install python3 and related libraries
# https://pkgs.alpinelinux.org/package/edge/main/x86/python3
RUN apk add python3
# make a directory for our application
RUN mkdir -p /opt/exampleapp
# move requirements file into the container
COPY . /opt/exampleapp/
# install the library dependencies for this application
RUN pip3 install -r /opt/exampleapp/requirements.txt
ENTRYPOINT ["python3"]
CMD ["/opt/exampleapp/exampleapp.py"]
```

This container is based on Alpine Linux. I appreciate the small size of the containers, and there is less extraneous software residing in the container. You will see several commands that may not be familiar, specifically the `apk` command. This is the command-line tool that helps install, update, and remove Alpine Linux packages. These commands update the package repository, upgrade all installed and pre-existing packages in the image, and then install Python 3 from packages.

If you are already familiar with Debian commands (such as `apt-get`) or Fedora/CentOS commands (such as `rpm`), then I recommend you use those base Linux containers for your own work.

The next two commands make a directory on the container at `/opt/exampleapp` to house our source code and copy it all into place. The `COPY` command adds everything from the local directory into the container, which is probably more than we need. You can create a file called `.dockerignore` in the future that will `ignore` a set of files based on patterns so that some common files that we don't want to be included will be ignored in the `COPY` command.

Next, you'll see a `RUN` command that installs the application dependencies, in this case from the file `requirements.txt`, which is included in the source repository. It is good practice to maintain your dependencies in a file like this, and the `pip` command was made to support doing exactly that.

The last two commands leverage `ENTRYPOINT` and `CMD` separately. For this simple example, I could have used just one or the other. Both are included to show how they can be used together, the `CMD` being essentially arguments passed to the executable defined in `ENTRYPOINT`.

Building the container

We will use the `docker build` command to create the container. In a Terminal window, change into the directory with the Dockerfile and run the following command:

```
docker build .
```

You should see output that looks something like the following:

```
Sending build context to Docker daemon      107kB
Step 1/9 : FROM alpine
 ---> 76da55c8019d
Step 2/9 : RUN apk update
 ---> Running in f72d5991a7cd
```

```
fetch http://dl-cdn.alpinelinux.org/alpine/v3.6/main/x86_64/APKINDEX.tar.gz
fetch
http://dl-cdn.alpinelinux.org/alpine/v3.6/community/x86_64/APKINDEX.tar.gz
v3.6.2-130-gfde2d8ebb8 [http://dl-cdn.alpinelinux.org/alpine/v3.6/main]
v3.6.2-125-g93038b573e
[http://dl-cdn.alpinelinux.org/alpine/v3.6/community]
OK: 8441 distinct packages available
 ---> b44cd5d0ecaa
Removing intermediate container f72d5991a7cd
```

Each step in the Dockerfile will be reflected by output of what's happening when Docker is building the image at that step, and with more complex Dockerfiles, the output can be quite extensive. As it finishes its build process, it will report an overall success or failure, and will also report the container IDs:

```
Step 8/9 : ENTRYPOINT python3
 ---> Running in 14c58ace8b14
 ---> 0ac8be8b042d
Removing intermediate container 14c58ace8b14
Step 9/9 : CMD /opt/exampleapp/exampleapp.py
 ---> Running in e769a65fedbc
 ---> b704504464dc
Removing intermediate container e769a65fedbc
Successfully built 4ef370855f35
```

When we build the container without any other information, it makes an image locally that we can play with (it has an ID), but it doesn't have a name or a tag. When you are choosing a name, you will generally want to consider where you are hosting your container images. In this case, I am using CoreOS's Quay.io service, which offers free hosting for open source container images.

To tag the image that we just created, we can use the `docker tag` command:

```
docker tag 4ef370855f35 quay.io/kubernetes-for-developers/flask
```

This tag contains three relevant parts. The first `quay.io` is the container registry. The second (`kubernetes-for-developers`) is the namespace for your container, and the third (`flask`) is the name of the container. We did not specify any specific tag for the container, so the `docker` command will use the latest.

You should use tags for releases or other points in time in your development that you want to be able to jump back to easily and leverage latest to represent your most recent development work, so let's also tag this as a specific version:

```
docker tag 4ef370855f35 quay.io/kubernetes-for-developers/flask:0.1.0
```

When you share an image with someone else, it is a very good idea to be explicit about which image you are working with. As a general rule, consider only using the code yourself, and whenever you share the image with any other people, use an explicit tag. The tag does not have to be a version, and although there are limits on its format, it can be nearly any string.

You use the `docker push` command to transfer the image to the container repository once it's been tagged. You will need to log in to your container repository first:

```
docker login quay.io
```

And then you can push the image:

```
docker push quay.io/kubernetes-for-developers/flask
```

The push refers to a repository, [`quay.io/kubernetes-for-developers/flask`]:

```
0b3b7598137f: Pushed
602c2b5ffa76: Pushed
217607c1e257: Pushed
40ca06be4cf4: Pushed
5fbd4bb748e7: Pushed
0d2acef20dc1: Pushed
5bef08742407: Pushed
latest: digest:
sha256:de0c5b85893c91062fcbec7caa899f66ed18d42ba896a47a2f4a348cbf9b591f
size: 5826
```

You will generally want to build your container with a tag from the start, rather than having to do the additional commands. To do that, you can add the tag information with the `-t <your_name>` option to the `build` command. For the examples in this book, I am using the name `kubernetes-for-developers`, so the command I have been using to build the example is:

```
docker build -t quay.io/kubernetes-for-developers/flask .
```

If you are following along with this example, use your own value where the preceding command has `quay.io/kubernetes-for-developers/flask` .. You should see output that looks as follows:

```
Sending build context to Docker daemon     107kB
Step 1/9 : FROM alpine
 ---> 76da55c8019d
Step 2/9 : RUN apk update
 ---> Using cache
 ---> b44cd5d0ecaa
```

```
Step 3/9 : RUN apk upgrade
 ---> Using cache
 ---> 0b1caea1a24d
Step 4/9 : RUN apk add python3
 ---> Using cache
 ---> 1e29fcb9621d
Step 5/9 : RUN mkdir -p /opt/exampleapp
 ---> Using cache
 ---> 622a12042892
Step 6/9 : COPY . /opt/exampleapp/
 ---> Using cache
 ---> 7f9115a50a0a
Step 7/9 : RUN pip3 install -r /opt/exampleapp/requirements.txt
 ---> Using cache
 ---> d8ef21ee1209
Step 8/9 : ENTRYPOINT python3
 ---> Using cache
 ---> 0ac8be8b042d
Step 9/9 : CMD /opt/exampleapp/exampleapp.py
 ---> Using cache
 ---> b704504464dc
Successfully built b704504464dc
Successfully tagged quay.io/kubernetes-for-developers/flask:latest
```

Take a moment to read through that output, and notice that in several places it reports `Using cache`. You may have also noticed that the command was faster than the first time you built the image.

That is because Docker attempts to reuse any layers that haven't changed so that it doesn't have to recreate that work. Since we just did all of those commands, it can use the layers from the cache it made while creating the previous image.

If you run the `docker images` command, you should now see it listed:

```
REPOSITORY                                   TAG        IMAGE ID       CREATED
SIZE
quay.io/kubernetes-for-developers/flask      0.1.0      b704504464dc   2 weeks
ago           70.1MB
quay.io/kubernetes-for-developers/flask      latest     b704504464dc   2 weeks
ago           70.1MB
```

As you continue with using container images to house and deploy your code, you will likely want to automate the process of creating the images. As a general pattern, a good build process would be:

- Get the code from source control
- `docker build`
- `docker tag`
- `docker push`

This is the process we are using in these examples, and you can automate these commands with whatever tooling is most comfortable for you. I recommend you set up something that can be run on a command line quickly and consistently.

Running your container

Now, let's run the container we just made. We will use the `kubectl run` command to specify the simplest deployment—just the container:

```
kubectl run flask --image=quay.io/kubernetes-for-developers/flask:latest --
port=5000 --save-config
deployment "flask" created
```

To see what this is doing, we need to ask the cluster for the current state of the resources we just created. When we use the `kubectl run` command, it will implicitly create a Deployment resource for us, and as you learned in the last chapter, a Deployment has a ReplicaSet within it, and a Pod within the ReplicaSet:

```
kubectl get deployments
NAME         DESIRED    CURRENT    UP-TO-DATE    AVAILABLE    AGE
flask        1          1          1             1            20h
kubectl get pods
NAME                         READY      STATUS      RESTARTS    AGE
flask-1599974757-b68pw       1/1        Running     0           20h
```

We can get details on this deployment by asking for the raw data associated with the Kubernetes deployment resource `flask`:

```
kubectl get deployment flask -o json
```

We could just as easily request the information in YAML format, or query a subset of these details leveraging JsonPath or the other capabilities of the kubectl command. The JSON output will be extensive. It will start with a key indicating apiVersion from Kubernetes, the kind of resource, and metadata about the resource:

```
{
    "apiVersion": "extensions/v1beta1",
    "kind": "Deployment",
    "metadata": {
        "annotations": {
            "deployment.kubernetes.io/revision": "1"
        },
        "creationTimestamp": "2017-09-16T00:40:44Z",
        "generation": 1,
        "labels": {
            "run": "flask"
        },
        "name": "flask",
        "namespace": "default",
        "resourceVersion": "51293",
        "selfLink":
"/apis/extensions/v1beta1/namespaces/default/deployments/flask",
        "uid": "acbb0128-9a77-11e7-884c-0aef48c812e4"
    },
```

Beneath this is usually the specification of the deployment itself, which has a lot of the core of what is running:

```
    "spec": {
        "replicas": 1,
        "selector": {
            "matchLabels": {
                "run": "flask"
            }
        },
        "strategy": {
            "rollingUpdate": {
                "maxSurge": 1,
                "maxUnavailable": 1
            },
            "type": "RollingUpdate"
        },
        "template": {
            "metadata": {
                "creationTimestamp": null,
                "labels": {
                    "run": "flask"
```

```
                    }
                },
                "spec": {
                    "containers": [
                        {
                            "image": "quay.io/kubernetes-for-
developers/flask:latest",
                            "imagePullPolicy": "Always",
                            "name": "flask",
                            "ports": [
                                {
                                    "containerPort": 5000,
                                    "protocol": "TCP"
                                }
                            ],
                            "resources": {},
                            "terminationMessagePath": "/dev/termination-log",
                            "terminationMessagePolicy": "File"
                        }
                    ],
                    "dnsPolicy": "ClusterFirst",
                    "restartPolicy": "Always",
                    "schedulerName": "default-scheduler",
                    "securityContext": {},
                    "terminationGracePeriodSeconds": 30
                }
            }
        },
```

And the last part is usually the status, which indicates the current state of the deployment, as of the time you made the request for the information:

```
"status": {
    "availableReplicas": 1,
    "conditions": [
        {
            "lastTransitionTime": "2017-09-16T00:40:44Z",
            "lastUpdateTime": "2017-09-16T00:40:44Z",
            "message": "Deployment has minimum availability.",
            "reason": "MinimumReplicasAvailable",
            "status": "True",
            "type": "Available"
        }
    ],
    "observedGeneration": 1,
    "readyReplicas": 1,
    "replicas": 1,
    "updatedReplicas": 1
```

```
        }
    }
```

Remember that when a Pod runs in Kubernetes, it is running in a sandbox, isolated from the rest of the world. Kubernetes does this intentionally, so you can specify how Pods are supposed to be connected and what can be accessed from outside the cluster. We will cover how to set up external access in a later chapter. In the meantime, you can leverage one of two commands with `kubectl` to get direct access from your development machine: `kubectl port-forward` or `kubectl proxy`.

These commands both work by making proxies from your local development machine into the Kubernetes cluster, providing you private and personal access to your running code. The `port-forward` command will open a specific TCP (or UDP) port and arrange all traffic to forward to your Pod in the cluster. The proxy command uses an HTTP proxy that already exists to forward HTTP traffic in and out of your Pod. Both of these commands rely on knowing the Pod name to make the connections.

Pod name

Since we are working with a web server, using a proxy would make the most sense, as it will forward HTTP traffic through a URL based on the name of the Pod. Before we do that, we will use the `port-forward` command, which will be more relevant if what you're writing doesn't use the HTTP protocol.

The key thing you will need is the name of the Pod that was created. When we ran `kubectl get pods` earlier, you probably noticed that the name wasn't just `flask`, but included some additional characters in the name: `flask-1599974757-b68pw`. When we invoked `kubectl run`, it created a deployment, which consists of a Kubernetes ReplicaSet wrapped around a Pod. The first part of the name (`flask`) is from the deployment, the second part (`1599974757`) is the unique name assigned to the ReplicaSet that was created, and the third part (`b68pw`) is the unique name assigned to the Pod that was created. If you run the following command:

```
kubectl get replicaset
```

The result will show you the replicasets:

```
NAME                 DESIRED    CURRENT    READY    AGE
flask-1599974757     1          1          1        21h
```

You can see that the ReplicaSet name is the first two parts of the Pod's name.

Port forwarding

Now we can use that name to ask `kubectl` to set up a proxy that will forward all traffic from a local port we specify to a port associated with the Pod we determine. Get the full name of the Pod that was created with your deployment by looking at the Pods using the following command:

```
kubectl get pods
```

In my example, the result was `flask-1599974757-b68pw`, which can then be used with the `port-forward` command:

```
kubectl port-forward flask-1599974757-b68pw 5000:5000
```

The output should be something like the following:

```
Forwarding from 127.0.0.1:5000 -> 5000
Forwarding from [::1]:5000 -> 5000
```

This is forwarding any and all traffic that gets created on your local machine at TCP port `5000` to TCP port `5000` on the Pod `flask-1599974757-b68pw`.

You will note that you don't have a Command Prompt back yet, which is because the command is actively running to keep this particular tunnel we've requested alive. If we cancel or quit the `kubectl` command, typically by pressing *Ctrl* + *C*, then port forwarding will immediately end. `kubectl proxy` works in the same fashion, so when you use commands such as `kubectl port-forward` or `kubectl proxy`, you will probably want to open another Terminal window to run that command in by itself.

While the command is still running, open a browser and put in this URL: `http://localhost:5000`. The response should come back that says `Index Page`. When we invoked the `kubectl run` command, I specifically choose port `5000` to match the default from Flask.

Proxy

The other command you can use to access your Pod is the `kubectl proxy` command. The proxy provides access not only to your Pod, but to all of the Kubernetes APIs as well. To invoke the proxy, run the following command:

```
kubectl proxy
```

And the output will show something akin to the following:

```
Starting to serve on 127.0.0.1:8001
```

Like the `port-forward` command, you won't get a prompt back in the Terminal window until the proxy terminates. While it is active, you can access Kubernetes REST API endpoints through this proxy. Open a browser and enter the URL `http://localhost:8001/`.

You should see a long list of URLs in JSON format, something akin to the following:

```
{
  "paths": [
    "/api",
    "/api/v1",
    "/apis",
    "/apis/",
    "/apis/admissionregistration.k8s.io",
    "/apis/admissionregistration.k8s.io/v1alpha1",
    "/apis/apiextensions.k8s.io",
    "/apis/apiextensions.k8s.io/v1beta1",
    "/apis/apiregistration.k8s.io",
```

These are accessing the Kubernetes infrastructure directly. One of those URL's is `/api/v1` - and although it wasn't listed specifically, it uses the Kubernetes API server to provide a proxy to Pods based on the name. When we invoked our `run` command, we didn't specify a namespace, so it used the default, which is called `default`. The URL pattern to see a Pod is:

```
http://localhost:8001/api/v1/proxy/namespaces/<NAME_OF_NAMESPACE>/pods/
<POD_NAME>/
```

And in the case of our Pod, this would be:

```
http://localhost:8001/api/v1/proxy/namespaces/default/pods/flask-159997
4757-b68pw/
```

If you open a URL in your browser created with the Pod name that your Kubernetes cluster assigned, it should show you the same output that you saw using the `port-forward` command.

How did the proxy know to connect to port 5000 on the container?

When you ran a container, Kubernetes did not magically know what TCP ports your code is listening on. When we created this deployment using the `kubectl run` command, we added the `--port=5000` option at the end of that command. That was used by Kubernetes to know that the program should be listening on port `5000` for HTTP traffic. If you look back at the output from the `kubectl get deployment -o json` command, you will see a section in there under the key containers that includes the image we provided, the name of the deployment, and a data structure indicating a default port for accessing the container: `5000`. If we had not provided the additional details, the proxy would have assumed we wanted to access the container at port `80`. Since nothing is running on port `80` with our development container, you would have seen an error akin to the following:

```
Error: 'dial tcp 172.17.0.4:80: getsockopt: connection refused'
Trying to reach: 'http://172.17.0.4/'
```

Getting logs from your application

There are more ways to interact with your code running in the container, which we'll cover in a future chapter. If the code you run does not listen on a TCP socket to provide HTTP traffic, or something equivalent, then you generally want to see the output that your code created to know that it's running.

Containers are specifically set up to capture any output to STDOUT and STDERR from the executable you've specified and capture that into logs, which can be retrieved with another `kubectl` command: `kubectl logs`. Like the `proxy` and `port-forward` commands, this command needs to know the name of the Pod you want to interact with.

Run the following command:

```
kubectl logs flask-1599974757-b68pw
```

And you should see some output akin to the following:

```
* Running on http://0.0.0.0:5000/ (Press CTRL+C to quit)
* Restarting with stat
* Debugger is active!
* Debugger PIN: 996-805-904
```

Example – Node.js/Express container image

This example follows the same pattern as the Python example, a simple Node.js application built with the Express library to walk through the details of how to use Kubernetes. If you are more familiar with JavaScript development, this example may be more meaningful. The sample application is directly from the Express documentation (`https://expressjs.com/en/starter/generator.html`).

You can get a download a copy of this code from GitHub at `https://github.com/kubernetes-for-developers/kfd-nodejs/tree/first_container`. Since we will evolve these files, the code referenced here is available at the `first_container` tag. If you want to use Git to retrieve these files, you can do so using the following commands:

```
git clone https://github.com/kubernetes-for-developers/kfd-nodejs
cd kfd-nodejs
git checkout tags/first_container
```

Like the Python example, we will start with the Dockerfile. As a reminder, this is what defines what gets built into a container, and how it happens. The goals of this Dockerfile are:

- Get and install any critical security patches for the underlying operating system
- Install the language or runtime that we'll need to use to run our code
- Install any dependencies for our code that aren't included directly in our source control
- Copy our code into the container
- Define how and what to run

```
FROM alpine
# load any public updates from Alpine packages
RUN apk update
# upgrade any existing packages that have been updated
RUN apk upgrade
# add/install python3 and related libraries
# https://pkgs.alpinelinux.org/package/edge/main/x86/python3
RUN apk add nodejs nodejs-npm
# make a directory for our application
WORKDIR /src
# move requirements file into the container
COPY package.json .
COPY package-lock.json .
# install the library dependencies for this application
RUN npm install --production
# copy in the rest of our local source
```

```
COPY . .
# set the debug environment variable
ENV DEBUG=kfd-nodejs:*
CMD ["npm", "start"]
```

Like the Python example, this container is based on Alpine Linux. You will see several commands that may not be familiar, specifically the `apk` command. As a reminder, this command is used to install, update, and remove Alpine Linux packages. These commands update the Alpine package repository, upgrade all installed and pre-existing packages in the image, and then install `nodejs` and `npm` from packages. Those steps basically bring us to a minimal container that can run a Node.js application.

The next commands make a directory in the container at `/src` to house our source code, copy in the `package.json` file, and then use `npm` to install the dependencies for running the code. The `--production` option used with the `npm install` command installs only those items listed in `package.json` that are needed for running the code - development dependencies are excluded. Node.js makes it easy and consistent to maintain your dependencies with its `package.json` format, and it is good practice to separate out dependencies needed in production from those needed in development.

The last two commands leverage `ENV` and `CMD`. This differs from the Python example where I used `CMD` and `ENTRYPOINT` to highlight how they work together. In this example, I use the `ENV` command to set the `DEBUG` environment variable to match the example instructions in the Express documentation. `CMD` then contains a command to start our code, which simply leverages `npm` to run the command defined in `package.json`, and uses the earlier `WORKDIR` command to set the local directory for that invocation.

Building the container

We use the same `docker build` command to create the container:

```
docker build .
```

You should see output that looks something like the following:

```
Sending build context to Docker daemon  197.6kB
Step 1/11 : FROM alpine
 ---> 76da55c8019d
Step 2/11 : RUN apk update
 ---> Using cache
 ---> b44cd5d0ecaa
```

As you saw with the Python-based example, every step in the Dockerfile is reflected with output showing you what happened as Docker was building the container image based on your instructions (the Dockerfile):

```
Step 9/11 : COPY . .
 ---> 6851a9088ce3
Removing intermediate container 9fa9b8b9d463
Step 10/11 : ENV DEBUG kfd-nodejs:*
 ---> Running in 663a2cd5f31f
 ---> 30c3b45c4023
Removing intermediate container 663a2cd5f31f
Step 11/11 : CMD npm start
 ---> Running in 52cf9638d065
 ---> 35d03a9d90e6
Removing intermediate container 52cf9638d065
Successfully built 35d03a9d90e6
```

As with the Python example, this builds a container with only an ID. This example also leverages Quay for hosting the images publicly, so we will take the image appropriately so we can upload it to Quay:

```
docker tag 35d03a9d90e6 quay.io/kubernetes-for-developers/nodejs
```

As with the Python example, the tag contains three relevant parts - quay.io is the container registry. The second (kubernetes-for-developers) is the namespace for your containers, and the third (nodejs) is the name of the container. The same commands as the Python example are used to upload the container, referencing nodejs instead of flask:

```
docker login quay.io
docker push quay.io/kubernetes-for-developers/nodejs

The push refers to a repository [quay.io/kubernetes-for-developers/nodejs]
0b6165258982: Pushed
8f16769fa1d0: Pushed
3b43ed4da811: Pushed
9e4ead6d58f7: Pushed
d56b3cb786f1: Pushedfad7fd538fb6: Pushing [==================>
]   11.51MB/31.77MB
5fbd4bb748e7: Pushing [===================================>      ]
2.411MB/3.532MB
0d2acef20dc1: Pushing [=================================================>]
1.107MB
5bef08742407: Pushing [=================>                        ]
1.287MB/3.966MB
```

And when it is complete, you should see something akin to the following:

```
The push refers to a repository [quay.io/kubernetes-for-developers/nodejs]
0b6165258982: Pushed
8f16769fa1d0: Pushed
3b43ed4da811: Pushed
9e4ead6d58f7: Pushed
d56b3cb786f1: Pushed
fad7fd538fb6: Pushed
5fbd4bb748e7: Pushed
0d2acef20dc1: Pushed
5bef08742407: Pushed
latest: digest:
sha256:0e50e86d27a4b29b5b10853d631d8fc91bed9a37b44b111111dcd4fd9f4bc723
size: 6791
```

Like the Python example, you may want to build and tag in the same command. For the Node.js example, that command would be:

```
docker build -t quay.io/kubernetes-for-developers/nodejs:0.2.0 .
```

This, if run immediately after you built the image, should display output that looks like the following:

```
Sending build context to Docker daemon  197.6kB
Step 1/11 : FROM alpine
 ---> 76da55c8019d
Step 2/11 : RUN apk update
 ---> Using cache
 ---> b44cd5d0ecaa
Step 3/11 : RUN apk upgrade
 ---> Using cache
 ---> 0b1caea1a24d
Step 4/11 : RUN apk add nodejs nodejs-npm
 ---> Using cache
 ---> 193d3570516a
Step 5/11 : WORKDIR /src
 ---> Using cache
 ---> 3a5d78afa1be
Step 6/11 : COPY package.json .
 ---> Using cache
 ---> 29724b2bd1b9
Step 7/11 : COPY package-lock.json .
 ---> Using cache
 ---> ddbcb9af6ffc
Step 8/11 : RUN npm install --production
 ---> Using cache
 ---> 1556a20af49a
```

```
Step 9/11 : COPY . .
 ---> Using cache
 ---> 6851a9088ce3
Step 10/11 : ENV DEBUG kfd-nodejs:*
 ---> Using cache
 ---> 30c3b45c4023
Step 11/11 : CMD npm start
 ---> Using cache
 ---> 35d03a9d90e6
Successfully built 35d03a9d90e6
Successfully tagged quay.io/kubernetes-for-developers/nodejs:latest
```

Again, it will be significantly faster as it was using Docker's cache of the image layers that were previously built.

If you run the `docker images` command, you should now see it listed:

```
REPOSITORY                                 TAG      IMAGE ID      CREATED
SIZE
quay.io/kubernetes-for-developers/nodejs   0.2.0    46403c409d1f  4 minutes
ago     81.9MB
```

> If you are pushing your own images to `quay.io` as a container repository, you may need to log in to the website and make the images public in addition to these commands. By default, `quay.io` will keep images private, even the public ones, until you approve their exposure on their website.

Running your container

Now, let's run the container we just made. We will use the `kubectl run` command as with the Python example, but replacing flask with `nodejs` to specify the container we just made and uploaded:

```
kubectl run nodejs --image=quay.io/kubernetes-for-developers/nodejs:0.2.0 -
-port=3000
deployment "nodejs" created
```

To see what it's doing, we need to ask the cluster for the current state of the resources we just created:

```
kubectl get deployments
NAME        DESIRED    CURRENT    UP-TO-DATE    AVAILABLE    AGE
nodejs      1          1          1             1            1d
kubectl get pods
NAME                       READY      STATUS       RESTARTS     AGE
nodejs-568183341-2bw5v     1/1        Running      0            1d
```

The `kubectl run` command works regardless of the language, and in the same fashion as the Python example. The simple deployment created in this case is named `nodejs`, and we can request the same kinds of information about it that we did with the Python example earlier:

```
kubectl get deployment nodejs -o json
```

The JSON output should will be fairly extensive, and will have multiple sections. At the top of the output will be `apiVersion`, `kind`, and `metadata` about the deployment:

```
{
    "apiVersion": "extensions/v1beta1",
    "kind": "Deployment",
    "metadata": {
        "annotations": {
            "deployment.kubernetes.io/revision": "1"
        },
        "creationTimestamp": "2017-09-16T10:06:30Z",
        "generation": 1,
        "labels": {
            "run": "nodejs"
        },
        "name": "nodejs",
        "namespace": "default",
        "resourceVersion": "88886",
        "selfLink":
"/apis/extensions/v1beta1/namespaces/default/deployments/nodejs",
        "uid": "b5d94f83-9ac6-11e7-884c-0aef48c812e4"
    },
```

Typically, underneath that will be `spec`, which has a lot of the core of what you're just asked to be run:

```
"spec": {
    "replicas": 1,
    "selector": {
        "matchLabels": {
            "run": "nodejs"
        }
    },
    "strategy": {
        "rollingUpdate": {
            "maxSurge": 1,
            "maxUnavailable": 1
        },
        "type": "RollingUpdate"
    },
    "template": {
        "metadata": {
            "creationTimestamp": null,
            "labels": {
                "run": "nodejs"
            }
        },
        "spec": {
            "containers": [
                {
                    "image": "quay.io/kubernetes-for-
developers/nodejs:0.2.0",
                    "imagePullPolicy": "IfNotPresent",

                    "name": "nodejs",
                    "ports": [
                        {
                            "containerPort": 3000,
                            "protocol": "TCP"
                        }
                    ],
                    "resources": {},
                    "terminationMessagePath": "/dev/termination-log",
                    "terminationMessagePolicy": "File"
                }
            ],
            "dnsPolicy": "ClusterFirst",
            "restartPolicy": "Always",
            "schedulerName": "default-scheduler",
            "securityContext": {},
```

```
                        "terminationGracePeriodSeconds": 30
                }
        }
},
```

And the final section is `status`, which indicates the current state (as of the request for this information) of the deployment:

```
"status": {
    "availableReplicas": 1,
    "conditions": [
        {
            "lastTransitionTime": "2017-09-16T10:06:30Z",
            "lastUpdateTime": "2017-09-16T10:06:30Z",
            "message": "Deployment has minimum availability.",
            "reason": "MinimumReplicasAvailable",
            "status": "True",
            "type": "Available"
        }
    ],
    "observedGeneration": 1,
    "readyReplicas": 1,
    "replicas": 1,
    "updatedReplicas": 1
}
}
```

When a Pod runs in Kubernetes, it is running in a sandbox, isolated from the rest of the world. Kubernetes does this intentionally, so you can specify what systems can communicate with each other, and what can be accessed from outside. For most clusters, the defaults for Kubernetes allow any Pod to communicate with any other Pod. Just like the Python example, you can leverage one of two commands with `kubectl` to get direct access from your development machine: `kubectl` port-forward or `kubectl` proxy.

Port forwarding

Now we can use that name to ask `kubectl` to set up a proxy that will forward all traffic from a local port we specify to a port associated with the Pod we determine. The Node.js example runs on a different port than the Python example (port 3000 instead of port 5000), so the command needs to be updated accordingly:

```
kubectl port-forward nodejs-568183341-2bw5v 3000:3000
```

The output should be something like the following:

```
Forwarding from 127.0.0.1:3000 -> 3000
Forwarding from [::1]:3000 -> 3000
```

This is forwarding any and all traffic that gets created on your local machine at TCP port 3000 to TCP port 3000 on the `nodejs-568183341-2bw5v` Pod.

Just as with the Python example, you don't get a Command Prompt back yet because the command is actively running to keep this particular tunnel alive. As a reminder, you can cancel or quit the `kubectl` command by pressing *Ctrl + C* and port forwarding will immediately end.

While the command is still running, open a browser and put in this URL: `http://localhost:3000`. The response should come back that says, `Index Page`. When we invoked the `kubectl run` command, I specifically choose port 3000 to match the default from Express.

Proxy

Since this is an HTTP-based application, we can also use the `kubectl proxy` command to get access to the responses from our code:

```
kubectl proxy
```

And the output will show something akin to the following:

```
Starting to serve on 127.0.0.1:8001
```

As a reminder, you won't get a prompt back in the Terminal window until the proxy terminates. Just as with the Python example, we can determine the URL to use that the proxy will use to forward to our container based on the Pod name and the namespace that we used when invoking the `kubectl run` command. Since we did not specify a namespace, it used the default, which is called `default`. The URL pattern for accessing the Pod is the same as the Python example:

```
http://localhost:8001/api/v1/proxy/namespaces/<NAME_OF_NAMESPACE>/pods/
<POD_NAME>/
```

And in the case of our Pod, this would be:

```
http://localhost:8001/api/v1/proxy/namespaces/default/pods/nodejs-56818
3341-2bw5v/
```

If you open a URL in your browser created with the Pod name that your Kubernetes cluster assigned, it should show you the same output that you saw using the `port-forward` command.

Getting logs from your application

Just like the Python example, the Node.js example sends some output to STDOUT. As the containers are specifically set up to capture any output to STDOUT and STDERR from the executable you've specified and capture that into logs, the same commands will work to show you the log output from the Node.js application:

```
kubectl logs nodejs-568183341-2bw5v
```

This should show you output akin to the following:

```
> kfd-nodejs@0.0.0 start /src
> node ./bin/www
Sat, 16 Sep 2017 10:06:41 GMT kfd-nodejs:server Listening on port 3000
GET / 304 305.615 ms - -
GET /favicon.ico 404 54.056 ms - 855
GET /stylesheets/style.css 200 63.234 ms - 111
GET / 200 48.033 ms - 170
GET /stylesheets/style.css 200 1.373 ms - 111
```

Tagging your container images

Using the :latest tag on Docker images is incredibly convenient, but it can easily lead to confusion as to what exactly is running. If you do use :latest, then it is a very good idea to also tell Kubernetes to always attempt to pull a new image when loading the container. We will see how to set this in Chapter 4, *Declarative Infrastructure*, when we talk about declaratively defining our applications.

An alternative is to make explicit tags, building with a tag, and also using docker tag to tag the image as latest for the convenience factor, but maintaining specific tags within the declarations that you check in to source control. For this example, the tag chosen is 0.2.0, using semantic versioning to represent a value to use with the container, and matched to a git tag as well.

The steps that were used while making this example were:

```
git tag 0.2.0
docker build -t quay.io/kubernetes-for-developers/nodejs:0.2.0 .
git push origin master --tags
docker push quay.io/kubernetes-for-developers/nodejs
```

Summary

In this chapter, we reviewed what makes up a container, how to store and share containers on the internet, and some of the commands you can use to create your own containers. We then used that knowledge to walk through an example in Python and another in Node.js, creating simple web-based services in both, building those into container images, and running them within Kubernetes. In our next chapter, we will dive deeper into how to interact with your code once it's been packaged into a container and will explore tips for taking full advantage of containers and Kubernetes during your development.

Interacting with Your Code in Kubernetes

3

In the last chapter, we walked through making container images, and created simple examples using Python and Node.js. In this chapter, we will expand on the brief introduction to interacting with your running code, and dig into further details on how to see how your code is operating, run additional commands, and get debugging from those Pods.

The sections for this chapter are:

- Practical notes for writing your software to run in a Pod
- Getting logs from your containers and Pods
- Interaction with a running Pod
- Kubernetes Concepts—labels and selectors
- Kubernetes Resource—service
- Discovering services from your Pod

Practical notes for writing software to run in a container

To use Kubernetes in your development process, one of the foundational requirements is running your code in a container. As you've seen, this adds a few steps to your development process. It also places a few more constraints around how you structure your code and interact with it, primarily so you can take advantage of the constraints to let Kubernetes do the work of running the processes, connecting them together, and coordinating any output. This is very different from many developers' habits of running one or more processes together, even with additional services needed for your application – such as databases or caches—on your local development machine.

This section provides some tips and suggestions on how to work with containers more effectively.

Getting options for your executable code

Aside from the ENTRYPOINT and CMD defined when you create your container, a container image can also define environment variables, usually via the ENV command when creating the container image. The ENTRYPOINT, CMD, and the environment variables can be overwritten or updated at execution time or when defining a deployment. Environment variables therefore become one of the most common ways of passing in configuration to your container.

Writing your software to utilize these environment variables will be important. As you create your software, make sure that you can take advantage of environment variables as well as command-line arguments in your code. Most languages have a library that will support options as either command-line arguments or environment variables.

In our next chapter, we will see how to set up configurations and pass them to your container at deployment time.

Practical notes for building container images

The following are suggestions and practical advice for maintaining your container images:

- Keep a Dockerfile in your source repository. If your application source is by itself in a Git repository, then including a Dockerfile in the repository along with it makes a great deal of sense. You can reference files to COPY or ADD from the relative directory of where your source is located. It's not uncommon to see a Dockerfile in the root of a repository, or if you're working from a monorepo with many projects, consider a Docker directory in the same directory as your project's source code:
    - If you want to take advantage of an automatic Docker build on Docker Hub, Quay, or another container repository, the automated system expects the Dockerfile to be in the root of your Git repository.

- Maintain a separate script (if needed) for creating the container image. Or more specifically, don't mix the process of creating your container image with code generation, compilation, testing, or validation. This keeps a clear separation of concerns from development tasks that you may need, depending on your language and framework. This will allow you to include it when and where you want to in an automation pipeline.
- It will be very tempting to add in additional tools to your base image to enable debugging, support new or additional diagnostic work, and so on. Make an explicit and conscious choice of what additional tooling you will (and won't) include within the image. I advise minimal additional tools, not just because they cause the image to be larger, but often the same tools that are so effective at debugging present an option for easier exploitation from hackers:
    - If you find you must add debugging tools into your image, consider making a second Dockerfile in a subdirectory that adds to the first and only includes the debugging tools you want to add. If you do this, I recommend you add a name `-debug` to the name of the image to make it clear that the image has the additional tooling installed.

- When you build your container image, build it with production usage in mind, and as a default. With containers, this is often represented with default values for environment variables that are made available in the container. In general, try not to include the dependencies needed for unit testing, development tasks, and so on in your container image:
  - In the case of Node.js, use the environment variable ENV=PROD, so that npm doesn't include development dependencies, or explicitly strip them away with a command line npm install —production.
- Treat the entire container you create as a read-only filesystem after you've created it. If you want to have some place to write local files, identify that location explicitly and set up a volume in your container for it.

Sending output from your program

kubectl logs (as well as the Docker equivalent: docker logs) defaults to combining stdout and stderr and passing anything presented as logs for the container. You may have also had experience with creating specific logging capabilities in your code to write logs to a file location on disk. In general, writing logs to a filesystem location is not encouraged for software running within a container, as to include it in general logging means that something has to read it again, which unnecessarily increases disk I/O.

If you want to have a means of supporting aggregated logging in your application, then you will typically want to have something external to your container and/or Pod defined to help capture, transport, and process those logs.

In general, if you write your programs to log to stdout and stderr, then containers and Kubernetes running those containers will generally help you to get access to those details more easily.

Logs

The most common method of getting information about how your code is working is generally through logs. Every language and development environment has its own pattern of how to expose those details, but at the very basics, it can be as simple as a print statement sending a line of text that will mean something to you to stdout. It is without a doubt the most consistent means across all programming languages of quick and simple debugging. When you deploy and run your code in Kubernetes, it maintains access to the logs from each Pod and container—where logs, in this case, are sending data to stdout and stderr.

If your existing pattern of development writes output to a specific file location, and maybe your framework includes the capability of rotating those log files as they grow, you may want to consider just sending data to stdout and/or stderr so that Kubernetes can make this coordination work.

Pods with more than one container

Our examples have been simple so far, with a single container in a Pod. A Pod can have more than one container at a time, and the command to get the logs can specify which container to use. If there is only one container, you don't need to specify which one to use.

If you need to specify a specific container, you can do so with either the -c option, or by adding it onto the logs command. For example, if you had a Pod named webapp with two containers, flask and background, and you wanted to see the logs from the background container, you could use the kubectl logs webapp background or kubectl logs webapp -c background commands.

Likewise, there's a shortcut for defining Pods and containers within a deployment. Rather than specifying the full Pod name based on the names assigned through Kubernetes, you can prefix the name of the Pod with just the deployment name. For example, if we had created a deployment with the kubectl run flask image=... command from our earlier examples, we could use the following command:

```
kubectl logs deployment/flask
```

This is rather than looking up the specific Pod name and then asking for the logs based on that name.

Streaming the logs

A common desire is to see a continuously flowing set of logs from your container, updated as the container provides the information. You can enable this with the -f option. For example, to see the updated logs from the Pod associated with the flask deployment, you can run the following command:

```
kubectl logs deployment/flask -f
```

As you interact with that service, or that service writes to stdout and does its normal logging, you will see the output streamed to your console.

Previous logs

The logs are generally specific to an active container. However, there is a common need to see what might have been in the logs if a container fails, or perhaps if you rolled out an update and something didn't work as expected. Kubernetes maintains a reference to the previous container for any Pod (if it exists), so that you can get this information when you need it. You can do this with the -p option, as long as the logs are available to Kubernetes.

Timestamps

Timestamps are also available for the log output, although not by default. You can get the log messages prefixed by a timestamp by adding the --timestamps option. For example:

```
kubectl logs deployment/flask --timestamps
```

You then may see the following:

```
2017-09-16T03:54:20.851827407Z  * Running on http://0.0.0.0:5000/ (Press
CTRL+C to quit)
2017-09-16T03:54:20.852424207Z  * Restarting with stat
2017-09-16T03:54:21.163624707Z  * Debugger is active!
2017-09-16T03:54:21.165358607Z  * Debugger PIN: 996-805-904
```

It is worthwhile to note that the timestamps are from the hosts that are running the containers, not your local machine, so the time zone on those logs will often not be the same time zone in which you reside. The timestamps all include full-time zone detail (typically set to the UTC-0 time zone) so the values can be converted easily.

More debugging techniques

There are several debugging techniques to work with your code deployed into an existing cluster. These include:

- Interactive deployment of a container image
- Attaching to a running Pod
- Running a second command within an existing Pod

Interactive deployment of an image

You can also use the `kubectl run` command to start an interactive session with a Pod. This can be exceptionally useful to log in and see what is available in a container image, or within the context of the software you've copied into a container image.

For example, if you wanted to run a shell to look around inside the base Alpine container image that I used for the Python example, you could run the following command:

```
kubectl run -i -t alpine-interactive --image=alpine -- sh
```

The `-i` option is what tells it to make the session interactive, and the `-t` option (which is almost always used with the `-i` option) indicates that it should allocate a TTY session (a Terminal session) for the interactive output. The trailing `-- sh` is an override to provide a specific command to be invoked with this session, in this case `sh`, asking to execute the shell.

When you invoke this command, it still sets up a deployment, and when you exit the interactive shell, the output will tell you how can you reattach to that same interactive shell. The output will look something like the following:

```
Session ended, resume using 'kubectl attach alpine-
interactive-1535083360-4nxj8 -c alpine-interactive -i -t' command when the
pod is running
```

If you want to kill that deployment, you will need to run the following command:

```
kubectl delete deployment alpine-interactive
```

This technique is immensely useful for getting a container image up and running within the Kubernetes cluster, and giving you shell access to interact with it. If you are used to using Python, Node.js, or similar dynamic languages, then the ability to get your libraries all loaded and a REPL active for you to interrogate or interact with to interactively poke at the running environment can be incredibly useful.

As an example, we can do this with the same Python image that we used for our Flask application. To bring it up as an interactive session that you can later delete, use the following command:

```
kubectl run -i -t python-interactive --image=quay.io/kubernetes-for-
developers/flask:latest --command -- /bin/sh
```

This command can take a little time to complete, as it will wait while Kubernetes downloads the image and starts it, using the command we put in (`/bin/sh`) instead of the entrypoint that we defined for it originally. In a short while, you should see some output in your Terminal window akin to the following:

```
If you don't see a command prompt, try pressing enter.
/ #
```

At this point, you can invoke Python and interact with the Python REPL directly, loading code and doing whatever you need. The following are some example commands to show you how this might work:

```
cd /opt/exampleapp
/opt/exampleapp # python3
Python 3.6.1 (default, May 2 2017, 15:16:41)
[GCC 6.3.0] on linux
Type "help", "copyright", "credits" or "license" for more information.
>>> import os
>>> os.environ
environ({'KUBERNETES_PORT': 'tcp://10.0.0.1:443',
'KUBERNETES_SERVICE_PORT': '443', 'HOSTNAME': 'python-
interactive-666665880-hwvvp', 'SHLVL': '1', 'OLDPWD': '/', 'HOME': '/root',
'TERM': 'xterm', 'KUBERNETES_PORT_443_TCP_ADDR': '10.0.0.1', 'PATH':
'/usr/local/sbin:/usr/local/bin:/usr/sbin:/usr/bin:/sbin:/bin',
'KUBERNETES_PORT_443_TCP_PORT': '443', 'KUBERNETES_PORT_443_TCP_PROTO':
'tcp', 'KUBERNETES_PORT_443_TCP': 'tcp://10.0.0.1:443',
'KUBERNETES_SERVICE_PORT_HTTPS': '443', 'PWD': '/opt/exampleapp',
'KUBERNETES_SERVICE_HOST': '10.0.0.1'})
>>> import flask
>>> help(flask.app)
Help on module flask.app in flask:
NAME
  flask.app
```

```
DESCRIPTION
  flask.app
  ~~~~~~~~~
This module implements the central WSGI application object.
:copyright: (c) 2015 by Armin Ronacher.
 :license: BSD, see LICENSE for more details.
CLASSES
  flask.helpers._PackageBoundObject(builtins.object)
  Flask
class Flask(flask.helpers._PackageBoundObject)
 |  The flask object implements a WSGI application and acts as the central
 |  object. It is passed the name of the module or package of the
 |  application. Once it is created it will act as a central registry for
 |  the view functions, the URL rules, template configuration and much more.
 |
 |  The name of the package is used to resolve resources from inside the
 |  package or the folder the module is contained in depending on if the
 |  package parameter resolves to an actual python package (a folder with
>>> exit()
/opt/exampleapp #
```

Once you are done interacting with this deployment, you can exit the shell by pressing *Ctrl + D* or by typing `exit`.

```
Session ended, resume using 'kubectl attach python-interactive-666665880-
hwvvp -c python-interactive -i -t' command when the pod is running
```

This is leaving the deployment running, so you can reattach to it using the preceding command, or you can delete the deployment and recreate it again when/if you want it. To delete it, you would use the following command:

```
kubectl delete deployment python-interactive
deployment "python-interactive" deleted
```

Attaching to a running Pod

If your pod is up and running, and you want to run some commands from within the context of that container image, you can attach an interactive session to it. You do this via the `kubectl attach` command. A Pod must be active for this command to work, so if you're trying to figure out why a Pod didn't start properly, this command probably won't help.

Attaching to a Pod will connect stdin into your process, and take anything from stdout and stderr and present it on the screen, so it's more like an interactive version of the kubectl logs -f command. Whatever you specified for the container will need to take stdin in order for this to be useful. You will also need to explicitly enable the TTY in order to connect to it. If you do not, you will frequently see the following as a first line of the output:

```
Unable to use a TTY - container flask did not allocate one
```

If you had created a deployment from the nodejs example earlier using the following command:

```
kubectl run nodejs --image=quay.io/kubernetes-for-developers/nodejs:latest
--port=3000
```

You could attach to this Pod using the following command:

```
kubectl attach deployment/express -i -t
```

This will return a warning message:

```
Unable to use a TTY - container flask did not allocate one
If you don't see a command prompt, try pressing enter.
```

And thereafter, when you interact with the service, you will see stdout streamed in the Terminal window.

This is most effective if your application prints its logs to stdout and you want to watch those logs while you interact with your code, for example by using a web browser. To use a web browser to interact with your running Pod, remember to use either the kubectl proxy or kubectl port-forward commands, typically from another Terminal window, to route access from your laptop to your Pod within the cluster.

In many cases, you will be better served by using the kubectl logs command that we described earlier with the -f option. The primary difference is if you have enabled your application to react to input from stdin and you ran it with stdin and a TTY defined, then you can interact with it directly by using the kubectl attach command.

Running a second process in a container

I frequently find it more useful to run an additional command in a Pod rather than attempting to attach to the Pod. You can do this with the kubectl exec command.

As of Kubernetes 1.8, `kubectl exec` doesn't support the deployment/name shortcut that we have used for the logs or attach commands, so you will need to specify the specific Pod name you want to interact with. If you just want to open an interactive shell in the Pod, you could run the following command:

```
kubectl get pods
```

```
NAME                     READY STATUS   RESTARTS AGE
flask-1908233635-d6stj 1/1   Running 0          1m
```

Using the name of the running pod, invoke `kubectl exec` to open an interactive shell within it:

```
kubectl exec flask-1908233635-d6stj -it -- /bin/sh

# ps aux
PID USER TIME COMMAND
    1 root 0:00 python3 /opt/exampleapp/exampleapp.py
   12 root 0:00 /bin/sh
   17 root 0:00 ps aux
```

You can also use this to invoke any command that's built into your container. For example, if you had a script or process that collected and exported diagnostic data, you might invoke that. Or, you could use a command such as `killall -HUP python3`, which will send a `HUP` signal to all `python3` processes that are running.

Kubernetes concepts – labels

In the first example, you saw how creating a deployment also created a ReplicaSet and related pods, in order to run your software.

Kubernetes has a very flexible mechanism for connecting and referencing objects that it manages. Rather than having a very strict hierarchy of what can be connected, the Kubernetes project uses short, definitive key/value pairs as set of tags on resources, called labels. There is a matching mechanism to query and find related labels, called Selectors.

Labels are fairly strictly defined in format, and are intended to group together resources in Kubernetes. They are not intended to identify a single or unique resource. They can be used to describe relevant information about a set of Kubernetes resources, be that a Pod, ReplicaSet, Deployment, and so on.

As we mentioned earlier, labels are key-value structures. The keys in labels are limited in size and may include an optional prefix, followed by a / character, and then the rest of the key. Prefixes, if supplied, are expected to be a DNS domain. Internal components and plugins to Kubernetes are expected to use prefixes to group and segregate their labels, and the prefix `kubernetes.io` is reserved for Kubernetes internal labels. If a prefix is not defined, then it is considered entirely under user control, and you need to maintain your own rules about consistency of what non-prefixed labels mean.

If you do want to use a prefix, it needs to be 253 characters or less. The key beyond the prefix has a maximum length of 63 characters. Keys can also only be specified with alphanumeric characters, as well as -, _, and .. Unicode and non-alpha-numeric characters aren't supported as labels.

Labels are intended to represent semantic information about a resource, and having multiple labels is not only acceptable, but expected. You will see labels used extensively in Kubernetes examples for a wide variety of purposes. Most common are dimensions of interest, such as:

- Environment
- Version
- Application name
- Tier of service

They can also be used to track any grouping that you're interested in based on your organization or development needs. Team, area of responsibility, or other semantic attributes are fairly common.

Organization of labels

Grouping your resources when you have more than "just a few" is critical to maintaining understanding of your system, as well as allowing you to think about the resources by their responsibility rather than individual names or IDs.

You should consider making and maintaining a living document with labels you use and their meaning and intentions. I prefer to do this in a `README.md` in the deploy directory where I keep the Kubernetes declarations, and find that whatever conventions you set are critical to understand, especially when you are working as part of a team. Even if you work alone, this is an excellent practice: what is obvious to you today may be completely obscure to *future you* in six months or even longer.

It is also your responsibility to keep clear the meaning of your own labels. Kubernetes does nothing to prevent you from confusing or reusing simplistic labels. A resource we will talk about later in this chapter called a service specifically uses labels to coordinate access to Pods, so keeping clear usage of those labels is very important. Reusing label keys across different Pods can lead to very unexpected results.

Kubernetes concepts – selectors

Selectors are used in Kubernetes to connect resources together based on the labels they have (or don't have). A selector is meant to provide a means to retrieve a set of resources in Kubernetes.

Most of the `kubectl` commands support a `-l` option that allows you to provide a selector to filter what it finds.

A Selector can be equality-based to represent specific values, or set-based to allow filtering and selection based on multiple values. Equality selectors use = or !=. Set selectors use `in`, `notin`, and `exists`. You can combine these in a selector to create more complex filters and selection criteria by appending the selectors together with a , between them.

For example, you might use a label `app` to represent a grouping of Pods that provide service to a specific application - in this case using the value `flask` and `tier` to represent the values of `front-end`, `cache`, and `back-end` tiers. A selector that would return all resources related to the app might be:

```
app=flask
```

And the selector that just returned the frontend resources supporting this application:

```
app=flask,tier in (front-end)
```

If you wanted to list all the Pods that matched the select `app=flask`, you could do so with the following command:

```
kubectl get pods -l app=flask
```

Viewing labels

The deployments we made earlier through the `kubectl run` commands put in place labels and used them as selectors. As you saw earlier, you can get all the underlying detail for a Kubernetes resource using the `kubectl get -o json` command.

A similar command is `kubectl describe`, which is intended to provide a human-readable overview of a resource and its recent history:

```
kubectl describe deployment flask
```

This will provide output akin to the following:

```
Name: flask
Namespace: default
CreationTimestamp: Sat, 16 Sep 2017 08:31:00 -0700
Labels: pod-template-hash=866287979
        run=flask
Annotations: deployment.kubernetes.io/revision=1
kubectl.kubernetes.io/last-applied-
configuration={"apiVersion":"apps/v1beta1","kind":"Deployment","metadata":{
"annotations":{},"labels":{"run":"flask"},"name":"flask","namespace":"defau
lt"},"spec":{"t...
Selector: app=flask
Replicas: 1 desired | 1 updated | 1 total | 1 available | 0 unavailable
StrategyType: RollingUpdate
MinReadySeconds: 0
RollingUpdateStrategy: 25% max unavailable, 25% max surge
Pod Template:
 Labels: app=flask
 Containers:
 flask:
 Image: quay.io/kubernetes-for-developers/flask:latest
 Port: 5000/TCP
 Environment: <none>
 Mounts: <none>
 Volumes: <none>
Conditions:
 Type Status Reason
 ---- ------ ------
 Available True MinimumReplicasAvailable
 Progressing True NewReplicaSetAvailable
OldReplicaSets: <none>
NewReplicaSet: flask-866287979 (1/1 replicas created)
Events:
 FirstSeen LastSeen Count From SubObjectPath Type Reason Message
 --------- -------- ----- ---- ------------- ------ ------ -------
 2d 2d 1 deployment-controller Normal ScalingReplicaSet Scaled up replica
set flask-866287979 to 1
```

You'll notice two labels in there, `run` and `pod-template-hash`, and a selector as well, `app=flask`. You can query for these exact labels using the `kubectl get` command line, for example:

```
kubectl get deployment -l run=flask
```

This will return the deployments matching that selector:

```
NAME       DESIRED   CURRENT   UP-TO-DATE   AVAILABLE   AGE
flask      1         1         1            1           2d
```

And the equivalent for pods, requesting by selector

```
kubectl get pods -l app=flask
```

This will return pods is matching the `app=flask` selector:

```
NAME                    READY    STATUS    RESTARTS   AGE
flask-866287979-bqg5w   1/1      Running   0          2d
```

Within this deployment, the Pod is referenced from the deployment using the selector `app=flask`.

NOTE: You can use selectors along with `kubectl get` to request multiple kinds of resources at once. For example, if you tagged all the relevant resources with `app=flask`, then you could use a command such as `kubectl get deployment,pod -l app=flask` to see both deployments and pods.

As you can see, there are some common label structures that are used implicitly when you create and run resources interactively. `kubectl run`, which creates deployments, uses the keys `run`, `pod-template-hash`, and `app` for specific meanings.

Labels can also be applied interactively to resources, after they already exist, using the `kubectl label` command. For example, to apply a label for enabled to a Pod, you might use the following command:

```
kubectl label pods your-pod-name enable=true
```

This lets you interactively group resources together, or provide a consistent means of rolling out, updating, or even removing sets of resources.

Listing resources with labels using kubectl

The `kubectl get` commands will show you basic information by default, typically the name and status of the resources you're looking for. You can extend the columns that it displays to include specific labels, which can often make it much easier to find what you are looking for when dealing with large numbers of different Pods, deployments, and ReplicaSets. `kubectl` takes an `-L` option with a comma-separated list of label keys to show as headers.

If you wanted to show the Pods along with the label keys `run` and `pod-template-hash`, the command would be:

```
kubectl get pods -L run,pod-template-hash
```

You then may see output like the following:

```
NAME READY STATUS RESTARTS AGE RUN POD-TEMPLATE-HASH
flask-1908233635-d6stj 1/1 Running 1 20h flask 1908233635
```

Automatic labels and selectors

Kubernetes includes a number of imperative commands that automatically create a number of resources for you. As these commands create the resources, they also apply their own conventions for labels and use those labels to tie the resources together. A perfect example of this is the command we have used several times now: `kubectl run`.

For example, when we used:

```
kubectl run flask --image=quay.io/kubernetes-for-developers/flask:latest
```

This created a deployment called `flask`. When the controller for the deployment was created, that in turn caused the creation of a ReplicaSet for that deployment, and the ReplicaSet controller in turn created a Pod. We saw earlier that the names of these resources were all related, and there are labels that relate them as well.

The deployment, `flask`, is created with the label `run=flask`, using the name of the `kubectl` command as the key, and the name we provided on the command line as a value. The deployment also has the selector `run=flask`, so that it can apply its controller rules to the relevant ReplicaSets and Pods that are created for it.

Looking at the ReplicaSet that was created, you will see the `run=flask` label as well as a label that corresponds to the name that was created for the ReplicaSet with the key `pod-template-hash`. This ReplicaSet also includes the same selectors to reference the Pods that are created for it.

And finally, the Pod has these same selectors, which is how the ReplicaSet and deployment know which resources within Kubernetes to interact with when needed.

Here is a table summarizing the labels and selectors that were automatically created with the preceding example:

	Deployment	ReplicaSet	Pod
Name	`flask`	`flask-1908233635`	`flask-1908233635-d6stj`
Labels	`run=flask`	`pod-template-hash=1908233635` `run=flask`	`pod-template-hash=1908233635` `run=flask`
Selectors	`run=flask`	`pod-template-hash=1908233635,run=flask`	

Kubernetes resources – service

So far, all the details we have explored have been related to a single container running within Kubernetes. The significant benefits of leveraging Kubernetes start to come into play when leveraging many containers running together. Being able to group together a set of Pods that all do the same thing, so that we can scale them and access them, is what the Kubernetes resource Service is all about.

A Service is the Kubernetes resource used to provide an abstraction through to your Pod (or Pods) that is agnostic of the specific instances that are running. Providing a layer between what one container (or set of containers) provides, such as a frontend web application, and another layer, such as a database, allows Kubernetes to scale them independently, update them, handle scaling issues, and more. A service also can contain a policy by which data should be transferred, so you might consider it a software load balancer within Kubernetes.

A Service is also the key abstraction used to expose Pods to each other, or your container outside the Kubernetes cluster. A service is the heart of how Kubernetes manages the coordination between sets of Pods, as well as traffic in and out of them.

An advanced use of Service also allows you to define a service for a resource entirely outside the cluster. This can allow you to have a consistent means of using services, regardless of whether the endpoint you need to run is from within Kubernetes or external to the cluster.

Kubernetes includes an expose command that can create a service based on a resource that is already operating within the cluster. For example, we could expose the `flask` deployment example we used earlier with the following command:

```
kubectl expose deploy flask --port 5000
service "flask" exposed
```

Most services will define a ClusterIP, and Kubernetes will handle all the dynamics of linking up the resources as Pods are created and destroyed that match to the relevant selectors. You can think of this like a simple load-balancer construct within Kubernetes, and it will forward traffic internally as Pods are available, and stop sending traffic to Pods that are failed or unavailable.

If you request the details of the service we just created with the `expose` command, you will see the ClusterIP listed:

```
kubectl get service flask

NAME TYPE CLUSTER-IP EXTERNAL-IP PORT(S) AGE
flask ClusterIP 10.0.0.168 <none> 5000/TCP 20h
```

Defining a service resource

The Service specification is fairly simple, documented for version 1.8 at `https://kubernetes.io/docs/api-reference/v1.8/#service-v1-core`. All resources within Kubernetes can be defined declaratively, which we will look at in more depth in `Chapter 4`, *Declarative Infrastructure*. Resources can also be defined using YAML as well as JSON. To look at the details of what can be included with a Service resource, we will look at the YAML specification for it. The core of the specification includes a name, a selector for the Pods that provide the service, and ports associated with the services.

For example, a simple service declaration for our `flask` Pod might be:

```
kind: Service
apiVersion: v1
metadata:
    name: service
spec:
  selector:
      run: flask
  ports:
  - protocol: TCP
    port: 80
    targetPort: 5000
```

This defines a service that selects the Pods to front using the selector `run: flask`, accepting any requests on TCP port `80` and forwarding them to port `5000` on the selected Pods. Services support both TCP and UDP. The default is TCP, so we didn't strictly need to include it. Additionally, targetPort can be a string referring to the name of a port and not just a port number, allowing significantly greater flexibility between services and the ability to move around the specific backend ports as development teams desire without needing as much careful coordination to keep the overall system operational.

A service can define (and redirect) multiple ports—for example, if you wanted to support both port `80` and `443` for access, you can define that on the service.

Endpoints

A service does not require a selector, and a service without a selector is how Kubernetes represents a service that's outside of the cluster for the other resources within. To enable this, you create a service without a selector as well as a new resource, an Endpoint, which defines the network location of the remote service.

If you are migrating services into Kubernetes and have some of those services external to the cluster, this provides one way to represent the remote system as a service internally, and if you move it into Kubernetes later, you wouldn't have to change how internal Pods connect or utilize that resource. This is an advanced feature of services, and does not also account for authorization. Another option is to not represent external services as service resources, and simply reference them in Secrets, a feature we will look at in more depth in the next chapter.

For example, if you had a remote TCP service running on the internet at port `1976` at the IP address `1.2.3.4`, you could define a Service and Endpoint to reference that `external-to-kubernetes` system:

```
kind: Service
apiVersion: v1
metadata:
  name: some-remote-service
spec:
  ports:
  - protocol: TCP
    port: 1976
    targetPort: 1976
```

This would work with the following `Endpoints` definition:

```
kind: Endpoints
apiVersion: v1
metadata:
  name: some-remote-service
subsets:
  - addresses:
      - ip: 1.2.3.4
    ports:
      - port: 1976
```

Service type – ExternalName

There is a variant to the preceding Endpoint definition that simply provides a DNS reference, called an `ExternalName` service. Like the `Endpoint` oriented service, it doesn't include a selector, but also does not include any port references. Instead, it simply defines an external DNS entry that can be used as a service definition.

The following example provides a Service interface inside Kubernetes to the external DNS entry `my.rest.api.example.com`:

```
kind: Service
apiVersion: v1
metadata:
  name: another-remote-service
  namespace: default
spec:
  type: ExternalName
  externalName: my.rest.api.example.com
```

Unlike the other services, which provide TCP and UDP (Layer 4 on the ISO network stack) forwarding, the `ExternalName` only provides a DNS response and does not manage any port forwarding or redirection.

Headless service

It is possible to create a service grouping that does not allocate an IP address or forward traffic, if there is a reason that you want to definitively control what specific pods you connect and communicate with. This kind of service is called a headless service. You can request this setup by explicitly setting ClusterIP to None within the service definition:

For example, a headless service might be:

```
kind: Service
apiVersion: v1
metadata:
    name: flask-service
spec:
  ClusterIP: None
  selector:
      app: flask
```

For these services, DNS entries will be created that point to the Pods backing the service, and that DNS will be automatically updated as Pods matching the selector come online (or disappear).

NOTE: Be aware that DNS caching could end up getting in the way if using a headless service. You should always check DNS records before making connections.

Discovering services from within your Pod

There are two means by which services are visible from within your Pods. The first is through environment variables that are added to all Pods in the same namespace as the service.

When you add a service (using `kubectl create`, or `kubectl apply`), the service is registered within Kubernetes and thereafter any Pods that are started will get environment variables set that reference the services. For example, if we created the preceding first example service, and then ran:

```
kubectl get services
```

We would see the service listed:

```
NAME              CLUSTER-IP      EXTERNAL-IP    PORT(S)    AGE
flask             10.0.0.61       <none>         80/TCP     2d
kubernetes        10.0.0.1        <none>         443/TCP    5d
```

If you looked inside that container, you would see environment variables associated with both services listed previously. Those environment variables are:

```
env
```

```
KUBERNETES_PORT=tcp://10.0.0.1:443
KUBERNETES_SERVICE_PORT=443
KUBERNETES_PORT_443_TCP_ADDR=10.0.0.1
KUBERNETES_PORT_443_TCP_PORT=443
KUBERNETES_PORT_443_TCP_PROTO=tcp
KUBERNETES_PORT_443_TCP=tcp://10.0.0.1:443
KUBERNETES_SERVICE_PORT_HTTPS=443
KUBERNETES_SERVICE_HOST=10.0.0.1
FLASK_SERVICE_PORT_80_TCP_ADDR=10.0.0.61
FLASK_SERVICE_PORT_80_TCP_PORT=80
FLASK_SERVICE_PORT_80_TCP_PROTO=tcp
FLASK_SERVICE_PORT_80_TCP=tcp://10.0.0.61:80
FLASK_SERVICE_SERVICE_HOST=10.0.0.61
FLASK_SERVICE_SERVICE_PORT=80
FLASK_SERVICE_PORT=tcp://10.0.0.61:80
```

(The preceding output has been re-ordered to make it easier to see the values and some extraneous environment variables have been removed.)

For each service, there are environment variables defined that provide the IP address, port, and protocol with a couple of name variations. Note that this IP address is not the IP address of any underlying Pods, but an IP address within the Kubernetes cluster that the service is managing as a single endpoint for accessing the selected Pods.

WARNING: Ordering is critical with services! If Pods exist prior to the Service being defined, then the environment variables for that service will not exist within those Pods. Restarting the Pods, or scaling them down to 0 and back up (forcing the containers to be killed and recreated) will resolve it, but in general it's best to always define and apply your service declarations first.

DNS for services

Not originally part of the core distribution, there is a cluster add-on that is now included for all clusters in version 1.3 (and later) that provides internal DNS services for Kubernetes. Minikube, for example, includes this add-on, and it is likely already running within your cluster.

A DNS entry is created and coordinates with every service defined, so that you can request the DNS entry for `<service>` or `<service>.<namespace>`, and the internal DNS services will provide you with a correct internal IP address.

For example, if we exposed the `flask` deployment with the `expose` command, the service would be listed in DNS from our containers. We could open an interactive Terminal to an existing Pod and check on that DNS:

```
kubectl exec flask-1908233635-d6stj -it -- /bin/sh

/ # nslookup flask
nslookup: can't resolve '(null)': Name does not resolve
Name: flask
Address 1: 10.0.0.168 flask.default.svc.cluster.local
```

The service gets an internal A record (address record in DNS) for every service at `<servicename>.<namespace>.svc.cluster.local`, and as a shortcut, they can generally be referenced within the Pods as `<servicename>.<namespace>.svc`, or more simply `<servicename>` for Pods that are all within the same namespace.

NOTE: Tacking on a namespace should only be done when you are explicitly trying to refer to a service in another namespace. Leaving the namespace off makes your manifest inherently more reusable, since you can stamp out an entire stack of services with static routing configuration into arbitrary namespaces.

Exposing services outside the cluster

Everything we have discussed so far has been about representing services inside the Kubernetes cluster. The service concept is also how applications are exposed outside of a cluster.

The default service type is ClusterIP, and we briefly touched upon the type `ExternalName`, which was added to Kubernetes 1.7 to provide an external DNS reference. There are two other types that are very common, `NodePort` and `LoadBalancer`, which are specifically oriented towards exposing a service outside of the Kubernetes cluster.

Service type – LoadBalancer

The `LoadBalancer` service type is not supported in all Kubernetes clusters. It is most commonly used with cloud providers such as Amazon, Google, or Microsoft, and coordinates with the cloud provider's infrastructure to set up an external `LoadBalancer` that will forward traffic into the service.

How you define these services is specific to your cloud provider, and slightly different between AWS, Azure, and Google. `LoadBalancer` service definitions may also include recommended annotations to help define how to handle and process SSL traffic. More details about the specifics for each provider can be found in the Kubernetes documentation. The documentation on the LoadBalancer definitions is available at `https://kubernetes.io/docs/concepts/services-networking/service/#type-loadbalancer`.

Service type – NodePort

When you are using a Kubernetes cluster on premises, or in our case in a virtual machine on your development machine with Minikube, NodePort is a common service type used to expose your services. NodePort relies on the underlying hosts upon which you run Kubernetes to be accessible on your local network, and exposes the service definition through a high-numbered port on all of the Kubernetes cluster nodes.

These services are exactly like the default ClusterIP services, with the exception that they have a type of `NodePort`. If we wanted to create such a service with the `expose` command, we could add a `--type=Nodeport` option to our earlier command, for example:

```
kubectl delete service flask

kubectl expose deploy flask --port 5000 --type=NodePort
```

This results in a definition that would look something like the following:

```
kubectl get service flask -o yaml

apiVersion: v1
kind: Service
metadata:
  creationTimestamp: 2017-10-14T18:19:07Z
  labels:
    run: flask
  name: flask
  namespace: default
  resourceVersion: "19788"
  selfLink: /api/v1/namespaces/default/services/flask
  uid: 2afdd3aa-b10c-11e7-b586-080027768e7d
spec:
  clusterIP: 10.0.0.39
  externalTrafficPolicy: Cluster
  ports:
  - nodePort: 31501
    port: 5000
    protocol: TCP
    targetPort: 5000
  selector:
    run: flask
  sessionAffinity: None
  type: NodePort
status:
  loadBalancer: {}
```

Notice `nodePort: 31501`. This is the port that the service is exposed on. With this enabled, where previously we had to use port-forward or a proxy to access our service, we can now do so directly through the service.

Minikube service

Minikube has a service command to make it very easy to both get and access this service. While you could get the IP address for your `minikube` host with `minikube ip` and put that together with the previous port, you could also use the `minikube service` command to make a combined URL in one command:

```
minikube service flask --url
```

This should return a value like this:

```
http://192.168.64.100:31505
```

And `minikube` has the helpful option of opening a browser window with your default if you use the following command:

```
minikube service flask

Opening kubernetes service default/flask in default browser...
```

If you had a service enabled, but no Pods are backing that service, then you would see a connection refused message.

You can list all the services exposed from your instance of `minikube` with the following:

```
minikube service list
```

You would then see output like the following:

```
|-------------|-----------------------|------------------------------|
| NAMESPACE   |        NAME           |            URL               |
|-------------|-----------------------|------------------------------|
| default     | flask                 | http://192.168.99.100:31501  |
| default     | kubernetes            | No node port                 |
| kube-system | kube-dns              | No node port                 |
| kube-system | kubernetes-dashboard  | http://192.168.99.100:30000  |
|-------------|-----------------------|------------------------------|
```

Example service – Redis

We will create an example service within Kubernetes, to show you how you can connect to services, and use them to architect your code. Redis (`https://redis.io`) is a super-flexible data store that you may already be familiar with, and it is easy to use from both Python and Node.js.

Redis is already available as a container, and it is easily found on the Docker Hub (`https://hub.docker.com/`) as a container image. There are several options available, with the relevant tags listed on the Docker Hub web page:

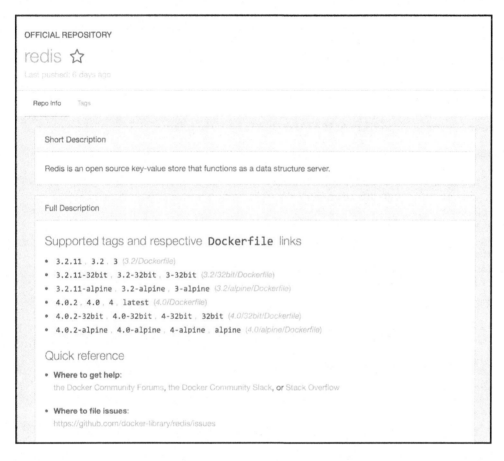

We can use this image with the `kubectl run` command to create a deployment, and then with the `kubectl expose` command to create a service to map to the Pods within the deployment:

```
kubectl run redis --image=docker.io/redis:alpine
```

We will create a deployment named `redis`, and through that deployment download the image and start running it. We can see the Pod operational:

```
kubectl get pods
```

```
NAME                   READY    STATUS     RESTARTS   AGE
flask-1908233635-d6stj  1/1     Running    1          1d
redis-438047616-3c9kt   1/1     Running    0          21s
```

You can run an interactive shell within this Pod using the `kubectl exec` command and interrogate the running instance of `redis` directly:

```
kubectl exec -it redis-438047616-3c9kt -- /bin/sh

/data # ps aux
PID   USER      TIME    COMMAND
    1 redis      0:22   redis-server
   24 root       0:00   /bin/sh
   32 root       0:00   ps aux
/data # which redis-server
/usr/local/bin/redis-server
/data # /usr/local/bin/redis-server --version
Redis server v=4.0.2 sha=00000000:0 malloc=jemalloc-4.0.3 bits=64
build=7f502971648182f2
/data # exit
```

We can expose this service both inside our cluster instance and outside of `minikube` using `NodePort`. The default port for `redis` is `6379`, so we will want to make sure to include that in our service:

```
kubectl expose deploy redis --port=6379 --type=NodePort

service "redis" exposed
```

If we then list the services available:

```
kubectl get services
```

```
NAME        TYPE        CLUSTER-IP    EXTERNAL-IP   PORT(S)          AGE
flask       NodePort    10.0.0.39     <none>        5000:31501/TCP   3h
kubernetes  ClusterIP   10.0.0.1      <none>        443/TCP          1d
redis       NodePort    10.0.0.119    <none>        6379:30336/TCP   15s
```

We will see `redis` exposed on port `30336` using `NodePort`. The `minikube service` command won't be immediately helpful here because redis isn't an HTTP-based API, but using `minikube ip` we can put together a command to interact with `redis` through its command-line interface:

```
minikube ip

192.168.99.100
```

To interact with `redis`, we can use the `redis-cli` command-line tool. If you don't have the tool, you can follow along with this example by downloading it from `https://redis.io/download`:

```
redis-cli -h 192.168.99.100 -p 30336

192.168.99.100:30336>
192.168.99.100:30336> ping
PONG
```

Finding the Redis service

WIth the Redis service up and running, we can now use it from our own Pod. As we mentioned previously, there are two ways to locate the service: an environment variable with a name based on the service will be set with the host IP and port, or you can use a DNS entry based on the name of the service.

The environment variables will only be set on Pods that are created after the service. If you still have the `flask` Pod up and running as per our previous example, then it will not show the environment variables. If we create a new Pod, even a temporary one, then it will include the service in the environment variables. This is because environment variables are set based on the state of Kubernetes at the time that the Pods are created and they are not updated during the life of the Pod.

DNS, however, is updated dynamically with the state of the cluster. While not instantaneous, this means that a DNS request will start returning as expected after the service is created. And because the DNS entries are predictable based on namespace and service name, they can easily be included in configuration data.

NOTE: Use DNS for service discovery, not environment variables, because DNS updates with your environment, but environment variables do not.

If you still have a Flask or Node.js Pod running, get the Pod name and open a shell within it:

```
kubectl get pods

NAME                        READY     STATUS      RESTARTS    AGE
flask-1908233635-d6stj      1/1       Running     1           2d
redis-438047616-3c9kt       1/1       Running     0           1d

kubectl exec flask-1908233635-d6stj -it -- sh
```

And then, we can look up the Redis service we just created in the default namespace, which should be listed as `redis.default`:

```
/ # nslookup redis.default
nslookup: can't resolve '(null)': Name does not resolve
Name:       redis.default
Address 1: 10.0.0.119 redis.default.svc.cluster.local
```

Using Redis from Python

Once we can access our Python Pod, we can invoke Python interactively and access Redis. Recall that when we created this Pod, we didn't include any Python libraries for Redis. For this example, we can install them on the fly, but that change will only be relevant for this single Pod, and for the duration of this Pod's life cycle. If the Pod dies, any changes (such as adding the Redis library) will be lost.

This makes a great tool for interactively and dynamically trying things out, but remember that you will need to incorporate any desired changes back into the process of creating the container as well.

Within the `flask` Pod, go to the code directory we set up and we can add the Redis library using PIP:

```
# cd /opt/exampleapp/
/opt/exampleapp # pip3 install redis
Collecting redis
  Downloading redis-2.10.6-py2.py3-none-any.whl (64kB)
    100% |████████████████████████████████| 71kB
```

```
803kB/s
Installing collected packages: redis
Successfully installed redis-2.10.6
```

Now, we can interactively try Redis from the Python interpreter:

```
/opt/exampleapp # python3
Python 3.6.1 (default, May  2 2017, 15:16:41)
[GCC 6.3.0] on linux
Type "help", "copyright", "credits" or "license" for more information.
>>> import redis
>>> redis_db = redis.StrictRedis(host="redis.default", port=6379, db=0)
>>> redis_db.ping()
True
>>> redis_db.set("hello", "world")
True
>>> redis_db.get("hello")
b'world'
```

To match this and enable this library for our Python code, we will want to add it to the `requirements.txt` file that is used by the Docker build process to install all the dependencies. We would then want to rebuild the container and push it to the registry, and then recreate the Pods so that the new image was used.

Updating the Flask deployment

The steps to this update process are:

- Update the code or dependencies in source control
- Build and tag a new Docker image
- Push the Docker image to the container repository
- Update the deployment resource in Kubernetes to use this new image

An example of stepping through this will highlight how you can start to roll out code updates, either directly or by adding additional services, to your application.

For this example, we will not change any code immediately, we just want to include the Redis Python library so that it's available. To do this, we would normally use PIP to install the library we want. With our Python example, we are installing all the required libraries with PIP through the dependency listing `requirements.txt`, which gets invoked during the Docker build process:

- Update the `requirements.txt` file to include Redis:

```
Flask==0.12.2
redis
```

> Not specifying a specific version is an indicator to PIP that you want it to locate the most recent version and install it. If you know the version of the `redis` library already, or want to pin it explicitly, you can add it, such as `==2.10.6` (akin to what was added with Flask previously).

- Rebuild the `docker` image:

```
docker build .
Sending build context to Docker daemon   162.8kB
Step 1/9 : FROM alpine
...
Removing intermediate container d3ee8e22a095
Successfully built 63635b37136a
```

> In this example, I am explicitly rebuilding without a tag, intending to add that one in a second step:

- Tag the `build`

> To tag a `build`, use a command like the following:

```
docker tag <image_id>
<container_repository>/<group_name>/<container_name>:<tag>
```

> The command I used for this example was:

```
docker tag 63635b37136a quay.io/kubernetes-for-developers/flask:0.1.1
```

> Once the build has the tag you'd like associated with it (in this case, we used `0.1.1`), you could tag this with more than one value if you wanted to reference the image in different ways. Once it is tagged, you need to make the images available to your cluster.

- Push the container image:

```
docker push quay.io/kubernetes-for-developers/flask:0.1.1

The push refers to a repository [quay.io/kubernetes-for-developers/flask]
34f306a8fb12: Pushed
801c9c3c42e7: Pushed
e94771c57351: Pushed
9c99a7f27402: Pushed
993056b64287: Pushed
439786010e37: Pushed
5bef08742407: Layer already exists
0.1.1: digest:
sha256:dc734fc37d927c6074b32de73cd19eb2a279c3932a06235d0a91eb66153110ff
size: 5824
```

Container tags do not need to be in a dot version format. In this case, I chose a tag that was simple and contextual, but also explicit rather than reusing `latest`, which could lead to some confusion over which `latest` we were running.

NOTE: Use tags that are meaningful, and avoid using `latest` as a tag when running Kubernetes. You will save yourself an immense amount of time debugging exactly which version is running if you use explicit tags at the start. Even something as simple as a Git hash or very explicit timestamp can be used as a tag.

Now, we can update the deployment to indicate that we want Kubernetes to use this new image we have created. Kubernetes supports several commands that will do what we want, such as `kubectl replace`, which will take a changed specification in YAML or JSON format, where you could change any of the values. There is an older command, `kubectl rolling-update`, but that only works with replication controllers.

NOTE: Replication controllers were an early version of ReplicaSet, and have been replaced by ReplicaSets and Deployments.

The `kubectl rolling-update` command has been replaced by a combination of `kubectl set` and `kubectl rollout`, which applies to deployments as well as some additional resources. The `kubectl set` command helps with frequent updates to some of the more common changes, such as changing an image in a deployment, environment variables defined within a deployment, and so on.

The `kubectl apply` command is similar to `kubectl replace`, taking a file (or set of files) and dynamically applying differences to all the kubernetes resources referenced. We will look deeper into using the `kubectl apply` command in the next chapter, where we will also look into maintaining the definitions of your application and its structure alongside your code as declarative files, rather than relying on the ordering and invocation of interactive commands.

As you can see, there are a lot of options to choose from; all of which boil down to changing the resources that are defined within Kubernetes to let it perform some action.

Let's take the most general option and use the `kubectl replace` command, stepping through the process to make it clear exactly what we are changing.

First, get the deployment we are changing:

```
kubectl get deploy flask -o yaml --export > flask_deployment.yaml
```

Now, open the `flask_deployment.yaml` file in a text editor and find the line that specifies the image. The current image version can be found in the file under `template -> spec -> containers`, and should read something like the following:

```
- image: quay.io/kubernetes-for-developers/flask:latest
```

Edit the file and change this to reference our updated tag:

```
- image: quay.io/kubernetes-for-developers/flask:0.1.1
```

And now, we can use the `kubectl replace` command to tell Kubernetes to update it:

```
kubectl replace -f flask_deployment.yaml
deployment "flask" replaced
```

This change will initiate an update of the resources associated with the deployment, in this case doing a rolling update or rollout. The deployment controller will automatically create a new ReplicaSet and Pod for the deployment, and terminate the old one once it is available. This process will also maintain the scale, or number of replicas running, during this process, and can take some time.

 Note: You should also be aware of the command `kubectl edit`, which allows you to specify a resource, such as a deployment/flask, and edit the YAML declaration for it directly. When you save the editor window that was opened with `kubectl edit`, it does the actions as the `kubectl replace` command previously.

You can use `kubectl get pods` to get a view of this happening:

```
kubectl get pods

NAME                        READY   STATUS              RESTARTS   AGE
flask-1082750864-nf99q      0/1     ContainerCreating   0          27s
flask-1908233635-d6stj      1/1     Terminating         1          2d
redis-438047616-3c9kt       1/1     Running             0          1d
```

Since there is only a single Pod with a single container, it will not take long to complete, and when it is done you will see something like the following:

```
kubectl get pods

NAME                        READY   STATUS    RESTARTS   AGE
flask-1082750864-nf99q      1/1     Running   0          1m
redis-438047616-3c9kt       1/1     Running   0          1d
```

You may notice that the replica-set hash has changed, as well as the Pod's unique identifier. If we now access this Pod with an interactive session, we can see that the library has been loaded. This time, we will use Python's interactive REPL directly:

```
kubectl exec flask-1082750864-nf99q -it -- python3

Python 3.6.1 (default, Oct  2 2017, 20:46:59)
[GCC 6.3.0] on linux
Type "help", "copyright", "credits" or "license" for more information.
>>> import redis
>>> redis_db = redis.StrictRedis(host="redis.default", port=6379, db=0)
>>> redis_db.ping()
True
>>> redis_db.get('hello')
b'world'
>>> exit()
```

Deployments and rollouts

Changing the image within a deployment initiates a rollout. A deployment rollout is an asynchronous process that takes time to complete, and is controlled by values defined within the deployment. If you look at the resource file that we dumped into YAML and updated, you will see the defaults that were created for the deployment when we made it with the `kubectl run` command.

Under `spec -> strategy`, you will see the default specification of how it will handle an update:

```
strategy:
  rollingUpdate:
    maxSurge: 1
    maxUnavailable: 1
  type: RollingUpdate
```

As of Kubernetes 1.8, there are two strategies available: `Recreate` and `RollingUpdate`. `RollingUpdate` is the default, and is intended for the primary use case of maintaining service availability while doing code updates. Recreate operates differently: killing all existing pods before creating new pods with updated versions, which may result in a short outage.

The `RollingUpdate` is controlled by two values: `maxUnavailable` and `maxSurge`, which serve to provide some controls so that you can have a minimum number of pods available to handle your service while the update rolls out. You can find details on these two controlling options in the documentation at `https://kubernetes.io/docs/concepts/workloads/controllers/deployment/`, along with some additional options that influence the rollout process.

Rollout history

Kubernetes also maintains a history (the length of which can also be controlled) for rollouts. You can see the state of a rollout, as well as its history, through the `kubectl rollout` command.

For example, to see the status of the rollout that we just did:

```
kubectl rollout status deployment/flask

deployment "flask" successfully rolled out
```

And you can view the history of the changes to the deployment with the following:

```
kubectl rollout history deployment/flask

deployments "flask"
REVISION   CHANGE-CAUSE
1          <none>
2          <none>
```

change-cause is tracked as an annotation on the deployment resource, which (as of Kubernetes 1.8) does not exist, since we created the deployment with the default kubectl run command. There is a --record=true option, which can be used with kubectl run, kubectl set, and several other commands that explicitly set these annotations. We will discuss annotations, more detail in the next chapter.

We can go ahead and create an annotation to match what we just did with the following command:

```
kubectl annotate deployment flask kubernetes.io/change-cause='deploying
image 0.1.1'

deployment "flask" annotated
```

Now, if we look at the history, you will see the following displayed:

```
kubectl rollout history deployment/flask

deployments "flask"
REVISION   CHANGE-CAUSE
1          <none>
2          deploying image 0.1.1
```

You can get more detailed information using the --revision option with the history command. For example:

```
kubectl rollout history deployment flask --revision=2
```

This would return something like the following:

```
deployments "flask" with revision #2
Pod Template:
  Labels: pod-template-hash=1082750864
  run=flask
  Annotations: kubernetes.io/change-cause=deploying image 0.1.1
  Containers:
   flask:
    Image: quay.io/kubernetes-for-developers/flask:0.1.1
    Port: <none>
   Environment: <none>
    Mounts: <none>
  Volumes: <none>
```

You can see the annotation that we just created as well as the container image version that we changed.

Rollout undo

The deployment resource includes the capability to revert back to a previous version. The simplest form of this is the `kubectl rollout undo` command. If you wanted to revert back to the Pods running at the previous image, you could use the following command:

```
kubectl rollout undo deployment/flask
```

This would reverse the process, doing the same steps except moving back to the earlier deployment resource configuration.

If you have multiple versions, you can roll back to a specific version with the `--revision` option. You can also watch the process updates with the `rollout status` command and the `-w` option. For example, if you just invoked the `undo` command, you could watch the progress with the following command:

```
kubectl rollout status deployment/flask -w

Waiting for rollout to finish: 0 of 1 updated replicas are available...
deployment "flask" successfully rolled out
```

The deployment history keeps rolling version numbers forward, even when you undo or roll back to a previous version. If you are familiar with using Git for source control, it is very similar to using the `git revert` command. If you looked at the history after an undo, you might see the following:

```
kubectl rollout history deployment/flask

deployments "flask"
REVISION   CHANGE-CAUSE
2          <none>
3          <none>
```

Updating with the kubectl set command

Updating the container image is a very common task. You may also update that value directly with the `kubectl set` command, as we mentioned previously. If the deployment resource has the `change-cause` annotation added, then using the `kubectl set` command will update the annotation as you make changes. For example:

```
# delete the deployment entirely
kubectl delete deployment flask
deployment "flask" deleted
```

```
# create a new deployment with the run command
kubectl run flask --image=quay.io/kubernetes-for-developers/flask:latest
deployment "flask" created

# add the initial annotation for change-cause
kubectl annotate deployment/flask kubernetes.io/change-cause='initial
deployment'
deployment "flask" annotated

# update the container version with kubectl set
kubectl set image deployment/flask flask=quay.io/kubernetes-for-
developers/flask:0.1.1
deployment "flask" image updated
```

If you now look at the history, it will include the changes made with the set command:

```
kubectl rollout history deployment/flask

deployments "flask"
REVISION   CHANGE-CAUSE
1          initial deployment
2          kubectl set image deployment/flask flask=quay.io/kubernetes-for-
developers/flask:0.1.1
```

As you create services and deployments with your code, you may find it convenient to quickly create deployments and update them with these commands.

Note: Another reason to avoid using the latest tag when referencing container images: updates to deployments require a change to the deployment specification. If you were just updating the image behind the deployment, the deployment would never know when to update it.

The rollouts that we have been describing so far are all idempotent and expect that you can change the containers seamlessly forward or back. This expects that the container images you are creating and deploying are stateless and don't have to manage existing persistent data. That will not always be the case, and Kubernetes is actively adding support for handling these more complex needs with a feature called StatefulSets, which we will discuss further in a future chapter.

Summary

In this chapter, we started with reviewing some practical notes about how to develop your code to run within a container. We reviewed options for getting logging from your program, and then some techniques for accessing the Pods when your code is running. We then reviewed the Kubernetes concepts of labels and selectors, showing how they are used on the commands we have used so far, and then looked at the Kubernetes service concept to expose sets of Pods (such as in a deployment) to each other, or external to a Kubernetes cluster. Finally, we ended the chapter by looking at deployment rollouts, and how you can roll out changes as well as see the history of those changes.

4
Declarative Infrastructure

Kubernetes is inherently a declarative system. In prior chapters, we have explored Kubernetes and some of its key concepts using commands such as `kubectl run` and `kubectl expose`. These commands are all imperative: do this thing now. Kubernetes does this by managing these resources as objects themselves. `kubectl` and the API server translate these requests into resource representations, and then store them, and it is the job of the various controllers to understand the current state and make it as requested.

We can take advantage of the declarative structures directly—all the Services, Pods, and more can be represented by either JSON or YAML files. In this chapter, we will move to define your applications as a declarative infrastructure. We will take the existing simple Kubernetes Pods and put them into declarations that you can manage alongside your code; stored in source control and deployed to run your software. We will also introduce ConfigMaps and Secrets, to allow you to define your configuration as well as your application structure, and explore how to use them.

The sections for this chapter include:

- Imperative versus declarative
- Declaring your first application
- Kubernetes resource—Annotations
- Kubernetes resource—ConfigMap
- Kubernetes resource—Secrets
- Python example with ConfigMap

Imperative versus declarative commands

Our examples thus far have focused on quick and imperative commands such as kubectl run to create a deployment that in turn runs our software. This is convenient for something quick, but does not easily expose the full flexibility of the API. To leverage all the options available via Kubernetes, it is often more effective to manage files that describe the deployment you want.

When using these files, you can use commands such as kubectl create, kubectl delete, and kubectl replace along with the -f option to specify the file to use. The imperative commands are easy and effective for simple setups, but you quickly need a sequence of commands that you repeat again and again to take full advantage of all the capabilities. You might be storing sets of these commands in a cheatsheet, but that can get cumbersome and isn't always clear.

Kubernetes offers a declarative mechanism as well, leveraging the kubectl apply command, which takes in files, reviews the current state, and manages the updates—creating, removing, and so on—as needed, while also keeping a simple audit log of the changes.

I recommend using the kubectl apply command for anything more complex than running a single process, which will likely be most of your developed services. You may not need the audit trails in development. You probably would in a staging/canary environment or in production, so being familiar and comfortable with them is advantageous to understand them.

Best of all, but keeping the description of your application in files, you can include them in source control, treating them like code. This gives you a consistent means of sharing that application structure among your team members, all of which can use it to provide a consistent environment.

The kubectl apply command has an -f option to specify a file or directory of files, as well as an -R option that will recursively descend directories if you are establishing a complex deployment.

As we go forward in this book, I will use declarative commands and configurations in YAML format (with comments) to describe and manipulate the Kubernetes resources. JSON can be used as well if you have a strong preference.

Note: If you would like a command-line tool to parse YAML, there is an equivalent to `jq` for JSON: `yq`. Our examples won't go into that much detail, but if you want to use the tool you can find more information about it at `https://yq.readthedocs.io`.

A wall of YAML

What do these configurations look like? The vast majority of them are managed in YAML format, and the options and configurations can seem overwhelming. Each resource in Kubernetes has its own format, and some of those formats are changing and under active development. You will notice that some of the APIs and object structures will actively reference either `alpha` or `beta` to indicate the state of maturity of those resources in the project. The project tends to use these terms in a very conservative manner:

- `alpha` tends to mean it is an early experiment and the data format may change, but something achieving the end goal will likely exist
- `beta` is more solid than purely experimental, and can likely be used in production loads, although the specific resource format hasn't been entirely locked down and may change slightly over Kubernetes releases

Be aware that alpha and beta APIs evolve as new releases of Kubernetes are made available. If you use an earlier version, it may become deprecated and ultimately unavailable. You will need to track these updates with the version of Kubernetes you are using.

The formal documentation for the resources, their options, and formats, are hosted at `https://kubernetes.io` under reference documentation. As I write this, the current released version is 1.8, and the reference documentation for that is available at `https://kubernetes.io/docs/api-reference/v1.8/`. This documentation is generated from the Kubernetes project source and updated each release, which generally comes out approximately every three months.

In addition to wading through the reference documentation, you can get the declaration from existing Kubernetes objects. When you request the Kubernetes resource using the `kubectl get` command you can add the `-o yaml --export` option.

The `-o yaml` option could instead be `-o json` if you prefer that format. `--export` will strip out some extraneous information that is specific to the current state and identity of the resource within Kubernetes, and won't benefit you to store externally.

Although the capability isn't quite complete with version 1.8, you should be able to ask for all resources in a namespace, store those configurations, and use those files to reproduce it exactly. In practice, there are a few bumps along the way, as the exported versions don't always have exactly what you want. At this point, it is far better to manage your own declaration files.

Finally, I recommend using YAML as the format for these declarations. You could use JSON, but YAML allows you to add comments into the declarations, which are immensely useful for others reading those files—a capability that the JSON format doesn't share.

Creating a simple deployment

Let's start by looking at what `kubectl run` created for us, and work from there. We created the earlier simple deployments with the following commands:

```
kubectl run flask --image=quay.io/kubernetes-for-developers/flask:0.1.1 --
port=5000
```

In the examples, we dumped the state of the declaration with the `kubectl get deployment flask -o json` command. Let's repeat that except using the `-o yaml --export` option:

```
kubectl get deployment flask -o yaml --export
```

The output should look something like the following:

```
apiVersion: extensions/v1beta1
kind: Deployment
metadata:
  annotations:
    deployment.kubernetes.io/revision: "1"
  creationTimestamp: null
  generation: 1
  labels:
    run: flask
  name: flask
  selfLink: /apis/extensions/v1beta1/namespaces/default/deployments/flask
spec:
  replicas: 1
  selector:
    matchLabels:
      run: flask
  strategy:
    rollingUpdate:
```

```
      maxSurge: 1
      maxUnavailable: 1
    type: RollingUpdate
  template:
    metadata:
      creationTimestamp: null
      labels:
        run: flask
    spec:
      containers:
      - image: quay.io/kubernetes-for-developers/flask:latest
        imagePullPolicy: Always
        name: flask
        ports:
        - containerPort: 5000
          protocol: TCP
        resources: {}
        terminationMessagePath: /dev/termination-log
        terminationMessagePolicy: File
      dnsPolicy: ClusterFirst
      restartPolicy: Always
      schedulerName: default-scheduler
      securityContext: {}
      terminationGracePeriodSeconds: 30
  status: {}
```

The general format of any Kubernetes resource will have the same top four objects:

- apiVersion
- kind
- metadata
- spec

If you are retrieving information from Kubernetes, you will see a fifth key: status. Status isn't expected to be defined by a user, and is provided by Kubernetes when retrieving objects to share their current state. If you miss the --export option on a kubectl get command, it will include status.

You will see metadata scattered throughout the objects, as the objects are related to each other and build conceptually on each other. The metadata is included per resource, even though it may be combined (as shown previously) into a single reference. For the deployment we created, it is using a declarative reference for a deployment, which wraps a ReplicaSet, which wraps a Pod.

You can see the formal definition of each of these at the following URLs:

- **Deployment:** `https://kubernetes.io/docs/api-reference/v1.8/#deployment-v1beta2-apps`
- **ReplicaSet** : `https://kubernetes.io/docs/api-reference/v1.8/#replicaset-v1beta2-apps`
- **Pod:** `https://kubernetes.io/docs/api-reference/v1.8/#pod-v1-core`

You may notice that ReplicaSet and Deployment are nearly identical. Deployment extends ReplicaSet and every instance of Deployment will have at least one ReplicaSet. Deployment includes declarative options (and the responsibility) for how to perform updates on running software. Kubernetes recommends that when you're deploying code, you use a Deployment over a ReplicaSet directly, in order to specify exactly how you want it to react as you update it.

Within the deployment `spec` (`https://kubernetes.io/docs/api-reference/v1.8/#deploymentspec-v1beta2-apps`), all the items under the key template are defined from the Pod template specification. You can view the details of the Pod template specification at `https://kubernetes.io/docs/api-reference/v1.8/#podtemplatespec-v1-core`.

If you take a look at the online documentation, you will see a large number of options that we're not specifying. When they aren't specified, Kubernetes will still fill in values using the defaults defined in the specification.

You can specify as completely, or as lightly, as you desire. The number of required fields is quite small. You typically only need to define the optional fields when you want a different value than the default. As an example, for a deployment, the required fields are a name and the image to be deployed.

I recommend keeping to a minimal set of declarations in YAML as you create them for your own code. This will support easier understanding of your resource declarations, and along with the liberal use of comments, should make the resulting files easy to understand.

Declaring your first application

Go ahead and pick one of the examples and create a deployment declaration, and try creating one using the declaration.

I recommend making a directory called `deploy`, and putting your declaration file within that. This is using the `flask` example:

```
flask.yml

apiVersion: apps/v1beta1
kind: Deployment
metadata:
  name: flask
  labels:
    run: flask
spec:
  template:
    metadata:
      labels:
          app: flask
    spec:
      containers:
      - name: flask
        image: quay.io/kubernetes-for-developers/flask:0.1.1
        ports:
        - containerPort: 5000
```

Remove the existing deployment before you try out your file:

```
kubectl delete deployment flask
```

It is a good practice to use the `--validate` option to have `kubectl` check the files, and you can use it with `--dry-run` to compare the file to anything existing in Kubernetes to let you know specifically what it will be doing. YAML is easy to read, and unfortunately even easier to make formatting mistakes due to its use of whitespace to define the structure. Using the `--validate` option, `kubectl` will warn you of missing fields or other problems. Without it, `kubectl` will often fail quietly, simply ignoring what it doesn't understand:

```
kubectl apply -f deploy/flask.yml --dry-run --validate
```

You should see results that look as follows:

```
deployment "flask" created (dry run)
```

If you happened to make a typo, you'll see an error reported in the output. I made an intentional typo in one of the keys, `metadata`, and the result was as follows:

```
error: error validating "deploy/flask.yml": error validating data: found
invalid field metdata for v1.PodTemplateSpec; if you choose to ignore these
errors, turn validation off with --validate=false
```

Once you are happy that the data validates and will work as you expect, you can create the object with the following command:

```
kubectl apply -f deploy/flask.yml
```

It is still easy to make minor mistakes that aren't immediately apparent, but become clear when you try and run the code. You can use the kubectl get command to inspect specific resources. I would encourage you to also use the kubectl describe command to see not only the state of the resources, but all related events from Kubernetes about it:

```
kubectl describe deployment/flask
```

```
 Name: flask
Namespace: default
CreationTimestamp: Sun, 22 Oct 2017 14:03:27 -0700
Labels: run=flask
Annotations: deployment.kubernetes.io/revision=1
 kubectl.kubernetes.io/last-applied-
configuration={"apiVersion":"apps/v1beta1","kind":"Deployment","metadata":{
"annotations":{},"labels":{"run":"flask"},"name":"flask","namespace":"defau
lt"},"spec":{"t...
Selector: app=flask
Replicas: 1 desired | 1 updated | 1 total | 1 available | 0 unavailable
StrategyType: RollingUpdate
MinReadySeconds: 0
RollingUpdateStrategy: 25% max unavailable, 25% max surge
Pod Template:
 Labels: app=flask
 Containers:
 flask:
 Image: quay.io/kubernetes-for-developers/flask:0.1.1
 Port: 5000/TCP
 Environment: <none>
 Mounts: <none>
 Volumes: <none>
Conditions:
 Type Status Reason
 ---- ------ ------
 Available True MinimumReplicasAvailable
 Progressing True NewReplicaSetAvailable
OldReplicaSets: <none>
NewReplicaSet: flask-2003485262 (1/1 replicas created)
Events:
 Type Reason Age From Message
 ---- ------ ---- ---- -------
 Normal ScalingReplicaSet 5s deployment-controller Scaled up replica set
flask-2003485262 to 1
```

Once you are comfortable with the declaration working as expected, store it in source control along with your code. The example sections of this book will move to using stored configurations, and the Python and Node.js examples will be updated in this and future chapters.

> If you want to create Kubernetes resources and then later manage them with the `kubectl apply` command, you should use the `--save-config` option when running the `kubectl run` or `kubectl create` commands. This will explicitly add in the annotations that `kubectl apply` expects to be there when it's run. If they aren't there, the commands will still operate correctly, but you'll get a warning:

```
Warning: kubectl apply should be used on resource created by either kubectl
create --save-config or kubectl apply
```

ImagePullPolicy

If you use `:latest` tags in your code while trying things, you may have noticed that the value of `imagePullPolicy` was set to `Always`:

```
imagePullPolicy: Always
```

This tells Kubernetes to always attempt to load new Docker images from container repositories. If you use a tag other than `:latest`, then the default (`IfNotPresent`) will only attempt to reload the container images if it can't find them in its local cache.

This is a technique that can be very useful while you are frequently updating your code. I recommend only using this when you are working by yourself, as sharing the knowledge of what exactly `:latest` means can be difficult and lead to a great deal of confusion.

> It is generally considered a bad practice to use the `:latest` tag in any staging or production deployment, simply because of the uncertainty of what it references.

Audit trail

When you use the `kubectl apply` command, it automatically maintains an audit trail for you in the Kubernetes resources as annotations. If you use the following command:

```
kubectl describe deployment flask
```

You'll see fairly readable output akin to the following:

```
Name: flask
Namespace: default
CreationTimestamp: Sat, 16 Sep 2017 08:31:00 -0700
Labels: run=flask
Annotations: deployment.kubernetes.io/revision=1
kubectl.kubernetes.io/last-applied-
configuration={"apiVersion":"apps/v1beta1","kind":"Deployment","metadata":{
"annotations":{},"labels":{"run":"flask"},"name":"flask","namespace":"defau
lt"},"spec":{"t...
Selector: app=flask
Replicas: 1 desired | 1 updated | 1 total | 1 available | 0 unavailable
StrategyType: RollingUpdate
MinReadySeconds: 0
RollingUpdateStrategy: 25% max unavailable, 25% max surge
Pod Template:
  Labels: app=flask
  Containers:
   flask:
    Image: quay.io/kubernetes-for-developers/flask:0.1.1
    Port: 5000/TCP
    Environment: <none>
    Mounts: <none>
  Volumes: <none>
Conditions:
  Type Status Reason
  ---- ------ ------
  Available True MinimumReplicasAvailable
  Progressing True NewReplicaSetAvailable
OldReplicaSets: <none>
NewReplicaSet: flask-866287979 (1/1 replicas created)
Events:
  FirstSeen LastSeen Count From SubObjectPath Type Reason Message
  --------- -------- ----- ---- ------------- -------- ------ ------
  2d 2d 1 deployment-controller Normal ScalingReplicaSetScaled up replica
set flask-866287979 to 1
```

The audit trail I mentioned is contained in the
annotation `kubectl.kubernetes.io/last-applied-configuration`—which includes
the last applied configuration. Because that annotation is fairly lengthy, it is clipped a bit in
this output. You can see the full details if you dump the entire object with the following
command:

```
kubectl get deployment flask -o json
```

The information we're interested in here is `metadata | annotations`
`kubectl.kubernetes.io/last-applied-configuration`. The full detail in that
annotation might look something like the following:

```
 ● ● ●                    1. heckj@greyberry: ~ (bash)
heckj 2 ~ 2 $  kubectl get deployment flask -o json
{
    "apiVersion": "extensions/v1beta1",
    "kind": "Deployment",
    "metadata": {
        "annotations": {
            "deployment.kubernetes.io/revision": "1",
            "kubectl.kubernetes.io/last-applied-configuration": "{\"apiVersion\":\"apps/v1beta1\",\"k
ind\":\"Deployment\",\"metadata\":{\"annotations\":{},\"labels\":{\"run\":\"flask\"},\"name\":\"flask
\",\"namespace\":\"default\"},\"spec\":{\"template\":{\"metadata\":{\"labels\":{\"app\":\"flask\"}},\
"spec\":{\"containers\":[{\"envFrom\":[{\"configMapRef\":{\"name\":\"flask-config\"}}],\"image\":\"qu
ay.io/kubernetes-for-developers/flask:0.2.0\",\"name\":\"flask\",\"ports\":[{\"containerPort\":5000}]
,\"volumeMounts\":[{\"mountPath\":\"/etc/flask-config\",\"name\":\"config\",\"readOnly\":true}]}],\"v
olumes\":[{\"configMap\":{\"name\":\"flask-config\"},\"name\":\"config\"}]}}}}\n"
        },
        "creationTimestamp": "2017-11-30T02:35:27Z",
        "generation": 1,
        "labels": {
            "run": "flask"
        },
        "name": "flask",
        "namespace": "default",
        "resourceVersion": "3132",
        "selfLink": "/apis/extensions/v1beta1/namespaces/default/deployments/flask",
        "uid": "1fed2bdb-d577-11e7-83ad-62e8baafc447"
    },
```

Kubernetes resource – Annotations

Where labels and selectors are used for grouping and selecting sets of Kubernetes resources,
Annotations provide a means of adding resource-specific metadata that can be accessed by
either Kubernetes or in the containers it runs.

As you just saw, `kubectl apply` automatically applies an annotation to track the last applied configuration state of a resource when it is invoked. In the last chapter, you might have noticed the annotation that the deployment controllers used to track revision, `deployment.kubernetes.io/revision`, and we spoke of the `kubernetes.io/change-cause` annotation that was used by `kubectl` to display the change history of deployment rollouts.

Annotations can be simple values or complex blocks (as in the case of `kubectl.kubernetes.io/last-applied-configuration`). The examples so far are Kubernetes tools using annotations to share information, although annotations are also used to share information in a container for an application to use.

You might use them to include information such as adding version control revision information, a build number, relevant human-readable contact information, and so forth.

Like labels, annotations can be added using an imperative `kubectl` command: `kubectl annotate`. In general, annotations use the same key mechanism that labels use, so any annotation that includes `kubernetes.io` in its prefix is something from the Kubernetes project.

Labels are intended to group and organize Kubernetes objects – Pods, Deployments, Services, and so on. Annotations are intended to provide additional information specific to an instance (or a couple of instances) generally as additional data within the annotation itself.

Exposing labels and annotations in Pods

Kubernetes can expose data about a Pod in a container directly, typically as files in a specific filesystem, which your code can read and use. Labels, annotations, and more can be made available as files in your container through the container specification, and using what Kubernetes calls the `downwardAPI`.

This can be a convenient way to expose annotation information such as build time, source code reference hash, and so forth in a container so that your runtime code can read and reference the information.

To make the Pods labels and annotations available, you define a volume mount for the container, and then specify the `downwardAPI` and items from it for the volume mount point.

Update the `flask` deployment file:

```
apiVersion: apps/v1beta1
kind: Deployment
metadata:
  name: flask
  labels:
    run: flask
  annotations:
    example-key: example-data
spec:
  template:
    metadata:
      labels:
          app: flask
    spec:
      containers:
      - name: flask
        image: quay.io/kubernetes-for-developers/flask:0.1.1
        ports:
        - containerPort: 5000
        volumeMounts:
          - name: podinfo
            mountPath: /podinfo
            readOnly: false
      volumes:
        - name: podinfo
          downwardAPI:
            items:
              - path: "labels"
                fieldRef:
                  fieldPath: metadata.labels
              - path: "annotations"
                fieldRef:
                  fieldPath: metadata.annotations
```

The details in the lower section identify a mount point—a directory structure that will be created inside the container. It also specifies that the volume should be using the `downwardAPI` with specific metadata; in this case, the labels and annotations.

When you specify a volume mount location, take care not to specify a location that already exists and has files (such as/and so on) or the container may have trouble operating as expected. The mount point doesn't throw an error—it just overlays on whatever might already exist in the container at that location.

You can apply this updated declaration with the following command:

```
kubectl apply -f ./flask.yml
```

Now we can open a shell to that running Pod, with a command like the following:

```
kubectl exec flask-463137380-d4bfx -it -- sh
```

And in that active shell, run the following:

```
ls -l /podinfo
```

```
total 0
lrwxrwxrwx    1 root      root             18 Sep 16 18:14 annotations ->
..data/annotations
lrwxrwxrwx    1 root      root             13 Sep 16 18:14 labels ->
..data/labels
```

```
cat /podinfo/annotations
```

```
kubernetes.io/config.seen="2017-09-16T18:14:04.024412807Z"
kubernetes.io/config.source="api"
kubernetes.io/created-
by="{\"kind\":\"SerializedReference\",\"apiVersion\":\"v1\",\"reference\":{
\"kind\":\"ReplicaSet\",\"namespace\":\"default\",\"name\":\"flask-46313738
0\",\"uid\":\"d262ca60-9b0a-11e7-884c-0aef48c812e4\",\"apiVersion\":\"exten
sions\",\"resourceVersion\":\"121204\"}}\n"
```

```
cat /podinfo/labels
```

```
app="flask"
pod-template-hash="463137380"
```

You can compare this to the annotations on the Pod itself through the following:

```
kubectl describe pod flask-463137380-d4bfx
```

```
Name: flask-463137380-d4bfx
Namespace: default
Node: minikube/192.168.64.3
Start Time: Sat, 16 Sep 2017 11:14:04 -0700
Labels: app=flask
pod-template-hash=463137380
Annotations: kubernetes.io/created-
by={"kind":"SerializedReference","apiVersion":"v1","reference":{"kind":"Rep
licaSet","namespace":"default","name":"flask-463137380","uid":"d262ca60-9b0
a-11e7-884c-0aef48c812e4","a...
Status: Running
IP: 172.17.0.5
```

```
Created By:     ReplicaSet/flask-463137380
Controlled By:  ReplicaSet/flask-463137380
```

A variety of data about the Pods can be exposed in the Pods, and the same data can be exposed to Pods via environment variables. The full set of data that can be exposed is detailed in the Kubernetes documentation (https://kubernetes.io/docs/tasks/inject-data-application/downward-api-volume-expose-pod-information/).

While it may seem convenient and obvious to use this mechanism to provide a means of passing in configuration data, Kubernetes provides additional capabilities specifically for providing configuration to code within containers, including the private configuration needed for passwords, access tokens, and other secrets.

Kubernetes resource – ConfigMap

When you create containers as read-only instances of your code, you quickly want a means to provide small changes in the form of flags or configuration. Perhaps, more importantly, you do not want to include private details such as API keys, passwords, or authentication tokens in your container images.

Kubernetes supports two resources to help and link in exactly this kind of information. The first is a ConfigMap, which can be used individually or across Pods for your application deployment, providing a single place to update and propagate configuration for your application. Kubernetes also supports the concept of a Secret, a far more locked down type of configuration that is more tightly controlled and exposed only where you need it.

For example, one might use a ConfigMap to control basic configuration of the example Redis deployment, and a Secret to distribute sensitive authentication credentials for clients to connect.

Creating a ConfigMap

You can create a ConfigMap using the kubectl create configmap command, with the data for the configuration set on the command line, or coming from one or more files that you have stored. It also supports loading a directory of files for convenience.

Creating from single key/value pairs on the command line is very simple, but probably the least convenient for managing configuration. For example, run the following command:

```
kubectl create configmap example-config --from-literal=log.level=err
```

This will create a ConfigMap named `example-config` with a single key/value pair. You can see the list of all configurations loaded with the following:

```
kubectl get configmap
```

```
NAME              DATA      AGE
example-config    0         2d
```

And view that ConfigMap using the following:

```
kubectl describe configmap example-config
```

```
Name: example-config
Namespace: default
Labels: <none>
Annotations: <none>
Data
====
log.level:
----
err
Events: <none>
```

And you can also request the raw data in YAML format:

```
kubectl get configmap example-config -o yaml --export
```

```
apiVersion: v1
data:
  log.level: err
kind: ConfigMap
metadata:
  creationTimestamp: null
  name: example-config
  selfLink: /api/v1/namespaces/default/configmaps/example-config
```

And you can also request the raw data in JSON format:

```
kubectl get configmap example-config -o json --export
```

```
{
    "apiVersion": "v1",
    "data": {
        "log.level": "err"
    },
    "kind": "ConfigMap",
    "metadata": {
        "creationTimestamp": null,
```

```
        "name":  "example-config",
        "selfLink":  "/api/v1/namespaces/default/configmaps/example-config"
    }
}
```

The values for configurations created from literals will generally be strings.

If you want to create configuration values that your code can parse as a different type (number, Boolean, and so on), then you will want to either specify those configurations as files or define them as blobs inside the ConfigMap objects in YAML or JSON.

If you would prefer to manage the configuration in separate files, they can have multiple lines in a simple `key=value` format, one configuration per line. The `kubectl create configmap <name> --from-file <filename>` command will load those, creating a `configmap` name based on the filename, each with all the relevant data from the files included within it. If you already have configuration files that you're working with, you can use this option to make ConfigMaps based on those files.

For example, if you wanted a configuration file, `config.ini`, that you wanted to load into a ConfigMap:

```
[unusual]
greeting=hello
onoff=true
anumber=3
```

You could use the following command to create an `iniconfig` ConfigMap:

```
kubectl create configmap iniconfig --from-file config.ini --save-config
```

Dumping that data back out as a ConfigMap:

```
kubectl get configmap iniconfig -o yaml --export
```

Should return you something akin to the following:

```
apiVersion: v1
data:
  config.ini: |
    [unusual]
    greeting=hello
    onoff=true
    anumber=3
kind: ConfigMap
metadata:
  name: iniconfig
  selfLink: /api/v1/namespaces/default/configmaps/iniconfig
```

The pipe symbol (|) in the YAML output defines a multiline input. These kinds of configurations won't be directly available as environment variables, as they are invalid for that format. They can be made available as files once you add them to your Pod specification. Adding them to your Pod specification is very similar to using the downward API to expose labels or annotations in a Pod's containers as files.

Managing ConfigMaps

Once you have created a ConfigMap, you can't overwrite it with another ConfigMap using the `kubectl create` command. You can delete it and recreate it, although a more effective option would be managing the configuration declarations like other Kubernetes resources, updating it with the `kubectl apply` command.

If you created an initial ConfigMap using the `kubectl create` command while you're trying out some ideas, you can start managing that configuration using the `kubectl apply` command in the same fashion we used previously with deployments: exporting the YAML and then using `kubectl apply` from within that file.

For example, to get and store the configuration we created earlier in a deploy directory, you might use the following command:

```
kubectl get configmap example-config -o yaml --export > deploy/example-
config.yml
```

In the 1.7 release of Kubernetes, there are a few fields added in the export that aren't strictly needed, but also won't hurt anything if you leave them in. Looking at the file, you should see something like the following:

```
apiVersion: v1
data:
  log.level: err
kind: ConfigMap
metadata:
  creationTimestamp: null
  name: example-config
  selfLink: /api/v1/namespaces/default/configmaps/example-config
```

The keys of `data`, `apiVersion`, `kind`, and metadata are all critical, but some of the subkeys under metadata aren't required. For instance, you could delete `metadata.creationTimestamp` and `metadata.selfLink`.

You now still have the ConfigMap resource in Kubernetes, so the first time you run `kubectl apply`, it will alert you that you're doing something a bit unexpected:

```
kubectl apply -f deploy/example-config.yml

Warning: kubectl apply should be used on resource created by either kubectl
create --save-config or kubectl apply
configmap "example-config" configured
```

You can get rid of this warning by using the `--save-config` option with your `kubectl create` commands, which will include the annotations that `kubectl apply` expects to be there.

At this point, `kubectl apply` has applied its diff and made the relevant updates. If you now retrieve the data from Kubernetes, it will have the annotations that `kubectl apply` adds when updating resources:

```
kubectl get configmap example-config -o yaml --export

apiVersion: v1
data:
  log.level: err
kind: ConfigMap
metadata:
  annotations:
    kubectl.kubernetes.io/last-applied-configuration: |
{"apiVersion":"v1","data":{"log.level":"err"},"kind":"ConfigMap","metadata"
:{"annotations":{},"name":"example-config","namespace":"default"}}
  creationTimestamp: null
  name: example-config
  selfLink: /api/v1/namespaces/default/configmaps/example-config
```

Exposing the configuration into your container images

There are two primary ways to expose configuration data into your container:

- Connecting the keys from one or more ConfigMaps into environment variables that are set for your Pod
- Kubernetes can map the data from one or more ConfigMaps into volumes that are mounted in your Pod

The primary difference is that environment variables are typically set once at the start of invoking your container and are generally simple string values, where as ConfigMaps mounted as data in volumes can be more complex and will get updated if you update the ConfigMap resource.

 Note that no mechanism exists to explicitly tells your container that a ConfigMap value has been updated. As of version 1.9, Kubernetes does not include any means to signal to Pods and Containers that something has updated.

Additionally, configuration data exposed as file mounts isn't updated immediately. There is a lag between updating the ConfigMap resource and seeing the changes reflected in the relevant Pods.

Environment variables

When defining a Pod specification, in addition to the mandatory name and image key, you can specify an `env` key. The environment key requires a name, and you can add a key that makes a reference using `valueFrom:` to get data from a ConfigMap.

For example, to expose our example configuration as an environment variable, you could add the following stanza to a Pod specification:

```
env:
  - name: LOG_LEVEL_KEY
    valueFrom:
      configMapKeyRef:
        name: example-config
        Key: log.level
```

You can include multiple environment variables in the Pod specification, and each can reference a different ConfigMap if you have your configuration split up into multiple pieces to make it easier (or more sensible) to administer.

You can also map the entirety of a ConfigMap that are all key/values into environment variables as a single block.

Instead of using individual keys under env, you can use `envFrom` and specify the ConfigMap, for example:

```
envFrom:
  - configMapRef:
      name: example-config
```

With this setup, every configuration data key/value will be loaded as an environment variable when the Pod starts.

> You can create keys in ConfigMap that are not legal to be environment variables, such as keys starting with a number. In those cases, Kubernetes will load all the other keys and record the failed keys in the event log, but otherwise not throw an error. You can use `kubectl get events` to see the failed messages, where it will show each key that it skipped because it was invalid.

If you want to use one of the ConfigMap values that the arguments passed to the command to run within a container, you can also do that. When you specify the environment variables by `env` and name, you can reference that variable elsewhere in the Pod specification using `$(ENVIRONMENT_VARIABLE_NAME)`.

For example, the following `spec` snippet uses the environment variable in the invocation of the container:

```
spec:
  containers:
    - name: test-container
      image: gcr.io/google_containers/busybox
      command: [ "/bin/sh", "-c", "echo $(LOG_LEVEL_KEY)" ]
      env:
        - name: LOG_LEVEL_KEY
          valueFrom:
            configMapKeyRef:
              name: example-config
              key: log.level
```

Exposing ConfigMap as files inside the container

Exposing ConfigMap data into files within a container is very similar to how annotations and labels are exposed into a container. There are two parts to the specification on a Pod. The first is defining a volume for the container, including a name for it, and the location for where it should be mounted:

```
volumeMounts:
  - name: config
    mountPath: /etc/kconfig
    readOnly: true
```

The second part is a volume description that references the same name for the volume and lists ConfigMap as a property to indicate where to get the values:

```
volumes:
  - name: config
    configMap:
      name: example-config
```

Once that specification is applied, the values will be available as files within the container:

```
ls -al /etc/kconfig/

total 12
drwxrwxrwx   3 root     root           4096 Sep 17 00:57 .
drwxr-xr-x   1 root     root           4096 Sep 17 00:57 ..
drwxr-xr-x   2 root     root           4096 Sep 17 00:57
..9989_17_09_00_57_49.704362876
lrwxrwxrwx   1 root     root             31 Sep 17 00:57 ..data ->
..9989_17_09_00_57_49.704362876
lrwxrwxrwx   1 root     root             16 Sep 17 00:57 log.level ->
..data/log.level

cat /etc/kconfig/log.level

Err
```

You can use either environment variables or config files to provide the configuration data to your application, just depending on which is easier or more comfortable for your needs. We will update the examples to use ConfigMaps and adding ConfigMaps to deployments as well as reference the values within the code for the sample applications.

Dependencies on ConfigMaps

If you start referencing a ConfigMap in a Pod specification, you are creating a dependency on that ConfigMap for your resources. For example, if you added some of the preceding examples to expose example-data as an environment variable, but hadn't added the example-config ConfigMap to Kubernetes, when you try to deploy or update the Pod, it will report an error.

If this happens, the error will generally be reported in `kubectl get pods` or will be visible in the event log:

```
kubectl get pods

NAME                     READY      STATUS
RESTARTS     AGE
flask-4207440730-xpq8t   0/1        configmaps "example-config" not found
0            2d

kubectl get events

LASTSEEN    FIRSTSEEN     COUNT      NAME                        KIND
SUBOBJECT                 TYPE       REASON                      SOURCE
MESSAGE
2d          2d            1          flask-4207440730-30vn0      Pod
Normal      Scheduled                default-scheduler          Successfully
assigned flask-4207440730-30vn0 to minikube
2d          2d            1          flask-4207440730-30vn0      Pod
Normal      SuccessfulMountVolume    kubelet, minikube          MountVolume.SetUp
succeeded for volume "podinfo"
2d          2d            1          flask-4207440730-30vn0      Pod
Normal      SuccessfulMountVolume    kubelet, minikube          MountVolume.SetUp
succeeded for volume "default-token-s40w4"
2d          2d            2          flask-4207440730-30vn0      Pod
spec.containers{flask}    Normal     Pulling                     kubelet,
minikube        pulling image "quay.io/kubernetes-for-
developers/flask:latest"
2d          2d            2          flask-4207440730-30vn0      Pod
spec.containers{flask}    Normal     Pulled                      kubelet,
minikube        Successfully pulled image "quay.io/kubernetes-for-
developers/flask:latest"
2d          2d            2          flask-4207440730-30vn0      Pod
spec.containers{flask}    Warning    Failed                      kubelet,
minikube        Error: configmaps "example-config" not found
2d          2d            2          flask-4207440730-30vn0      Pod
Warning     FailedSync               kubelet, minikube          Error syncing pod
2d          2d            1          flask-4207440730            ReplicaSet
Normal      SuccessfulCreate         replicaset-controller      Created pod:
flask-4207440730-30vn0
2d          2d            1          flask                       Deployment
Normal      ScalingReplicaSet        deployment-controller      Scaled up replica
set flask-4207440730 to 1
```

If you add the ConfigMap after the fact, the Pod will start when the resource it needs is available.

Kubernetes resource – Secrets

ConfigMaps are great for general configuration, but are easily visible—which may not be desired. For some configuration, such as passwords, authorization tokens, or API keys, you often want a more controlled mechanism to protect those values. That's what the resource Secrets are designed to solve.

Secrets are generally created (and managed) individually, and internally Kubernetes stores this data using base64 encoding.

You can create a secret on the command line by first writing the values into one or more files, and then specifying those files in the create command. Kubernetes will take care of doing all the relevant base64 encoding and storing them away. For example, if you wanted to store a database username and password, you might do the following:

```
echo -n "admin" > username.txt
echo -n "sdgp63lkhsgd" > password.txt
kubectl create secret generic database-creds --from-file=username.txt --
from-file=password.txt
```

Note that in naming the secret's name, you can use any alphanumeric character, a - or ., but an underscore is not allowed.

If you use the following command:

```
kubectl get secrets
```

You can see the Secret we just created:

NAME	TYPE	DATA	AGE
database-creds	Opaque	2	2d
default-token-s40w4	kubernetes.io/service-account-token	3	5d

And by using the following:

```
kubectl describe secret database-creds

Name: database-creds
Namespace: default
Labels: <none>
Annotations: <none>
```

```
Type: Opaque
Data
====
password.txt: 18 bytes
username.txt: 11 bytes
```

You see the secret reported as type `Opaque` and just the number of bytes associated with the data.

You can still get the secret using the following:

```
kubectl get secret database-creds -o yaml --export
```

This will reveal the `base64` encoded values:

```
apiVersion: v1
data:
  password.txt: 4oCcc2RncDYzbGtoc2dk4oCd
  username.txt: 4oCcYWRtaW7igJ0=
kind: Secret
metadata:
  creationTimestamp: null
  name: database-creds
  selfLink: /api/v1/namespaces/default/secrets/database-creds
type: Opaque
```

And if you `base64` decode the value, you will see the original version:

```
echo "4oCcc2RncDYzbGtoc2dk4oCd" | base64 --decode
```

"sdgp631khsgd"

Be aware that anyone with access to your Kubernetes cluster resources can retrieve and view these secrets. Additionally, I do not recommend that you manage secrets like the rest of the declaration, stored in source control. Doing so exposes those secrets (in `base64` form) in your source control system.

Exposing Secrets into a container

We can expose Secrets to a Pod in a very similar fashion to exposing ConfigMaps. Like ConfigMaps, you can choose to expose a Secret as an environment variable, or as a file mounted within a volume, specified by the Pod.

The format for exposing a secret looks identical to exposing a ConfigMap value, except that it uses `secretKeyRef` instead of `configMapRef` in the specification.

As an example, to expose the preceding example secret password as an environment variable, you might use the following in a Pod specification:

```
env:
  - name: DB_PASSWORD
    valueFrom:
      secretKeyRef:
        name: database-creds
        key: password.txt
```

Then looking within the container, the environment variables container DB_PASSWORD:

```
kubectl exec flask-509298146-ql1t9 -it -- sh

env | grep DB

DB_PASSWORD="sdgp631khsgd"
```

A better path is to leverage the capability that Kubernetes includes for mounting secrets to be exposed as files inside the container. The configuration is very similar to exposing ConfigMap values, only defining the Secret as a volume property in the spec rather than ConfigMap.

In the specification, you need to define a volumeMount for the container, which indicates its location in the container:

```
volumeMounts:
  - name: secrets
    mountPath: "/secrets"
```

And then define how the contents of that volume get populated from secrets:

```
volumes:
  - name: secrets
    secret:
      secretName: database-creds
      items:
      - key: password.txt
        path: db_password
```

After deploying with this configuration, the container has a /secrets/db_password file with the contents from our secret:

```
/ # ls -l /secrets/
total 0
lrwxrwxrwx    1 root      root                 18 Sep 17 00:49 db_password ->
..data/db_password
```

```
/ # ls -l /secrets/db_password
lrwxrwxrwx    1 root     root          18 Sep 17 00:49
/secrets/db_password -> ..data/db_password

/ # cat /secrets/db_password
"sdgp63lkhsgd"
```

Secrets and security – how secret are the secrets?

Reasonably so, but not cryptographically secure, at least in Kubernetes 1.8. If you are looking at the secrets from a security perspective, the constraints on secrets are better than leaving values in ConfigMap, but the security profile has significant limits.

At the heart, the data for secrets is stored in plain-text (albiet encoded text) in etcd 3.0, which underpins Kubernetes 1.8. It does not use encryption at rest, or symmetric keys to preserve (and access) the secrets. If you are running your own Kubernetes cluster, be aware that an unsecured etcd represents a significant weakness in the overall security of the cluster.

For many applications and use cases, this is perfectly acceptable, but if you need to accommodate a higher security profile in your development and production environments, then you will want to look at tooling to work in conjunction with Kubernetes. The most commonly discussed alternative/extension is Vault, an open source project from HashiCorp. You can find more details about Vault at `https://www.vaultproject.io`.

The Kubernetes project also isn't standing still in regards to secrets and secret management, improving on their features as well. With the 1.7 release, Kubernetes included **Role-Based Access Control (RBAC)**, and the project is maintaining and developing against a roadmap that will improve Kubernetes, capabilities around its security profile, as well as supporting easier coordination with external sources of secrets management (such as Vault) in the future.

Example – Python/Flask deployment with ConfigMap

This example builds on our earlier Python/Flask example. This extension will add a ConfigMap that uses both environment variables and structured files, as well as code updates to consume and use those values.

To start, add a ConfigMap with both top-level values and a deeper configuration. The top values will be exposed as environment variables, and the multiline YAML will be exposed as a file inside the container:

```
# CONFIGURATION FOR THE FLASK APP
kind: ConfigMap
apiVersion: v1
metadata:
  name: flask-config
data:
  CONFIG_FILE: "/etc/flask-config/feature.flags"
  feature.flags: |
    [features]
    greeting=hello
    debug=true
```

This ConfigMap is mapped with updates to the Pod specification of the deployment with the `envFrom` key and as a volume to provide the file mapping:

```
spec:
  containers:
  - name: flask
    image: quay.io/kubernetes-for-developers/flask:latest
    ports:
    - containerPort: 5000
    envFrom:
    - configMapRef:
        name: flask-config
    volumeMounts:
      - name: config
        mountPath: /etc/flask-config
  volumes:
    - name: config
      configMap:
        name: flask-config
```

This update makes a dependency on having a ConfigMap named `flask-config` on the Deployment. If the ConfigMap isn't loaded and we try to load just that updated Deployment, it will not update the Deployment until that ConfigMap is available. To avoid the situation of accidentally missing a file, you can put both the ConfigMap and Deployment Spec in the same YAML file, separated by `---` on a new line. Then, you can deploy multiple resources in the order you specify when using the `kubectl apply` command.

You may also keep each resource in a separate file, if that is easier to understand or manage, primarily depending on your preference. The `kubectl apply` command includes options to reference all files in a directory, including recursively–so order and structure the files; however, it makes the most sense to manage them yourself.

To match this example, the code at `https://github.com/kubernetes-for-developers/kfd-flask` has a tag that you can use to update all the files at once:

```
git checkout 0.2.0
```

(If you skipped the earlier example, you may need to clone the repository first: `git clone https://github.com/kubernetes-for-developers/kfd-flask`)

With the code updated, deploy the updates:

```
kubectl apply -f deploy/
```

Once deployed, you may use `kubectl exec` to run an interactive shell in the Pod and inspect the deployment and what has been exposed.

SIDEBAR – JSONPATH

We might look up the specific Pod using a command like the following:

```
kubectl get pods -l app=flask
```

This will find just the pods matching the `app=flask` selector and print out human-readable output akin to the following:

```
NAME                      READY    STATUS     RESTARTS    AGE
flask-2376258259-p1cwb    1/1      Running    0           8m
```

This same data is available in a structured form (JSON, YAML, and so on) that we can parse with tools such as jq. Kubectl includes two additional options to make it a more convenient tool—you can use JSONPATH or GO_TEMPLATE to dig out specific values. With JSONPATH built into the kubectl client instead of doing the preceding two-step process to get the Pod name, you can directly get the specific details we want to use, which is the name:

```
kubectl get pods -l app=flask -o jsonpath='{.items[*].metadata.name}'
```

This should return the following:

```
flask-2376258259-p1cwb
```

This can be easily embedded into a shell command using $() to execute it inline. This ends up being a much more complex command, but it takes care of the step where we ask Kubernetes what the relevant Pod name is, which is critical for many of the interaction commands.

As an example, we can open an interactive shell within the Pod associated with this deployment using the following command:

```
kubectl exec $(kubectl get pods -l app=flask \
-o jsonpath='{.items[*].metadata.name}') \
-it -- /bin/sh
```

This gets the name of the Pod and embeds that into kubectl exec to run an interactive session with the /bin/sh command.

Once you have this session open, you can see the environment variables that have been set with the following:

```
env
```

This will show you all the environment variables set, one of which should be the following:

```
CONFIG_FILE=/etc/flask-config/feature.flags
```

You can see the more complex configuration data:

```
cat $CONFIG_FILE
[features]
greeting=hello
debug=true
```

We crafted the ConfigMap to have the correct location for this file based on what we put into the Deployment specification. If we change the Deployment Spec, but not the ConfigMap, the location embedded within the environment variable CONFIG_FILE will then be incorrect.

With Kubernetes Deployment, ConfigMap, and Service specifications in YAML, there is a lot of duplicate data that is not abstracted out. From a developer's perspective, this will feel awkward, violating the do not repeat yourself mantra that is commonly respected. There is a lot of repetition and places for small changes to unfortunately impact on the deployment specification.

The Kubernetes project is evolving the means of interacting with these files, with efforts to make generating the relevant configurations more with projects that are still early in development. As Kubernetes continues to mature, this should evolve to have more code-like qualities when defining the resource declarations.

Using the ConfigMap within Python/Flask

Within Python, you can view environment variables using os.environ, for example:

```
import os
os.environ.get('CONFIG_FILE')
```

You can set a default value when using os.environ.get in your code to handle a case when the environment variable isn't set:

```
import os
os.environ.get('CONFIG_FILE','./feature.flags')
```

We set the CONFIG_FILE environment variable here to show you how it could be done, but it is not strictly necessary to read the configuration file–more a convenience to allow you to override that value if desired.

Python also includes a module to parse and read INI-style configuration files, like the one we added in ConfigMap. Continuing with the example:

```
from configparser import SafeConfigParser
from pathlib import Path
# initialize the configuration parser with all the existing environment
variables
parser = SafeConfigParser(os.environ)
```

From here, ConfigParser has loaded a section named DEFAULT with all the environment variables, and we could retrieve one of them:

```
Python 3.6.1 (default, May  2 2017, 15:16:41)
[GCC 6.3.0] on linux
Type "help", "copyright", "credits" or "license" for more information.
>>> import os
>>> from configparser import SafeConfigParser
>>> from pathlib import Path
>>> # initialize the configuration parser with all the existing environment
variables
... parser = SafeConfigParser(os.environ)
>>> parser.get('DEFAULT', 'CONFIG_FILE')
'/etc/flask-config/feature.flags'
```

We can extend the parser with a section based on the INI file stored in that ConfigMap, which is exposed on the filesystem at /etc/flask-config/feature.flags with the following code:

```
# default location of ./feature.flags is used if the environment variable
isn't set
config_file = Path(os.environ.get('CONFIG_FILE','/opt/feature.flags'))
# verify file exists before attempting to read and extend the configuration
if config_file.is_file():
    parser.read(os.environ.get('CONFIG_FILE'))
```

And now the parser will be loaded with the DEFAULT section from the environment variables, and the 'features' section from the ConfigMap data:

```
>>> parser.sections()
['features']
>>> parser.getboolean('features', 'debug')
True
```

And the ConfigParser enables you to include defaults in your code as well:

```
>>> parser.getboolean('features', 'something-else', fallback=False)
False
```

We then use that kind of code to set debugging enabled or disabled based on that ConfigMap:

```
if __name__ == '__main__':
    debug_enable = parser.getboolean('features', 'debug', fallback=False)
    app.run(debug=debug_enable, host='0.0.0.0')
```

You can find more details on how to leverage Python 3's ConfigParser at `https://docs.python.org/3/library/configparser.html`.

Summary

In this chapter, we looked at how to take advantage of the declarative nature of Kubernetes in detail and managing our application through specification files. We also looked at Annotations, ConfigMap, and Secrets and how those can be created and then used from within Pods. We closed the chapter with updating our Python and Node.js applications to use ConfigMaps to run the example code we set up previously, and looked briefly at how to leverage the built-in `JSONPATH` within `kubectl` to make that tool more immediately powerful at providing the specific information you want.

Pod and Container Lifecycles

5

With Kubernetes being a declarative system, the lifecycle and hooks that are offered for Pods and Containers are the points where your code can take actions. Pods have a lifecycle, as do containers, and Kubernetes offers a number of places where you can provide explicit feedback to the system to have it operate as you'd like. In this chapter, we will dig into the expected lifecycle, hooks available to use, and examples of how to use them.

The topics will include:

- Pod lifecycle
- Container lifecycle
- Probes
- Container hook: post-start and pre-stop
- Initialization containers
- How to handle a graceful shutdown

Pod lifecycle

The lifecycle of a Pod is an aggregate of several components, as a Pod has a number of moving parts that can be in a variety of states as it operates. The representation of the lifecycle is how Kubernetes manages running your code for you, in conjunction with the control and feedback loops that work from the various controllers.

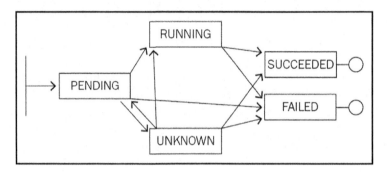

The states of a Pod's lifecycle are:

- **Pending**: The Pod has been created through the API, and is in the process of being scheduled, loaded, and run on one of the Nodes
- **Running**: The Pod is fully operational and the software is running within the cluster
- **Succeeded (or) Failed**: The Pod has finished operation (normally or crashed)
- **There is a fourth state**: Unknown, which is a fairly rare occurrence and is typically only seen when there's a problem internal to Kubernetes where it doesn't know the current state of containers, or is unable to communicate with its underlying systems to determine that state

If you are working with long-running code in Containers, then most of the time will be spent in running. If you are making use of shorter, batch-oriented code within Kubernetes using Job or CronJob, then the final status (Succeeded or Failed) may be what you are interested in.

Container lifecycle

Containers also have a state that is managed individually for them, since each Pod can have one or more Containers. The Container states are simpler and quite direct:

- Waiting

- Running
- Terminated

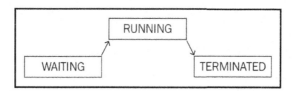

The container states will all have a timestamp associated with them, indicating when the cluster recorded the container in that state. If more than one state has been processed through, there will also be a last state field. As containers are fairly ephemeral, it is fairly common to see a previous state of Terminated, which includes information about when the container started, when it finished, its exit code, and a string entry about why it terminated called Reason.

The following is an example of the container states after your Pod has been processing a while (and in this example, after it had been updated a couple of times):

```
                                    1. heckj@greyberry: ~ (bash)
heckj      $  kubectl describe pod flask-78867f5567-wvzvr
Name:           flask-78867f5567-wvzvr
Namespace:      default
Node:           minikube/192.168.64.11
Start Time:     Wed, 20 Dec 2017 16:11:04 -0800
Labels:         app=flask
                pod-template-hash=3442391123
Annotations:    kubernetes.io/created-by={"kind":"SerializedReference","apiVersion":"v1","reference":{"kind":"ReplicaSet","namespace":"defa
ult","name":"flask-78867f5567","uid":"6f72b81d-e5e3-11e7-89d4-b29f363a60d7","...
Status:         Running
IP:             172.17.0.5
Controlled By:  ReplicaSet/flask-78867f5567
Containers:
  flask:
    Container ID:   docker://589fc05b0fd6bd6c50f62acd268e041a2c35321549d7de14817e05d1df0bc14b
    Image:          quay.io/kubernetes-for-developers/flask:0.3.0
    Image ID:       docker-pullable://quay.io/kubernetes-for-developers/flask@sha256:4cb1f7cb386894b2d2160b096bf90b5fb94493a19f91cfc59293dd
6fc59f0d84
    Port:           5000/TCP
    State:          Running
      Started:      Wed, 20 Dec 2017 16:13:11 -0800
    Last State:     Terminated
      Reason:       Completed
      Exit Code:    0
      Started:      Wed, 20 Dec 2017 16:12:47 -0800
      Finished:     Wed, 20 Dec 2017 16:13:09 -0800
    Ready:          True
```

You can see the additional details in a human-readable format within the output of the `kubectl describe pod` command, which is often most convenient for quickly understanding what's happening within the Pod.

The states all have additional information within them to provide detail on what's happening. There is a formal PodStatus object available via the API. Each state has additional details that are available, and more generally the status object includes a list of conditions that are commonly exposed and visible in the output of describe or the raw YAML.

Using the `kubectl get pod ... -o yaml` command, you can see the data in a machine-parsable form, and see that there's an additional detail that isn't also exposed in the `describe` command. In the following screenshot, you can see the output related to the Pod and container states, including the conditions, container states, and related timestamps:

Conditions are added to the state of a Kubernetes object as the object goes through its lifecycle.

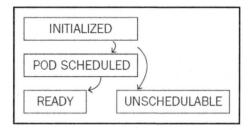

Within the Pod state pending, there are two conditions that are commonly added: `Initialized` and `PodScheduled`. If the cluster is unable to run the requested Pod, then you may see the condition `Unschedulable` instead of `PodScheduled`. When the Pod is in the state of Running, there is also the condition **Ready** that is relevant and affects Kubernetes' management of your code.

Deployments, ReplicaSets, and Pods

Pods are not the only Kubernetes resources that takes advantage of, and expose, conditions. Deployments also use conditions to represent detail such as to the progress of a rollout of a code update, and the overall availability of the deployment.

The two conditions you will see when using Deployments are:

- Progressing
- Available

Available will be true when the minimum number of replicas of the underlying Pods is available (the default is 1). Progressing will be set when the ReplicaSets and their related Pods are created and as they come available.

Kubernetes uses a consistent pattern in how its internal resources are related to each other. As we discussed in an earlier chapter, Deployments will have associated ReplicaSets, and ReplicaSets will have associated Pods. You can visualize this like a chain of objects, with the higher level being responsible for watching and maintaining the state of the next level down:

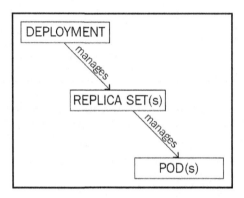

We have been focusing on Pod states and their lifecycle because that is where the code is represented and actually running. In most cases, you will be creating a deployment that will, in turn, have its own state and conditions. That will, in turn, create a ReplicaSet, and the ReplicaSet will create the Pod or Pods.

When a Pod is being created, the system will attempt to first create the API resource itself, and then it will attempt to find a place to run it within the cluster. When the resource has been created, the Initialized condition is added to the status. When the cluster has identified where to run the Pod, the PodScheduled condition will be added. If the cluster can't find a location to run the Pod as you've described, then the Unschedulable condition is added to the status.

Getting a snapshot of the current state

You can see the current snapshot of what Kubernetes knows about the state of your code using the `kubectl describe` or `kubectl get` command. If you are just trying to see the state for yourself interactively, then the `kubectl describe` command is the most valuable. Remember that Kubernetes manages a chain of objects related to running your code, so if you want to see a full snapshot, you will want to look at the status of each of the objects: deployment, ReplicaSet, and Pods. In practice, looking at the state of deployment and then jumping down to Pods will often provide you with any detail you want.

You can see these details of what Kubernetes is doing with your code by looking at the raw data for your Pod using `kubectl get pod`, or by using the `describe` command. You want to look for `Status` and `Conditions`. For example, when we earlier created a `nodejs` application deployment, the chain of objects created:

```
kubectl get deploy
NAME    DESIRED CURRENT UP-TO-DATE AVAILABLE AGE
nodejs 1        1          1          1          8h

kubectl get rs
NAME                   DESIRED CURRENT READY AGE
nodejs-6b9b87d48b 1        1          1     8h

kubectl get pod
NAME                        READY STATUS   RESTARTS AGE
nodejs-6b9b87d48b-ddhjf 1/1    Running 0            8h
```

You can see the snapshot of its current state using the `kubectl describe` command to look at the deployment:

```
kubectl describe deploy nodejs
```

This will present information that looks like this:

```
                              1. heckj@greyberry: ~/src/kfd-nodejs (bash)
heckj  ~   src  kfd-nodejs  master  $  kubectl describe deploy nodejs
Name:                   nodejs
Namespace:              default
CreationTimestamp:      Thu, 21 Dec 2017 05:08:57 -0800
Labels:                 run=nodejs
Annotations:            deployment.kubernetes.io/revision=1
                        kubectl.kubernetes.io/last-applied-configuration={"apiVersion":"apps/v1beta1","kind":"Deployment","metadata":{
"annotations":{},"labels":{"run":"nodejs"},"name":"nodejs","namespace":"default"},"spec":{...
Selector:               app=nodejs
Replicas:               1 desired | 1 updated | 1 total | 1 available | 0 unavailable
StrategyType:           RollingUpdate
MinReadySeconds:        0
RollingUpdateStrategy:  25% max unavailable, 25% max surge
Pod Template:
  Labels:   app=nodejs
  Containers:
   nodejs:
    Image:  quay.io/kubernetes-for-developers/nodejs:0.2.0
    Port:   3000/TCP
    Environment Variables from:
      nodejs-config  ConfigMap  Optional: false
    Environment:    <none>
    Mounts:
      /etc/nodejs-config from config (ro)
  Volumes:
   config:
    Type:       ConfigMap (a volume populated by a ConfigMap)
    Name:       nodejs-config
    Optional:   false
Conditions:
  Type          Status  Reason
  ----          ------  ------
  Available     True    MinimumReplicasAvailable
  Progressing   True    NewReplicaSetAvailable
OldReplicaSets:  <none>
NewReplicaSet:   nodejs-6b9b87d48b (1/1 replicas created)
Events:
  Type    Reason            Age   From                  Message
  ----    ------            ----  ----                  -------
  Normal  ScalingReplicaSet 8h    deployment-controller Scaled up replica set nodejs-6b9b87d48b to 1
heckj  ~   src  kfd-nodejs  master  $
```

And you can use `kubectl describe` to get additional details by looking at the ReplicaSet:

```
kubectl describe rs nodejskubectl describe deploy nodejs
```

```
1. heckj@greyberry: ~/src/kfd-nodejs (bash)
heckj    ~  src  kfd-nodejs  master  $  kubectl describe rs nodejs
Name:            nodejs-6b9b87d48b
Namespace:       default
Selector:        app=nodejs,pod-template-hash=2656438046
Labels:          app=nodejs
                 pod-template-hash=2656438046
Annotations:     deployment.kubernetes.io/desired-replicas=1
                 deployment.kubernetes.io/max-replicas=2
                 deployment.kubernetes.io/revision=1
Controlled By:   Deployment/nodejs
Replicas:        1 current / 1 desired
Pods Status:     1 Running / 0 Waiting / 0 Succeeded / 0 Failed
Pod Template:
  Labels:  app=nodejs
           pod-template-hash=2656438046
  Containers:
   nodejs:
    Image:   quay.io/kubernetes-for-developers/nodejs:0.2.0
    Port:    3000/TCP
    Environment Variables from:
      nodejs-config  ConfigMap  Optional: false
    Environment:     <none>
    Mounts:
      /etc/nodejs-config from config (ro)
  Volumes:
   config:
    Type:      ConfigMap (a volume populated by a ConfigMap)
    Name:      nodejs-config
    Optional:  false
Events:
  Type    Reason          Age   From                  Message
  ----    ------          ----  ----                  -------
  Normal  SuccessfulCreate  8h  replicaset-controller  Created pod: nodejs-6b9b87d48b-ddhjf
```

And finally, use it one more time to look at the Pods created by the Deployment and ReplicaSet:

```
kubectl describe pod nodejs
```

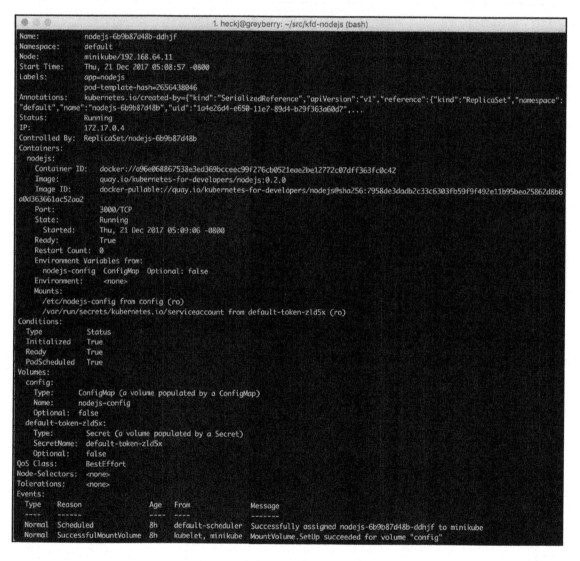

The events that are listed at the bottom of the output from `kubectl describe` will show you the sequence of what happened related to the Pod.

If you want to use the status in a script, or otherwise use a program to parse the output, then you can use the `kubectl get` command, specifying a data format for the output such as YAML. For example, the same Pod output in YAML might be retrieved using the following command:

```
kubectl get pod nodejs-6b9b87d48b-lcgvd -o yaml
```

The lower portion of the output under the key status will hold the state-snapshot information:

```
status:
  conditions:
  - lastProbeTime: null
    lastTransitionTime: 2017-12-21T13:42:38Z
    status: "True"
    type: Initialized
  - lastProbeTime: null
    lastTransitionTime: 2017-12-21T13:42:41Z
    status: "True"
    type: Ready
  - lastProbeTime: null
    lastTransitionTime: 2017-12-21T13:42:38Z
    status: "True"
    type: PodScheduled
  containerStatuses:
  - containerID: docker://c6a43a8226cb4a01aa2d3a546595104cbbe3874a9bf4c477226743840a5fa025
    image: quay.io/kubernetes-for-developers/nodejs:0.2.0
    imageID: docker-pullable://quay.io/kubernetes-for-developers/nodejs@sha256:7958de3dadb2c33c6303fb59f9f492e11b95bea25862d8b6a0d3636
61ac52aa2
    lastState: {}
    name: nodejs
    ready: true
    restartCount: 0
    state:
      running:
        startedAt: 2017-12-21T13:42:40Z
  hostIP: 192.168.64.11
  phase: Running
  podIP: 172.17.0.4
  qosClass: BestEffort
  startTime: 2017-12-21T13:42:38Z
```

While not shown in the output from `kubectl describe`, each condition is tracked with a last updated time, a time when it last changed, a type, and a status. In addition, each container is listed with its own state.

The list of Pod conditions that you could see could grow with future versions of Kubernetes, and today includes the following:

- **PodScheduled**: Transitioned to true when the Pod has been scheduled on a Node and the process to start loading it onto the node has begun.
- **Initialized**: Initialized will be marked true when all containers for the Pod have been loaded, and after any initialization containers defined have run to completion.
- **Ready**: The Pod has been loaded and started per the specification. This value won't be marked as true until the readiness probe and the liveness probe have completed successfully (if either or both are defined).
- **Unschedulable**: This condition will only be listed and asserted when the Kubernetes cluster is unable to match available resources to the Pod's needs.

Sometimes the states (such as `Succeeded` or `Failed`) will also include a `Reason`, which includes some text output intended to make it easier to understand what happened. And as you can see from the preceding output, timestamps are included for all the state changes. Since this is a snapshot in time, the timestamps can provide breadcrumb clues to understand the order of what happened, and how long ago it happened.

As a final note, the events associated with the Pod will often provide useful descriptive notes of what has happened (or failed to happen) while your Pod was starting. Utilizing all the details provided from describe, Pod status, conditions, and events, provides the best status updates external to the Pod's logs themselves.

The lifecycle of Pods also includes hooks or feedback mechanisms that you can specify to allow your application to provide feedback on how it is doing. One of these mechanisms, the condition `Ready`, you have seen previously. Kubernetes lets your application provide specific feedback on if it is ready to accept traffic, and if it is healthy. These feedback mechanisms are called **probes**, and can be optionally defined in your Pod specification.

Probes

The two probes enabled in Kubernetes are the liveness probe and readiness Probe. They are complimentary, but different in intent and usage, and can be defined for each container within a Pod. In both cases, they provide a means for your code to influence how Kubernetes manages the containers.

Liveness probe

The most basic probe is the Liveness probe. If defined, it provides a command or URL that Kubernetes can use to determine whether a Pod is still operational. If the call succeeds, Kubernetes will assume the container is healthy; if it fails to respond, then the Pod can be handled as the `restartPolicy` is defined. The result is binary: either the probe succeeds, and Kubernetes believes your Pod is running, or it fails, so Kubernetes believes your Pod is no longer functional. In the latter case, it will check with the defined RestartPolicy to choose what to do.

The default value for `restartPolicy` is `Always`, meaning if a container within the Pod fails, Kubernetes will always attempt to restart it. Other values that you can define include `OnFailure` and `Never`. When a container is restarted, Kubernetes will track how often that occurs and will slow down the frequency of restarts if they are happening in quick succession, capped at a maximum of five minutes between restart attempts. The number of restarts is tracked and visible as `restartcount` in the output of `kubectl describe`, and the key `restartCount` in the data output from `kubectl get`.

If a liveness probe isn't explicitly defined, the probe is assumed to succeed and the container is automatically set to live. If the container itself were to crash or exit, Kubernetes would react and restart it as per the `restartPolicy`, but no other active checks are taking place. This allows you to handle a scenario where your code has frozen or deadlocked and is no longer responding, even though the process continues to run.

A liveness probe can be defined to check the health of the Pod through one of three methods:

- `ExecAction`: This invokes a command within the Pod to get a response, and the result of the exit code of that command invocation is what's used in the liveness check. A result of anything other than 0 represents a failure.

- `TCPSocketAction`: This attempts to open a socket, but doesn't manipulate or interact with the socket beyond attempting to open it. If the socket opens, the probe is successful, and if it fails or fails after a timeout, then the probe fails.
- `HTTPGetAction`: Similar to the socket option, this makes an HTTP connection to your Pod as a URI specified, and the response code of the HTTP request is what is used to determine the success/failure of the liveness probe.

There are a number of variables that can configure the specifics of this probe as well:

- `activeDeadlineSeconds` (not set by default): This value is most commonly used with Jobs rather than long-running Pods to put a maximum cap on how long the job will be allowed to operate. This number will include any time taken by initialization containers, which will be discussed further later in this chapter.
- `initialDelaySeconds` (not set by default): This allows you to specify the number of seconds before starting probe checks. This is not set by default, so effectively defaults to 0 seconds.
- `timeoutSeconds` (defaults to 1): This provides a timeout in case the command or URL request takes a significant period of time to return. If the timeout expires before the command returns, it is presumed to have failed.
- `periodSeconds` (defaults to 10): This defines the frequency of how often Kubernetes will run the probe - either invoking the command, checking the socket availability, or making the URL request.
- `successThreshold` (defaults to 1): This is the number of times that the probe needs to return success in order to set the state of the container to `active`.
- `failureThreshold` (defaults to 3): This is the minimum number of consecutive failures of the probe that will trigger marking the container as unhealthy.

If you define a URL to request and leave everything else to defaults, the normal pattern will require three failure responses—a timeout or non-200 response code—before it will consider the container `dead` and apply the `restartPolicy`. Each check by default is 10 seconds apart, so your container could be dead for up to 30 seconds with these defaults before the system applies the `restartPolicy`.

If you are using an HTTP-based probe, you have a number of additional variables that can be defined while making the HTTP request:

- `host`: Defaults to the Pod IP address.
- `scheme`: HTTP or https. Kubernetes 1.8 defaults to HTTP

- `path`: Path of the URI request.
- `HttpHeaders`: Any custom headers to be included in the request.
- `port`: Port on which to make the HTTP request.

Readiness probe

The second probe available is the readiness probe, most often used in parallel with the liveness probe. The readiness probe is expected to respond positively only when your application is ready and able to service normal requests. For example, if you want to wait until your database is fully operational, or pre-load some caches that can take a few seconds, you probably don't want to return a positive response for a readiness probe until those operations have completed.

Like the liveness probe, if it is not defined, the system assumes that as soon as your code is running that it is also ready to accept requests. If you have code that takes a few seconds to get fully operational, then it is very worthwhile to define and utilize a readiness probe, as this will work with any Services to automatically update Endpoints so that traffic isn't routed to an instance when it is unable to service traffic.

The same options are available for configuring a readiness probe, one of `ExecAction`, `TCPSocketAction`, or `HTTPGetAction`. As with the liveness probe, the same variables can be used to tune the frequency of probe requests, timeouts, and a number of successes and/or failures to trigger a state change. If you modified the values in your liveness probe, then you probably do not want to set your readiness probe to be any more frequent than your liveness probe.

As a reminder, when a readiness probe fails, a container isn't automatically restarted. If you want that functionality, you should be using the liveness probe. The readiness probe is specifically set up to allow a Pod to indicate that it can't yet process traffic, but it expects it will be able to shortly. As the probe updates, the Pod status will be updated to set Ready to be positive or negative, and the related Ready condition will also be updated. As this happens, any services that are using this pod will get notified of those updates and will change to send traffic (or not) based on the readiness value.

You can view the readiness probe as an implementation of the circuit breaker pattern, and a means of load shedding. While running with multiple copies of a Pod, if one instance gets overloaded or has some temporary condition, it can respond negatively to the readiness probe and the service mechanism within Kubernetes will direct any further requests to the other Pods.

Adding a probe to our Python example

Like previous examples, the code is available in GitHub in the `https://github.com/ kubernetes-for-developers/kfd-flask` project. `I won't show all the changes, but you can check out the code from branch 0.3.0 using this command:` `git checkout 0.3.0`. `The Docker images built from this code are likewise available under the 0.3.0 tag from the` `quay.io` `repository.`

In this update, the project includes a secondary deployment of Redis to match some of the concepts from the previous chapter. The specification for the deployment has also been updated to specifically add a liveness probe and a readiness probe. The updated deployment specification now reads:

```
apiVersion: apps/v1beta1
kind: Deployment
metadata:
  name: flask
  labels:
  run: flask
spec:
  template:
    metadata:
      labels:
        app: flask
    spec:
      containers:
      - name: flask
        image: quay.io/kubernetes-for-developers/flask:0.3.0
        imagePullPolicy: Always
        ports:
        - containerPort: 5000
        envFrom:
        - configMapRef:
          name: flask-config
        volumeMounts:
        - name: config
          mountPath: /etc/flask-config
          readOnly: true
```

```
        livenessProbe:
          httpGet:
            path: /alive
            port: 5000
          initialDelaySeconds: 1
          periodSeconds: 5
        readinessProbe:
          httpGet:
            path: /ready
            port: 5000
          initialDelaySeconds: 5
          periodSeconds: 5
      volumes:
      - name: config
        configMap:
          name: flask-config
```

The probes are in bold. Both probes are using the same port as the rest of the application (`5000`), and their own respective endpoints. The liveness probe is set to delay one second before starting to check, and the readiness probe is set to delay five seconds before starting to check, and both are set to a slightly tighter frequency of five seconds.

The Python code has also been updated, primarily to implement the methods that respond to `/alive` and `/ready` for the liveness and readiness probes, respectively.

The liveness probe is the simplest, replying with a static response that just preserves the validation that the underlying flask code is responding to HTTP requests:

```
@app.route('/alive')
def alive():
    return "Yes"
```

The readiness probe extends on this pattern, but verifies that an underlying service (Redis in this case) is available and responding before replying positively. This code doesn't actually rely on Redis, but in your own code you may rely on a remote service being available and have some method that will indicate if that service is both available and responsive. As mentioned earlier, this is effectively an implementation of the circuit breaker pattern, and along with the service construct, allows Kubernetes to help direct load to instances that can respond.

In this case, we take advantage of the `redis ping()` capability, exposed in the Python library:

```
@app.route('/ready')
def ready():
    if redis_store.ping():
        return "Yes"
    else:
        flask.abort(500)
```

The other updates in the code initialize the `redis_store` variable in the code, and add the DNS entry to the matching service into a `configMap` so the application code can use it.

Running the Python probes example

If you check out the `0.3.0` branch, you can investigate this code and run it locally in your own instance of Minikube or another Kubernetes cluster. To check out the code:

```
git clone https://github.com/kubernetes-for-developers/kfd-flask

cd kfd-flask

git checkout 0.3.0

kubectl apply -f deploy/
```

The final command will create the service and deployment `redis-master`, and the service, `configmap`, and deployment for the Python/flask code. If you then use the `kubectl describe` command, you can see the probes defined and their values:

```
kubectl describe deployment flask
```

```
[deck] [src] [ktg-flask [0.3.0] [?]> kubectl describe deploy flask
Name:                   flask
Namespace:              default
CreationTimestamp:      Thu, 21 Dec 2017 06:57:42 -0800
Labels:                 run=flask
Annotations:            deployment.kubernetes.io/revision=1
                        kubectl.kubernetes.io/last-applied-configuration={"apiVersion":"apps/v1beta1","kind":"Deployment","metadata":{
"annotations":{},"labels":{"run":"flask"},"name":"flask","namespace":"default"},"spec":{"t...
Selector:               app=flask
Replicas:               1 desired | 1 updated | 1 total | 1 available | 0 unavailable
StrategyType:           RollingUpdate
MinReadySeconds:        0
RollingUpdateStrategy:  25% max unavailable, 25% max surge
Pod Template:
  Labels:  app=flask
  Containers:
   flask:
    Image:      quay.io/kubernetes-for-developers/flask:0.3.0
    Port:       5000/TCP
    Liveness:   http-get http://:5000/alive delay=1s timeout=1s period=5s #success=1 #failure=3
    Readiness:  http-get http://:5000/ready delay=5s timeout=1s period=5s #success=1 #failure=3
    Environment Variables from:
      flask-config  ConfigMap  Optional: false
    Environment:   <none>
    Mounts:
      /etc/flask-config from config (ro)
  Volumes:
   config:
    Type:       ConfigMap (a volume populated by a ConfigMap)
    Name:       flask-config
    Optional:   false
Conditions:
  Type          Status  Reason
  ----          ------  ------
  Available     True    MinimumReplicasAvailable
  Progressing   True    NewReplicaSetAvailable
OldReplicaSets:   <none>
NewReplicaSet:    flask-78867f5567 (1/1 replicas created)
Events:
  Type    Reason           Age   From                   Message
  ----    ------           ---   ----                   -------
  Normal  ScalingReplicaSet 8h   deployment-controller  Scaled up replica set flask-78867f5567 to 1
```

You can also look at the logs for the single flask Pod that's operational and see the requests being processed:

```
kubectl log deployment/flask

 * Running on http://0.0.0.0:5000/ (Press CTRL+C to quit)
 * Restarting with stat
 * Debugger is active!
 * Debugger PIN: 177-760-948
172.17.0.1 - - [21/Dec/2017 14:57:50] "GET /alive HTTP/1.1" 200 -
172.17.0.1 - - [21/Dec/2017 14:57:53] "GET /ready HTTP/1.1" 200 -
172.17.0.1 - - [21/Dec/2017 14:57:55] "GET /alive HTTP/1.1" 200 -
172.17.0.1 - - [21/Dec/2017 14:57:58] "GET /ready HTTP/1.1" 200 -
172.17.0.1 - - [21/Dec/2017 14:58:00] "GET /alive HTTP/1.1" 200 -
172.17.0.1 - - [21/Dec/2017 14:58:03] "GET /ready HTTP/1.1" 200 -
172.17.0.1 - - [21/Dec/2017 14:58:05] "GET /alive HTTP/1.1" 200 -
172.17.0.1 - - [21/Dec/2017 14:58:08] "GET /ready HTTP/1.1" 200 -
```

```
172.17.0.1 - - [21/Dec/2017 14:58:10] "GET /alive HTTP/1.1" 200 -
172.17.0.1 - - [21/Dec/2017 14:58:13] "GET /ready HTTP/1.1" 200 -
172.17.0.1 - - [21/Dec/2017 14:58:15] "GET /alive HTTP/1.1" 200 -
172.17.0.1 - - [21/Dec/2017 14:58:18] "GET /ready HTTP/1.1" 200 -
172.17.0.1 - - [21/Dec/2017 14:58:20] "GET /alive HTTP/1.1" 200 -
172.17.0.1 - - [21/Dec/2017 14:58:23] "GET /ready HTTP/1.1" 200 -
172.17.0.1 - - [21/Dec/2017 14:58:25] "GET /alive HTTP/1.1" 200 -
172.17.0.1 - - [21/Dec/2017 14:58:28] "GET /ready HTTP/1.1" 200 -
172.17.0.1 - - [21/Dec/2017 14:58:30] "GET /alive HTTP/1.1" 200 -
172.17.0.1 - - [21/Dec/2017 14:58:33] "GET /ready HTTP/1.1" 200 -
172.17.0.1 - - [21/Dec/2017 14:58:35] "GET /alive HTTP/1.1" 200 -
172.17.0.1 - - [21/Dec/2017 14:58:38] "GET /ready HTTP/1.1" 200 -
172.17.0.1 - - [21/Dec/2017 14:58:40] "GET /alive HTTP/1.1" 200 -
172.17.0.1 - - [21/Dec/2017 14:58:43] "GET /ready HTTP/1.1" 200 -
172.17.0.1 - - [21/Dec/2017 14:58:45] "GET /alive HTTP/1.1" 200 -
172.17.0.1 - - [21/Dec/2017 14:58:48] "GET /ready HTTP/1.1" 200 -
...
```

Adding a probe to our Node.js example

Adding example probes to the Node.js/express-based application follows exactly the same pattern as the Python application. And like the Python example, the code and specifications for this are available at GitHub under the `https://github.com/kubernetes-for-developers/kfd-nodejs` project, associated with branch `0.3.0`.

The probes add nearly the same specification to the Node.js deployment:

```
livenessProbe:
  httpGet:
    path: /probes/alive
    port: 3000
  initialDelaySeconds: 1
  periodSeconds: 5
readinessProbe:
  httpGet:
    path: /probes/ready
    port: 3000
  initialDelaySeconds: 5
  periodSeconds: 5
```

In this case, the probes are requesting against the same HTTP responses that the application provides, and the same port. The URI paths are longer, taking advantage of the application's structure, which uses a single bit of code for routes under a specific URI, so we are able to bundle the readiness and liveness probes into a single new `probes.js` router.

The main application is updated to create a probes router and bind it in on application start, and then the code within the router itself provides the responses.

The code for `probes.js` is as follows:

```javascript
var express = require('express');
var router = express.Router();
var util = require('util');
var db = require('../db');

/* GET liveness probe response. */
router.get('/alive', function(req, res, next) {
  res.send('yes');
});

/* GET readiness probe response. */
router.get('/ready', async function(req, res, next) {
  try {
    let pingval = await db.ping()
    if (pingval) {
      res.send('yes');
    } else {
      res.status(500).json({ error: "redis.ping was false" })
    }
  } catch (error) {
    res.status(500).json({ error: error.toString() })
  }
});

module.exports = router;
```

Like the preceding Python example, the liveness probe returns a static response, and is just used to validate that express is still responding to HTTP requests. The readiness probe is more involved, wrapping `db.ping()` in an asynchronous wait/catch and checking the value. If it's negative, or an error occurs, then we return a `500` response. If it's positive, then we return a static positive result.

Using `kubectl describe deployment nodejs` will show the configuration with the probes operational, very much like the Python example, and `kubectl log nodejs-65498dfb6f-5v7nc` will show the requests from the probes being responded to:

```
GET /probes/alive 200 1.379 ms - 3
Thu, 21 Dec 2017 17:43:51 GMT express:router dispatching GET /probes/ready
Thu, 21 Dec 2017 17:43:51 GMT express:router query : /probes/ready
Thu, 21 Dec 2017 17:43:51 GMT express:router expressInit : /probes/ready
Thu, 21 Dec 2017 17:43:51 GMT express:router logger : /probes/ready
```

```
Thu, 21 Dec 2017 17:43:51 GMT express:router jsonParser : /probes/ready
Thu, 21 Dec 2017 17:43:51 GMT express:router urlencodedParser :
/probes/ready
Thu, 21 Dec 2017 17:43:51 GMT express:router cookieParser : /probes/ready
Thu, 21 Dec 2017 17:43:51 GMT express:router serveStatic : /probes/ready
Thu, 21 Dec 2017 17:43:51 GMT express:router router : /probes/ready
Thu, 21 Dec 2017 17:43:51 GMT express:router dispatching GET /probes/ready
Thu, 21 Dec 2017 17:43:51 GMT express:router trim prefix (/probes) from url
/probes/ready
Thu, 21 Dec 2017 17:43:51 GMT express:router router /probes : /probes/ready
Thu, 21 Dec 2017 17:43:51 GMT express:router dispatching GET /ready
GET /probes/ready 200 1.239 ms - 3
Thu, 21 Dec 2017 17:43:54 GMT express:router dispatching GET /probes/alive
Thu, 21 Dec 2017 17:43:54 GMT express:router query : /probes/alive
Thu, 21 Dec 2017 17:43:54 GMT express:router expressInit : /probes/alive
Thu, 21 Dec 2017 17:43:54 GMT express:router logger : /probes/alive
Thu, 21 Dec 2017 17:43:54 GMT express:router jsonParser : /probes/alive
Thu, 21 Dec 2017 17:43:54 GMT express:router urlencodedParser :
/probes/alive
Thu, 21 Dec 2017 17:43:54 GMT express:router cookieParser : /probes/alive
Thu, 21 Dec 2017 17:43:54 GMT express:router serveStatic : /probes/alive
Thu, 21 Dec 2017 17:43:54 GMT express:router router : /probes/alive
Thu, 21 Dec 2017 17:43:54 GMT express:router dispatching GET /probes/alive
Thu, 21 Dec 2017 17:43:54 GMT express:router trim prefix (/probes) from url
/probes/alive
Thu, 21 Dec 2017 17:43:54 GMT express:router router /probes : /probes/alive
Thu, 21 Dec 2017 17:43:54 GMT express:router dispatching GET /alive
GET /probes/alive 200 1.361 ms - 3
```

We can test the operation of the readiness probe by terminating the Redis service. If we invoke the following command:

```
kubectl delete deployment redis-master
```

Fairly shortly, the results of kubectl get pods will show the Pod alive, but not ready:

```
kubectl get pods
NAME                        READY STATUS       RESTARTS AGE
nodejs-65498dfb6f-5v7nc     0/1   Running      0        8h
redis-master-b6b8774f9-sjl4w 0/1  Terminating 0        10h
```

While the `redis-master` deployment is shut down, you can get some interesting details from the Node.js deployment. Use `kubectl describe` to show the deployment:

```
kubectl describe deploy nodejs
```

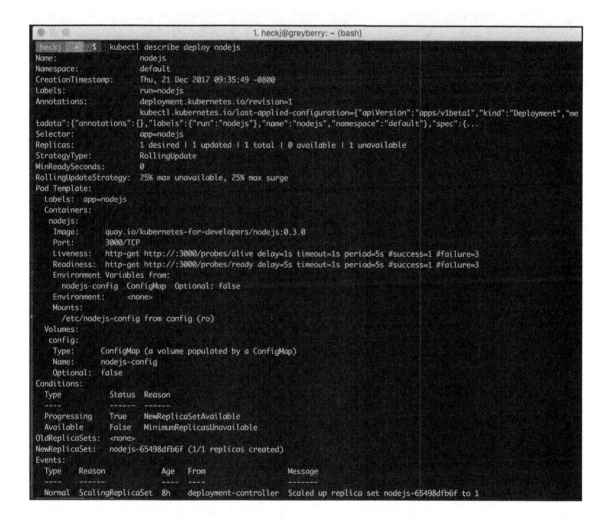

And use `kubectl describe` to look at the related Pods as well:

```
kubectl describe pod nodejs
```

```
                              1. heckj@greyberry: ~ (bash)
Namespace:      default
Node:           minikube/192.168.64.11
Start Time:     Thu, 21 Dec 2017 09:35:49 -0800
Labels:         app=nodejs
                pod-template-hash=2105489629
Annotations:    kubernetes.io/created-by={"kind":"SerializedReference","apiVersion":"v1","reference":{"kind":"ReplicaSet","namespace":"default","name"
:"nodejs-65498dfb6f","uid":"62275ba0-e675-11e7-89d4-b29f363a60d7",...
Status:         Running
IP:             172.17.0.4
Controlled By:  ReplicaSet/nodejs-65498dfb6f
Containers:
  nodejs:
    Container ID:   docker://afafad6b3301b64906a8bc370fa661451bcccd04ad0fae32f62c4aa03ce85b12
    Image:          quay.io/kubernetes-for-developers/nodejs:0.3.0
    Image ID:       docker-pullable://quay.io/kubernetes-for-developers/nodejs@sha256:c3b15726b49bf0e59d7d333c2aba053461bfbeea0f46ae0945eec34cadf0fa74
    Port:           3000/TCP
    State:          Running
      Started:      Thu, 21 Dec 2017 09:35:56 -0800
    Ready:          False
    Restart Count:  0
    Liveness:       http-get http://:3000/probes/alive delay=1s timeout=1s period=5s #success=1 #failure=3
    Readiness:      http-get http://:3000/probes/ready delay=5s timeout=1s period=5s #success=1 #failure=3
    Environment Variables from:
      nodejs-config  ConfigMap  Optional: false
    Environment:       <none>
    Mounts:
      /etc/nodejs-config from config (ro)
      /var/run/secrets/kubernetes.io/serviceaccount from default-token-zld5x (ro)
Conditions:
  Type           Status
  Initialized    True
  Ready          False
  PodScheduled   True
```

Note that `Condition Ready` is now `false`, and the status of the Node.js container has a state of `Running, but Ready of False`.

If the Redis deployment is recreated or restored, then the services will all come back online as you would expect.

Container lifecycle hooks

Kubernetes also provides some hooks within the lifecycle of each container that can be used at setup and teardown time for containers. These are called container lifecycle hooks, and are defined for each container, rather than for the Pod overall. When you want to configure some additional functionality specific to the container when you have multiple containers per Pod, these can be extremely useful.

The two hooks you can define for each container are post-start and pre-stop. The post-start and pre-stop hooks are intended to be invoked at least once, but Kubernetes does not make any guarantees that these hooks will be invoked only once. This means while it is likely rare, the post-start or pre-stop hooks may be invoked more than once.

Neither of these hooks accept parameters, and are defined in the same fashion as a container's run command. When used, they are expected to be self-contained, relatively short running commands that always return. When these hooks are being invoked, Kubernetes suspends management of the container until the hook completes and returns. Because of this, it is critical that executables invoked for these hooks don't hang or run indefinitely, as Kubernetes doesn't have a means of watching for this scenario and responding to a failure to complete or return a value.

In the case of post-start, the container state won't be moved to the Running state until the post-start hook. The post-start hook is also not guaranteed to be invoked either before or after the main command for the container is invoked. In the case of pre-stop, the container won't be terminated until the pre-stop hook completes and is returned.

These two hooks can be invoked using one of two handlers: Exec and HTTP. Exec runs a specific command inside the container and in the same process space as the container, much like using a `kubectl exec` invocation. The HTTP handler sets up for an HTTP request against the container. In either case, if the hook returns a failure code the container is killed.

The logs from these hooks are not exposed in Pod events or logging. If the handler fails, it broadcasts an event that can be seen with the `kubectl describe` command. These two events are `FailedPostStartHook` and `FailedPreStopHook`, respectively.

The pre-stop hook can be very useful when you want an external command to be invoked to cleanly shut down a running process, such as invoking `nginx -s quit`. This can be especially useful if you're using someone else's code, especially if it has a more complex shutdown process than responding correctly to the SIGTERM signal. We will discuss how to gracefully shut down Kubernetes a bit later in this chapter.

The post-start hook is often useful when you want to create a semaphore file within the container, or invoke an HTTP request call whenever the container starts. More often, the need is for initialization or pre-condition validation before your main code starts, and there is another option to use for that functionality: initialization containers.

Initialization containers

Initialization containers are containers that can be defined on your Pod, and will be invoked in the specific sequence that they are defined prior to your main container (or containers) being started. Initialization containers became a normal part of Pod specification in Kubernetes version 1.6.

These containers can use the same container image and simply have alternate commands, but they can also use entirely different images, leveraging the Kubernetes Pod guarantees of shared network and filesystem mounts to do initialization and setup work prior to the main container operating. These containers also use namespaces, so they can be given specific access that the main container doesn't have; consequently, they can be given access to Kubernetes Secrets that the main container cannot access.

Initialization containers are expected to have code that runs to completion and exits with a success response. As mentioned previously, these containers are also invoked in sequence, and will not run in parallel; each one has to complete before the next one will be started. When the containers have all completed, Kubernetes initializes the Pod and runs the defined container (or containers). If an initialization container fails, then the Pod is presumed to have failed and the whole kit is terminated (or more specifically, handled per the `restartPolicy`).

Initialization containers allow you to do all kinds of setup prior to your main process being run. Some examples of what you might do include writing configuration files that the main Pod container needs to have, verifying that a service is available and active prior to starting the main container, retrieving and initializing content such as pulling data from a Git repository or file service, for the main container to use, or even just enforcing a delay prior to starting the main container or containers.

While the initialization containers are running, the Pod status will show `Init:` followed by some initialization container-specific state. If everything is going well and as expected, it will report the number of initialization containers that are listed and how many have been run to completion. If an initialization container fails, then `Init:` will be followed by `Error` or `CrashLoopBackOff`.

Initialization containers are specified in the Pod specification at the same level as the main container or containers and as a list, each with its own name, image, and command to invoke. For example, we could add an `init` container to our Python flask specification that will only return when Redis is up and available. An example of that might be the following:

```
spec:
  template:
    metadata:
      labels:
          app: flask
    spec:
      containers:
      - name: flask
        image: quay.io/kubernetes-for-developers/flask:0.2.0
        ports:
        - containerPort: 5000
        envFrom:
        - configMapRef:
            name: flask-config
        volumeMounts:
          - name: config
            mountPath: /etc/flask-config
            readOnly: true
      volumes:
        - name: config
          configMap:
            name: flask-config
      initContainers:
      - name: init-myservice
        image: busybox
        command: ['sh', '-c', 'until nslookup redis-master; do echo waiting
for redis; sleep 2; done;']
```

In this case, the initialization container code is just a loop written in the shell that checks to see if there is a response to the DNS entry `redis-master`, and it runs indefinitely until that succeeds. If you were to look at the Pod prior to the `redis-master` service being established and having a relevant DNS entry, you would see the status of that Pod listed with `Init:0/1`.

For example, `kubectl get pods`:

```
NAME                READY STATUS    RESTARTS AGE
flask-f48f89687-8p8nj 0/1   Init:0/1 0        8h
```

kubectl describe deploy/flask

```
Namespace:      default
Node:           minikube/192.168.64.11
Start Time:     Thu, 21 Dec 2017 07:06:03 -0800
Labels:         app=flask
                pod-template-hash=904945243
Annotations:    kubernetes.io/created-by={"kind":"SerializedReference","apiVersion":"v1","reference":{"kind":"ReplicaSet","namespace":
"default","name":"flask-f48f89687","uid":"765fba5d-e660-11e7-89d4-b29f363a60d7","a...
Status:         Pending
IP:             172.17.0.4
Controlled By:  ReplicaSet/flask-f48f89687
Init Containers:
  init-myservice:
    Container ID:   docker://323de183ae2ac75b1ccdd99de61ab317395a44a63ea198096aecf546b545500d
    Image:          busybox
    Image ID:       docker-pullable://busybox@sha256:bbc3a03235220b170ba48a157dd097dd1379299370e1ed99ce976df0355d24f0
    Port:           <none>
    Command:
      sh
      -c
      until nslookup redis; do echo waiting for redis; sleep 2; done;
    State:          Running
      Started:      Thu, 21 Dec 2017 07:06:07 -0800
    Ready:          False
    Restart Count:  0
    Environment:    <none>
    Mounts:
      /var/run/secrets/kubernetes.io/serviceaccount from default-token-zld5x (ro)
Containers:
  flask:
    Container ID:
    Image:          quay.io/kubernetes-for-developers/flask:0.3.0
    Image ID:
    Port:           5000/TCP
    State:          Waiting
      Reason:       PodInitializing
    Ready:          False
    Restart Count:  0
    Liveness:       http-get http://:5000/alive delay=1s timeout=1s period=5s #success=1 #failure=3
    Readiness:      http-get http://:5000/ready delay=5s timeout=1s period=5s #success=1 #failure=3
    Environment Variables from:
      flask-config  ConfigMap  Optional: false
    Environment:    <none>
    Mounts:
      /etc/flask-config from config (ro)
      /var/run/secrets/kubernetes.io/serviceaccount from default-token-zld5x (ro)
Conditions:
  Type           Status
  Initialized    False
  Ready          False
  PodScheduled   True
```

You may notice that this output doesn't match the previous example; the command in the preceding output is looking for a DNS response to `redis`, where we named the service `redis-service`.

In this case, the initialization container will never complete and the Pod will remain in `pending` status indefinitely. In this case, you will need to manually delete the deployment, or if you make a modification that allows it to work, you will need to manually delete the Pods that are stuck initializing, as they won't otherwise be cleaned up.

Once the initialization container has completed successfully, you can see the results in the `kubectl describe` output from the Pod, or again via the data exposed with the `kubectl get` command.

The following is an extended example of the output that you will see from `kubectl describe`.

```
                          1. heckj@greyberry: ~/src/kfd-flask (bash)
Namespace:      default
Node:           minikube/192.168.64.11
Start Time:     Thu, 21 Dec 2017 07:26:09 -0800
Labels:         app=flask
                pod-template-hash=1504235051
Annotations:    kubernetes.io/created-by={"kind":"SerializedReference","apiVersion":"v1","reference":{"kind":"ReplicaSet","namespace":"
default","name":"flask-5948679495","uid":"454bd09f-e663-11e7-89d4-b29f363a60d7"},...
Status:         Running
IP:             172.17.0.4
Controlled By:  ReplicaSet/flask-5948679495
Init Containers:
  init-myservice:
    Container ID:  docker://54a3192886c8ab667b441b511177d15f656f0f746d0b7475d7821b64b2068f10
    Image:         busybox
    Image ID:      docker-pullable://busybox@sha256:bbc3a03235220b170ba48a157dd097dd1379299370e1ed99ce976df0355d24f0
    Port:          <none>
    Command:
      sh
      -c
      until nslookup redis-service; do echo waiting for redis-service; sleep 2; done;
    State:          Terminated
      Reason:       Completed
      Exit Code:    0
      Started:      Thu, 21 Dec 2017 07:26:11 -0800
      Finished:     Thu, 21 Dec 2017 07:26:11 -0800
    Ready:          True
    Restart Count:  0
    Environment:    <none>
    Mounts:
      /var/run/secrets/kubernetes.io/serviceaccount from default-token-zld5x (ro)
Containers:
  flask:
    Container ID:  docker://4a5a36df1a431107153027fbbccd46039b809e0379b0e54f3485c0cce46b6e52
    Image:         quay.io/kubernetes-for-developers/flask:0.3.0
    Image ID:      docker-pullable://quay.io/kubernetes-for-developers/flask@sha256:4cb1f7cb386894b2d2160b096bf90b5fb94493a19f91cfc592
93dd6fc59f0d84
    Port:          5000/TCP
    State:          Running
      Started:      Thu, 21 Dec 2017 07:26:13 -0800
    Ready:          True
    Restart Count:  0
    Liveness:       http-get http://:5000/alive delay=1s timeout=1s period=5s #success=1 #failure=3
    Readiness:      http-get http://:5000/ready delay=5s timeout=1s period=5s #success=1 #failure=3
    Environment Variables from:
      flask-config  ConfigMap  Optional: false
    Environment:    <none>
    Mounts:
      /etc/flask-config from config (ro)
      /var/run/secrets/kubernetes.io/serviceaccount from default-token-zld5x (ro)
```

The output of `describe` extends beyond a single Terminal page; you should continue to scroll down to see the following:

```
Conditions:
  Type            Status
  Initialized     True
  Ready           True
  PodScheduled    True
Volumes:
  config:
    Type:         ConfigMap (a volume populated by a ConfigMap)
    Name:         flask-config
    Optional:     false
  default-token-zld5x:
    Type:         Secret (a volume populated by a Secret)
    SecretName:   default-token-zld5x
    Optional:     false
QoS Class:        BestEffort
Node-Selectors:   <none>
Tolerations:      <none>
Events:
  Type    Reason                 Age   From               Message
  ----    ------                 ----  ----               -------
  Normal  Scheduled              8h    default-scheduler  Successfully assigned flask-5948679495-pl8pf to minikube
  Normal  SuccessfulMountVolume  8h    kubelet, minikube  MountVolume.SetUp succeeded for volume "config"
  Normal  SuccessfulMountVolume  8h    kubelet, minikube  MountVolume.SetUp succeeded for volume "default-token-zld5x"
  Normal  Pulling                8h    kubelet, minikube  pulling image "busybox"
  Normal  Pulled                 8h    kubelet, minikube  Successfully pulled image "busybox"
  Normal  Created                8h    kubelet, minikube  Created container
  Normal  Started                8h    kubelet, minikube  Started container
  Normal  Pulling                8h    kubelet, minikube  pulling image "quay.io/kubernetes-for-developers/flask:0.3.0"
  Normal  Pulled                 8h    kubelet, minikube  Successfully pulled image "quay.io/kubernetes-for-developers/flask:0.3.0"
  Normal  Created                8h    kubelet, minikube  Created container
  Normal  Started                8h    kubelet, minikube  Started container
heck]  ~  src  kfd-flask  0.3.0  $
```

Quick interactive testing

If you are trying to make a quick one-liner initialization container, it's often useful to try out a command interactively, especially if you're using a very minimal container such as `busybox`. The commands you want may not be available, so it's best to try it out quickly to verify it can work as you expect.

To run a `busybox` container interactively, and delete it all when it's complete, you can use a command such as the following:

```
kubectl run tempinteractive -it --rm --restart=Never --image=busybox --
/bin/sh
```

And then try out this command within the container:

```
                         1. heckj@greyberry: ~/src/kfd-flask (bash)
heckj  ⬚~ ⬚src ⬚kfd-flask ⬚0.3.0 ⬚$ ⬚kubectl run tempinteractive -it --rm --restart=Never --image=busybox -- /bin/sh
If you don't see a command prompt, try pressing enter.
/ # until nslookup redis-service; do echo waiting for redis-service; sleep 2; done;
Server:    10.96.0.10
Address 1: 10.96.0.10 kube-dns.kube-system.svc.cluster.local

Name:      redis-service
Address 1: 10.108.129.68 redis-service.default.svc.cluster.local
/ # echo $?
0
/ # exit
```

Handling a graceful shutdown

With the lifecycle hooks, we mentioned the pre-stop hook that can be defined and enabled, but if you're writing your own code, then you may find it just as easy to respect the SIGTERM signal that Kubernetes uses to tell containers to shut down.

If you aren't familiar with SIGTERM, it is one of the functions that Linux supports from the kernel—a means of sending an interrupt to a running process. The process can listen for these signals, and you can choose how they respond when they are received. There are two signals that you can't `ignore` and the operating system will enforce, regardless of what you implement: SIGKILL and SIGSTOP. The signal that Kubernetes uses when it wants to shut down a container is SIGTERM.

The kind of events where you will receive this signal aren't just on error or user-invoked deletion, but also when you roll out a code update leveraging the rolling update mechanism that deployment uses. It can also happen if you take advantage of any of the autoscaling features, which can dynamically increase (and decrease) the number of replicas within a `replicaSet`.

When you respond to the signal, you will generally want to save any needed state, close any connections, and then terminate your application.

If you are creating a service that others will use through Kubernetes as well, then one of the first things you might want to do is change an internal variable that will trigger any readiness probe to respond with `false`, sleep for a few seconds, and then do any finalization and termination. That will allow the service construct within Kubernetes to redirect any further connections, and all active connections can be completed, drained, and shut down politely.

Once Kubernetes sends the signal, it starts a timer. The default value of that timer is 30 seconds, and it can be defined on your Pod specification with the value `terminateGracePeriodSeconds` if you need or want a longer value. If the container hasn't exited by the time that timer expires, Kubernetes will attempt to force it using the SIGKILL signal.

If you have invoked `kubectl delete deploy nodejs`, for example, and then seen the Pods remaining for a while with the status `Terminating`, that is what was happening.

SIGTERM in Python

As an example, if you want to handle SIGTERM in Python, then you can import the signal module and reference a handler to do whatever you want. For example, a simple shut down immediately and exit bit of code might be:

```
import signal
import sys

def sigterm_handler(_signo, _stack_frame):
    sys.exit(0)

signal.signal(signal.SIGTERM, sigterm_handler)
```

The signal handler logic can be as complex, or as simple, as your code requires.

SIGTERM in Node.js

As an example, if you want to handle SIGTERM in Node.js, then you can use the process module that is implicitly created in every Node.js process to handle the signals and to exit the application. To match the preceding Python example, a simple shut down immediately and exit bit of code might be as follows:

```
/**
 * SIGTERM handler to terminate (semi) gracefully
 */
process.on(process.SIGTERM, function() {
    console.log('Received SIGTERM signal, now shutting down...');
    process.exit(0);
})
```

Summary

In this chapter, we started with looking at the Pod lifecycle and status details in depth, expanding to show multiple ways of revealing relevant details, and describing what Kubernetes does beneath the covers while running your software. We then looked at the feedback loops that your program can provide with liveness and readiness probes, and reviewed examples of enabling those in both Python and Node.js. Following on from the probes and how your code can interact with Kubernetes cleanly, we looked at the common cases for startup and initialization, and graceful shutdown.

In the next chapter, we look at how to use Kubernetes and open source to provide basic observability for your applications, specifically monitoring and logging.

6

Background Processing in Kubernetes

Kubernetes includes support for one-off (also known as batch) computation work, as well as supporting common use cases for asynchronous background work. In this chapter, we look at the Kubernetes concept of job, and its neighbor, CronJob. We also look at how Kubernetes handles and supports persistence, and some of the options that are available within Kubernetes. We then look at how Kubernetes can support asynchronous background tasks and the ways those can be represented, operated, and tracked by Kubernetes. We also go over how to set up worker codes operating from a message queue.

Topics covered in this chapter include:

- Job
- CronJob
- A worker queue example with Python and Celery
- Persistence with Kubernetes
- Stateful Sets
- **Custom Resource Definitions (CRDs)**

Job

Most of what we have covered so far has been focused on continuous, long-running processes. Kubernetes also has support for shorter, discrete runs of software. A job in Kubernetes is focused on a discrete run that is expected to end within some reasonably-known timeframe, and report a success or failure. Jobs use and build upon the same construct as the long-running software, so they use the pod specification at their heart, and add the concept of tracking the number of successful completions.

The simplest use case is to run a single pod to completion, letting Kubernetes handle any failures due to a node failure or reboot. The two optional settings you can use with jobs are parallelism and completion. Without specifying parallelism, the default is 1 and only one job will be scheduled at a time. You can specify both values as integers to run a number of jobs in parallel to achieve multiple completions, and you can leave completions unset if the job is working from a work queue of some form.

It is important to know that the settings for completions and parallelism aren't guarantees – so the code within your pods needs to be tolerant of multiple instances running. Likewise, the job needs to be tolerant of a container restarting in the event of a container failure (for example, when using the `restartPolicy OnFailure`), as well as handling any initialization or setup that it needs if on restart it finds itself running on a new pod (which can happen in the event of node failure). If your job is using temporary files, locks, or working off a local file to do its work, it should verify on startup what the state is and not presume the files will always be there, in the event of a failure during processing.

When a job runs to completion, the system does not create any more pods, but does not delete the pod either. This lets you interrogate the pod state for success or failure, and look at any logs from the containers within the pod. Pods that have run to completion will not show up in a simple run of `kubectl get pods`, but will appear if you use the `-a` option. It is up to you to delete completed jobs, and when you use `kubectl delete` to remove the job, the associated pod will be removed and cleaned up as well.

As an example, let's run an example job to look at how this works. A simple job that simply prints `hello world` can be specified with the following YAML:

```
apiVersion: batch/v1
kind: Job
metadata:
  name: helloworld
spec:
  template:
    metadata:
      name: helloworld
    spec:
      containers:
      - name: simple
        image: busybox
        command: ["/bin/echo", "'hello world'"]
      restartPolicy: Never
```

And then you can run this job using either `kubectl create` or `kubectl apply`:

```
kubectl apply -f simplejob.yaml
```

The expected command of `kubectl get jobs` will show you the jobs that exist and their current state. Since this job is so simple, it will likely complete before you can run a command to see its current state:

```
kubectl get jobs
```

NAME	DESIRED	SUCCESSFUL	AGE
helloworld	1	1	3d

And like pods, you can use the `kubectl describe` command to get more detailed state and output:

```
kubectl describe job helloworld
```

```
Name:           helloworld
Namespace:      default
Selector:       controller-uid=cdafeb57-e7c4-11e7-89d4-b29f363a60d7
Labels:         controller-uid=cdafeb57-e7c4-11e7-89d4-b29f363a60d7
                job-name=helloworld
Annotations:    kubectl.kubernetes.io/last-applied-
configuration={"apiVersion":"batch/v1","kind":"Job","metadata":{"annotation
s":{},"name":"helloworld","namespace":"default"},"spec":{"backoffLimit":4,"
template":{"met...
Parallelism:    1
Completions:    1
Start Time:     Sat, 23 Dec 2017 01:36:50 -0800
Pods Statuses:  0 Running / 1 Succeeded / 0 Failed
Pod Template:
  Labels:  controller-uid=cdafeb57-e7c4-11e7-89d4-b29f363a60d7
           job-name=helloworld
  Containers:
   simple:
    Image:  busybox
    Port:   <none>
    Command:
      /bin/echo
      'hello world'
    Environment:  <none>
    Mounts:       <none>
  Volumes:        <none>
Events:
  Type    Reason           Age   From            Message
  ----    ------           ----  ----            -------
  Normal  SuccessfulCreate 3d    job-controller  Created pod:
```

```
helloworld-2b2xt
```

If you run the command `kubectl get pods`, you won't see the pod `helloworld-2b2xt` in the list of pods, but running `kubectl get pods -a` will show the pods, including completed or failed pods that still exist:

NAME	READY	STATUS	RESTARTS	AGE
helloworld-2b2xt	0/1	Completed	0	3d

If you just want to see for yourself what the state of the pod was, using `kubectl describe` to get the details will show you the information in human, readable form:

```
kubectl describe pod helloworld-2b2xt
```

An example of this is the following:

If you are making a simple job with a shell script like in this example, it's easy to make a mistake. In those cases, the default will be for Kubernetes to retry running the pod repeatedly, leaving pods in a failed state in the system for you to see. Having a backoff limit, in this case, can limit the number of times the system retries your job. If you don't specify this value, it uses the default value of six tries.

A job with a simple mistake in the command might look like the following:

```
kubectl describe job helloworld

Name:           helloworld
Namespace:      default
Selector:       controller-uid=6693f83a-e7c7-11e7-89d4-b29f363a60d7
Labels:         controller-uid=6693f83a-e7c7-11e7-89d4-b29f363a60d7
                job-name=helloworld
Annotations:    kubectl.kubernetes.io/last-applied-
configuration={"apiVersion":"batch/v1","kind":"Job","metadata":{"annotation
s":{},"name":"helloworld","namespace":"default"},"spec":{"template":{"metad
ata":{"name":"h...
Parallelism:    1
Completions:    1
Start Time:     Sat, 23 Dec 2017 01:55:26 -0800
Pods Statuses:  0 Running / 0 Succeeded / 6 Failed
Pod Template:
  Labels:   controller-uid=6693f83a-e7c7-11e7-89d4-b29f363a60d7
            job-name=helloworld
  Containers:
   simple:
    Image:  busybox
    Port:       <none>
    Command:
      /bin/sh
      echo
      'hello world'
    Environment:    <none>
    Mounts:         <none>
   Volumes:         <none>
Events:
  Type      Reason              Age     From            Message
  ----      ------              ----    ----            -------
  Normal    SuccessfulCreate    3d      job-controller  Created pod:
helloworld-sz6zj
  Normal    SuccessfulCreate    3d      job-controller  Created pod:
helloworld-vtzh7
  Normal    SuccessfulCreate    3d      job-controller  Created pod:
helloworld-2gh74
  Normal    SuccessfulCreate    3d      job-controller  Created pod:
```

```
helloworld-dfggg
  Normal    SuccessfulCreate        3d    job-controller  Created pod:
helloworld-z2llj
  Normal    SuccessfulCreate        3d    job-controller  Created pod:
helloworld-69d4t
  Warning   BackoffLimitExceeded    3d    job-controller  Job has reach the
specified backoff limit
```

And looking at the `pods`:

```
kubectl get pods -a
```

NAME	READY	STATUS	RESTARTS	AGE
helloworld-2gh74	0/1	Error	0	3d
helloworld-69d4t	0/1	Error	0	3d
helloworld-dfggg	0/1	Error	0	3d
helloworld-sz6zj	0/1	Error	0	3d
helloworld-vtzh7	0/1	Error	0	3d
helloworld-z2llj	0/1	Error	0	3d

The logs for each pod will be available, so you can diagnose what went wrong.

If you do make a mistake, then you may be tempted to make a quick modification to the job specification and use `kubectl apply` to fix the error. Jobs are considered immutable by the system, so you will get an error if you try to make a quick fix and apply it. When you are working with jobs, it is better to delete the job and create a new one.

Jobs are not tied to the life cycle of other objects in Kubernetes, so if you are thinking about using one to initialize data in a persistence store, remember that you will need to coordinate running that job. In cases where you want some logic checked every time before a service starts to preload data, you may be better off using an initialization container, as we explored in the last chapter.

Some common cases that work well for jobs are loading a backup into a database, making a backup, doing some deeper system introspection or diagnostics, or running out-of-band cleanup logic. In all these cases, you want to know that the function you wrote ran to completion, and that it succeeded. And in the case of failure, you may want to retry, or simply know what happened via the logs.

CronJob

CronJobs are an extension that build on jobs to allow you to specify a recurring schedule for when they run. The name pulls from a common Linux utility for scheduling recurring scripts called `cron`. CronJobs were alpha as of Kubernetes version 1.7, and moved to beta in version 1.8, and remain in beta as of version 1.9. Remember that Kubernetes specifications may change, but tend to be fairly solid and have expected utility with beta, so the v1 release of CronJobs may be different, but you can likely expect it to be pretty close to what's available as of this writing.

The specification is highly related to a job, with the primary difference being the kind is CronJob and there is a required field schedule that takes a string representing the timing for running this job.

The format for this string is five numbers, and wildcards can be used. The fields represent:

- Minute (0–59)
- Hour (0–23)
- Day of Month (1–31)
- Month (1–12)
- Day of Week (0–6)

A `*` or? a character can be used in any of these fields to represent that any value is acceptable. A field can also include a `*/` and a number, which indicates a recurring instance at some interval, specified by the associated number. Some examples of this format are:

- `12 * * * *`: Run every hour at 12 minutes past the hour
- `*/5 * * * *`: Run every 5 minutes
- `0 0 * * 0`: Run every Saturday at midnight

There are also a few special strings that can be used for common occurrences that are a bit more human readable:

- `@yearly`
- `@monthly`
- `@weekly`
- `@daily`
- `@hourly`

A CronJob has five additional fields that you can specify, but which are not required. Unlike jobs, CronJobs are mutable (just like pods, deployments, and so on), so these values can be changed or updated after the CronJob is created.

The first is `startingDeadlineSeconds`, which, if specified, will put a limit on when a job can be started if Kubernetes doesn't meet its specified deadline of when to start the job. If the time exceeds `startingDeadlineSeconds`, that iteration will be marked as a failure.

The second is `concurrencyPolicy`, which controls whether Kubernetes allows multiple instances of the same job to run concurrently. The default for this is `Allow`, which will let multiple jobs run at the same time, with alternate values of `Forbid` and `Replace`. `Forbid` will mark the following job as a failure if the first is still running, and `Replace` will cancel the first job and attempt to run that same code again.

The third field is `suspended`, which defaults to `False`, and can be used to suspend any further invocations of jobs on the schedule. If a job is already running and `suspend` is added to the CronJob specification, that current job will run to completion, but any further jobs won't be scheduled.

The fourth and fifth fields are `successfulJobsHistoryLimit` and `failedJobsHistoryLimit`, which default to values of 3 and 1 respectively. By default, Kubernetes will clean up old jobs beyond these values, but retain the recent success and failures, including the logs, so they can be inspected as you wish.

When you create a CronJob, you will also want to choose (and define in your specification) a `restartPolicy`. A CronJob doesn't allow for the default value of `Always`, so you will want to choose between `OnFailure` and `Never`.

A simple CronJob that prints `hello world` every minute might look like the following:

```
apiVersion: batch/v1beta1
kind: CronJob
metadata:
  name: helloworld
spec:
  schedule: "*/1 * * * *"
  jobTemplate:
    spec:
      template:           spec:
          containers:
          - name: simple
            image: busybox
            command: ["/bin/sh", "-c", "echo", "'hello world'"]
          restartPolicy: OnFailure
```

After creating this job with `kubectl apply -f cronjob.yaml`, you can see the summary output with `kubectl get cronjob`:

NAME	SCHEDULE	SUSPEND	ACTIVE	LAST SCHEDULE	AGE
helloworld	*/1 * * * *	False	1	3d	3d

Or, see more detailed output with `kubectl describe cronjob helloworld`:

```
Name:                    helloworld
Namespace:               default
Labels:                  <none>
Annotations:             kubectl.kubernetes.io/last-applied-
configuration={"apiVersion":"batch/v1beta1","kind":"CronJob","metadata":{"a
nnotations":{},"name":"helloworld","namespace":"default"},"spec":{"jobTempl
ate":{"spec":{"...
Schedule:                */1 * * * *
Concurrency Policy:      Allow
Suspend:                 False
Starting Deadline Seconds: <unset>
Selector:                <unset>
Parallelism:             <unset>
Completions:             <unset>
Pod Template:
  Labels:    <none>
  Containers:
   simple:
    Image:   busybox
    Port:     <none>
    Command:
      /bin/sh
      -c
      echo
      'hello world'
    Environment:    <none>
    Mounts:         <none>
  Volumes:          <none>
Last Schedule Time:    Sat, 23 Dec 2017 02:46:00 -0800
Active Jobs:           <none>
Events:
  Type      Reason           Age    From               Message
  ----      ------           ----   ----               -------
  Normal    SuccessfulCreate 3d     cronjob-controller Created job
helloworld-1514025900
  Normal    SawCompletedJob  3d     cronjob-controller Saw completed job:
helloworld-1514025900
```

```
    Normal  SuccessfulCreate  3d      cronjob-controller  Created job
helloworld-1514025960
    Normal  SawCompletedJob   3d      cronjob-controller  Saw completed job:
helloworld-1514025960
```

As you might guess from this output, the CronJob is actually creating jobs to the schedule you define, and from the template in the specification. Each job gets its own name based on the name of the CronJob, and can be viewed independently:

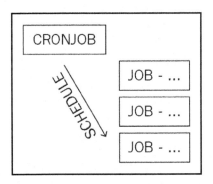

You can see the jobs that are created on the schedule defined from the preceding CronJob, by using the `kubectl get jobs` command:

```
kubectl get jobs
```

NAME	DESIRED	SUCCESSFUL	AGE
helloworld-1514025900	1	1	3d
helloworld-1514025960	1	1	3d
helloworld-1514026020	1	1	3d

And you can view the pods that were created and run to completion from each of those jobs, leveraging the `-a` option with `kubectl get pods`:

```
kubectl get pods -a
```

NAME	READY	STATUS	RESTARTS	AGE
helloworld-1514025900-5pj4r	0/1	Completed	0	3d
helloworld-1514025960-ckshh	0/1	Completed	0	3d
helloworld-1514026020-gjrfh	0/1	Completed	0	3d

A worker queue example with Python and Celery

Where the CronJob is well positioned to run repeated tasks at a specific schedule, another common need is to process a series of work items more or less constantly. A job is well oriented to running a single task until it is complete, but if the volume of things you need to process is large enough, it may be far more effective to maintain a constant process to work on those items.

A common pattern to accommodate this kind of work uses a message queue, as shown here:

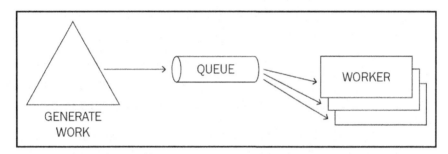

With a message queue, you can have an API frontend that creates the work to be run asynchronously, move that into a queue, and then have a number of worker processes pull from the queue to do the relevant work. Amazon has a web-based service supporting exactly this pattern of processing called **Simple Queue Service** (**SQS**). A huge benefit of this pattern is decoupling the workers from the request, so you can scale each of those pieces independently, as required.

You can do exactly the same within Kubernetes, running the queue as a service and workers connecting to that queue as a deployment. Python has a popular framework, Celery, that carries out background processing from a message, supporting a number of queue mechanisms. We will look at how you can set up an example queue and worker process, and how to leverage a framework such as Celery within Kubernetes.

Celery worker example

Celery has been in development and use since 2009, long before Kubernetes existed. It was written expecting to be deployed on multiple machines. This translates reasonably well to containers, which our example will illustrate. You can get more details about Celery at: http://docs.celeryproject.org/en/latest/.

In this example, we will set up a service with a deployment of RabbitMQ and a separate deployment of our own container, **celery-worker**, to process jobs from that queue:

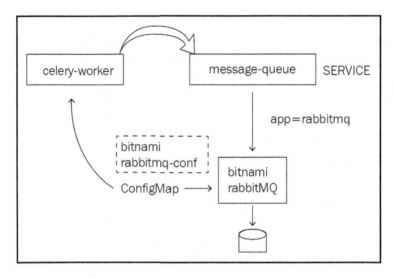

The deployments and source code for this example are available on GitHub at `https://github.com/kubernetes-for-developers/kfd-celery/`. You can get this code by using the following commands:

```
git clone https://github.com/kubernetes-for-developers/kfd-celery -b 0.4.0
cd kfd-celery
```

RabbitMQ and configuration

This example uses a container that includes RabbitMQ from Bitnami. The source for that image is available at `https://github.com/bitnami/bitnami-docker-rabbitmq`, and the container images are hosted publicly on DockerHub at `https://hub.docker.com/r/bitnami/rabbitmq/`.

RabbitMQ has a large number of options that can be used with it, and a variety of ways to deploy it, including in clusters to support HA. For this example, we are using a single RabbitMQ replica within a deployment to back a service called `message-queue`. We also set up a `ConfigMap` with some of the variables that we might want to adjust for a local setting, although in this example, the values are the same as the defaults within the container. The deployment does use a persistent volume to enable persistence for the queue in the event of a failure. We will go into persistent volumes and how to use them later in this chapter.

The ConfigMap we create will be used by both the RabbitMQ container and our worker deployment. The ConfigMap is called queue-config.yaml and reads as follows:

```
---
apiVersion: v1
kind: ConfigMap
metadata:
  name: bitnami-rabbitmq-config
data:
  RABBITMQ_USERNAME: "user"
  RABBITMQ_PASSWORD: "bitnami"
  RABBITMQ_VHOST: "/"
  RABBITMQ_NODE_PORT_NUMBER: "5672"
  RABBITMQ_MANAGER_PORT_NUMBER: "15672"
  WORKER_DEBUG_LEVEL: "info"
```

To deploy it, you can use this command:

```
kubectl apply -f deploy/queue-config.yaml

configmap "bitnami-rabbitmq-config" created
```

The ConfigMap was created based on the documentation for the Bitnami RabbitMQ container, which supports setting a number of configuration items through environment variables. You can see all the details that the container could take at the Docker Hub web page, or at the source in GitHub. In our case, we set some of the most common values.

Note: You would probably want to set username and password more correctly with secrets instead of including the values in a ConfigMap.

You can see the specification for the deployment:

```
                    2. heckj@greyberry: ~/src/kfd-celery (vim)
34 kind: Deployment
35 metadata:
36   name: rabbitmq
37 spec:
38   replicas: 1
39   template:
40     metadata:
41       labels:
42         app: rabbitmq
43         role: master
44         tier: queue
45     spec:
46       containers:
47       - name: rabbitmq
48         image: bitnami/rabbitmq:3.7
49         envFrom:
50         - configMapRef:
51             name: bitnami-rabbitmq-config
52         ports:
53         - name: queue
54           containerPort: 5672
55         - name: queue-mgmt
56           containerPort: 15672
57         livenessProbe:
58           exec:
59             command:
60             - rabbitmqctl
61             - status
62           initialDelaySeconds: 120
63           timeoutSeconds: 5
64           failureThreshold: 6
65         readinessProbe:
66           exec:
67             command:
68             - rabbitmqctl
69             - status
70           initialDelaySeconds: 10
71           timeoutSeconds: 3
72           periodSeconds: 5
73         volumeMounts:
74         - name: rabbitmq-storage
75           mountPath: /bitnami
76       volumes:
77       - name: rabbitmq-storage
78         persistentVolumeClaim:
79           claimName: rabbitmq-pv-claim
```

And this is how to deploy the instance:

```
kubectl apply -f deploy/rabbitmq.yml

service "message-queue" created
persistentvolumeclaim "rabbitmq-pv-claim" created
deployment "rabbitmq" created
```

Celery worker

To create a worker, we made our own container image very similar to the Flask container. The Dockerfile uses Alpine Linux and explicitly loads Python 3 onto that image, then installs the requirements from a `requirements.txt` file and adds in two Python files. The first, `celery_conf.py`, is the Python definition for a couple of tasks taken directly from the Celery documentation. The second, `submit_tasks.py`, is a short example that is meant to be run interactively to create work and send it over the queue. The container also includes two shell scripts: `run.sh` and `celery_status.sh`.

In all of these cases, we used environment variables that we source from the preceding `ConfigMap` to set up the logging output from the worker, as well as the host, username, and password for communicating with RabbitMQ within Kubernetes.

The Dockerfile uses the `run.sh` script as its command, so that we can use this shell script to set up any environment variables and invoke Celery. Because Celery was originally written as a command-line tool, using a shell script to set up and invoke what you want is very convenient. Here is a closer look at `run.sh`:

```
You, a few seconds ago | 2 authors (Joe Heck and others)
1    #!/bin/sh
2
3    # echo all the commands invoked within this shell to STDOUT
4    # so we can see what is being run in the logs
5    set -x
6
7    # make sure we exit this wrapper script with a failure if any of the commands
8    # we invoke fail to return properly
9    set -e
10        Joe Heck, 3 hours ago • adding a probe script and related updates
11   # apply a default debug level of info if
12   # not overridden in the environment variables
13   DEBUG_LEVEL=${WORKER_DEBUG_LEVEL:-info}
14
15   # make sure we're in the correct local directory for celery to
16   # module load celery_conf within python...
17   cd /opt/app
18
19   # initiate the celery worker
20   /usr/bin/celery -A celery_conf worker -l ${DEBUG_LEVEL}
21
```

The script sets two shell script options, -e and -x. The first, (-e), is to make sure that if we make a typo or a command in the script returned an error, the script itself will return an error. The second, (-x), echoes the commands invoked in the script to STDOUT, so we can see that in the container log output.

The next line with DEBUG_LEVEL uses the shell to look for a default environment variable: WORKER_DEBUG_LEVEL. If it's set, it will use it, and WORKER_DEBUG_LEVEL was added earlier to the ConfigMap. If the value isn't set, this will use a default of info in its place, so if the value is missing from the ConfigMap, we will still have a reasonable value here.

As mentioned earlier, Celery was written as a command-line utility and takes advantage of Python's module loading to do its work. Python module loading includes working from the current directory, so we explicitly change to the directory containing the Python code. Finally, the script invokes the command to start a Celery worker.

We use a similar structure in the script, celery_status.sh, which is used to provide an exec command used in both liveness and readiness probes for the worker container, with the key idea being if the command celery status returns without an error, the container is communicating effectively with RabbitMQ and should be fully able to process tasks.

The code that contains the logic that will be invoked is all in celery_conf.py:

```
1    #!/usr/bin/env python3
2
3    import os
4    from celery import Celery
5    from celery.utils.log import get_task_logger
6    logger = get_task_logger(__name__)
7
8    # set username and password for broker, with overrides from environment variables
9    rabbitmq_user = os.environ.get('RABBITMQ_USERNAME','user')
10   rabbitmq_password = os.environ.get('RABBITMQ_PASSWORD','bitnami')
11   rabbitmq_vhost = os.environ.get('RABBITMQ_VHOST','/')
12
13   # Get Kubernetes-provided address of the broker service
14   broker_service_host = os.environ.get('MESSAGE_QUEUE_SERVICE_HOST','message-queue')
15   # could also use DNS name: 'message-queue'|'message-queue.default.svc.cluster.local'
16   # for our default
17
18   broker_url = 'amqp://%s:%s@%s/%s' % (rabbitmq_user,
19           rabbitmq_password, broker_service_host, rabbitmq_vhost)
20   app = Celery('tasks', broker=broker_url, backend='amqp')
21
22   @app.task
23   def add(x, y):
24       logger.info('Adding {0} + {1}'.format(x, y))
25       return x + y
26
27   @app.task(bind=true)
28   def dump_context(self, x, y)
29       logger.info('Executing task id {0.id}, args: {0.args!r} kwargs: {0.kwargs!r}'.format(
30               self.request))
```

You can see that we again make use of environment variables to get the values needed to communicate with RabbitMQ (a hostname, username, password, and vhost) and assemble these from environment variables with defaults, if they're not provided. The hostname default (message-queue) also matches the service name in our service definition that fronts RabbitMQ, giving us a stable default. The remainder of the code comes from the Celery documentation, supplying two sample tasks that we can import and use separately as well.

You can deploy the worker using this command:

```
kubectl apply -f deploy/celery-worker.yaml
```

This should report the deployment created, such as:

```
deployment "celery-worker" created
```

And now, you should have two deployments running together. You can verify this with `kubectl get pods`:

```
NAME                            READY   STATUS    RESTARTS   AGE
celery-worker-7c59b58df-qptlc   1/1     Running   0          11m
rabbitmq-6c656f667f-rp2zm       1/1     Running   0          14m
```

To watch the system a bit more interactively, run this command:

```
kubectl log deploy/celery-worker -f
```

This will stream the logs from the `celery-worker`, for example:

```
● ● ●                    1. heckj@greyberry: ~/src/kfd-celery (kubectl)
heckj  ~  src  kfd-celery  0.4.0  $  kubectl log deploy/celery-worker -f
W1229 16:26:07.469537   20092 cmd.go:353] log is DEPRECATED and will be removed in a future versio
n. Use logs instead.
+ set -e
+ DEBUG_LEVEL=info
+ cd /opt/app
+ /usr/bin/celery -A celery_conf worker -l info
/usr/lib/python3.6/site-packages/celery/platforms.py:795: RuntimeWarning: You're running the worke
r with superuser privileges: this is
absolutely not recommended!

Please specify a different user using the -u option.

User information: uid=0 euid=0 gid=0 egid=0

  uid=uid, euid=euid, gid=gid, egid=egid,
/usr/lib/python3.6/site-packages/celery/backends/amqp.py:68: CPendingDeprecationWarning:
    The AMQP result backend is scheduled for deprecation in     version 4.0 and removal in version
  v5.0.     Please use RPC backend or a persistent backend.

  alternative='Please use RPC backend or a persistent backend.')
[2017-12-30 00:12:54,383: INFO/MainProcess] Connected to amqp://user:**@10.102.51.154:5672//
[2017-12-30 00:12:54,399: INFO/MainProcess] mingle: searching for neighbors
[2017-12-30 00:12:55,428: INFO/MainProcess] mingle: all alone
[2017-12-30 00:12:55,475: INFO/MainProcess] celery@celery-worker-7c59b58df-qptlc ready.
```

This will display the logs from the `celery-worker` deployment, as they happen. Open a second Terminal window and invoke the following command to run a temporary pod with an interactive shell:

```
kubectl run -i --tty \
--image quay.io/kubernetes-for-developers/celery-worker:0.4.0 \
--restart=Never --image-pull-policy=Always --rm testing /bin/sh
```

Within the shell, you can now run the script to generate some tasks for the worker to process:

```
python3 submit_tasks.py
```

An example of this script is:

```python
#!/usr/bin/env python3

import random
import syslog
import time

from celery_conf import add
from celery_conf import dump_context

while True:
    x = random.randint(1, 10)
    y = random.randint(1, 10)
    res = add.delay(x, y)
    dump_context.apply_async(args=[x, y])
    time.sleep(5)
    if res.ready():
        res.get()
```

This script will run indefinitely, invoking the two sample tasks in the worker, roughly every five seconds, and in the window that is showing you the logs, you should see the output update with logged results from the Celery worker:

Persistence with Kubernetes

So far, all our examples, and even code, have been essentially stateless. In the last chapter, we introduced a container using Redis, but didn't specify anything special for it. By default, Kubernetes will assume any resources associated with a pod are ephemeral, and if the node fails, or a deployment is deleted, all the associated resources can and will be deleted with it.

That said, almost all the work we do requires storing and maintaining state somewhere—a database, an object store, or even a persistent, in-memory queue. Kubernetes includes support for persistence, and as of this writing, it's still changing and evolving fairly rapidly.

Volumes

The earliest support in Kubernetes was for volumes, which can be defined by the cluster administrator, and we've already seen some variations of this construct with the configuration being exposed into a container using the Downward API back in `Chapter 4`, *Declarative Infrastructure*.

Another kind of volume that can be easily used is `emptyDir`, which you can use in a pod specification to create an empty directory, and mount it to one or more of the containers in your pod. This is typically created on whatever storage the local node has available, but includes an option to specify a medium of *memory*, which you can use to make a temporary memory-backed filesystem. This takes up more memory on the node, but creates a very fast, ephemeral file system for use by your pods. If your code wants to use some scratch space on disk, maintain a periodic checkpoint, or load ephemeral content, this can be a very good way of managing that space.

As we specified in the configuration, when you use a volume, you specify it under volumes and make a related entry under `volumeMounts` that indicates where you're using it on each container.

We can modify our Flask example application to have a cache space that is a memory-backed temporary space:

```
spec:
  containers:
  - name: flask
    image: quay.io/kubernetes-for-developers/flask:0.3.0
    imagePullPolicy: Always
    ports:
    - containerPort: 5000
    volumeMounts:
      - name: config
        mountPath: /etc/flask-config
        readOnly: true
      - name: cache-volume
        mountPath: /opt/cache
  volumes:
    - name: config
      configMap:
        name: flask-config
    - name: cache-volume
      emptyDir:
        medium: Memory
```

If we deploy this version of the specification and open an interactive shell in the container, you can see /opt/cache listed as a volume of type tmpfs:

```
df -h

Filesystem                    Size     Used Available Use% Mounted on
overlay                       15.3G    1.7G     12.7G  12% /
tmpfs                       1000.1M       0   1000.1M   0% /dev
tmpfs                       1000.1M       0   1000.1M   0% /sys/fs/cgroup
tmpfs                       1000.1M       0   1000.1M   0% /opt/cache
/dev/vda1                     15.3G    1.7G     12.7G  12% /dev/termination-
log
/dev/vda1                     15.3G    1.7G     12.7G  12% /etc/flask-config
/dev/vda1                     15.3G    1.7G     12.7G  12% /etc/resolv.conf
/dev/vda1                     15.3G    1.7G     12.7G  12% /etc/hostname
/dev/vda1                     15.3G    1.7G     12.7G  12% /etc/hosts
shm                           64.0M       0     64.0M   0% /dev/shm
tmpfs                       1000.1M   12.0K  1000.1M   0%
/run/secrets/kubernetes.io/serviceaccount
tmpfs                       1000.1M       0   1000.1M   0% /proc/kcore
tmpfs                       1000.1M       0   1000.1M   0% /proc/timer_list
tmpfs                       1000.1M       0   1000.1M   0% /proc/timer_stats
tmpfs                       1000.1M       0   1000.1M   0% /sys/firmware
```

If we had specified the volume without the medium of type Memory, the directory would show up on the local disk instead:

```
df -h

Filesystem                    Size     Used Available Use% Mounted on
overlay                       15.3G    1.7G     12.7G  12% /
tmpfs                       1000.1M       0   1000.1M   0% /dev
tmpfs                       1000.1M       0   1000.1M   0% /sys/fs/cgroup
/dev/vda1                     15.3G    1.7G     12.7G  12% /dev/termination-
log
/dev/vda1                     15.3G    1.7G     12.7G  12% /etc/flask-config
/dev/vda1                     15.3G    1.7G     12.7G  12% /opt/cache
/dev/vda1                     15.3G    1.7G     12.7G  12% /etc/resolv.conf
/dev/vda1                     15.3G    1.7G     12.7G  12% /etc/hostname
/dev/vda1                     15.3G    1.7G     12.7G  12% /etc/hosts
shm                           64.0M       0     64.0M   0% /dev/shm
tmpfs                       1000.1M   12.0K  1000.1M   0%
/run/secrets/kubernetes.io/serviceaccount
tmpfs                       1000.1M       0   1000.1M   0% /proc/kcore
tmpfs                       1000.1M       0   1000.1M   0% /proc/timer_list
tmpfs                       1000.1M       0   1000.1M   0% /proc/timer_stats
tmpfs                       1000.1M       0   1000.1M   0% /sys/firmware
```

If you are using volumes on a cloud provider, then you can use one of their persistent volumes. In these cases, you need to have created a persistent disk at the cloud provider that is accessible to the nodes where you have your Kubernetes cluster, but this allows you to have data exist beyond the lifetime of any pod or node. The volumes for each cloud provider are specific to each provider, for example, `awsElasticBlockStore`, `azureDisk`, or `gcePersistentDisk`.

 There are a number of other volume types available, and most of these depend on how your cluster was set up and what might be available in that setup. You can get a sense of all the supported volumes from the formal documentation for volumes at `https://kubernetes.io/docs/concepts/storage/volumes/`.

PersistentVolume and PersistentVolumeClaim

If you want to use persistent volumes, independent of the specific location where you have built your cluster, you probably want to take advantage of two newer Kubernetes resources: `PersistentVolume` and `PersistentVolumeClaim`. These separate the specifics of how volumes are provided and allow you to specify more of how you expect those volumes to be used, with both falling under the idea of dynamic volume provisioning—meaning that when you deploy your code into Kubernetes, the system should make any persistent volumes available from disks that have already been identified. The Kubernetes administrator will need to specify at least one, and possibly more, storage classes, which are used to define the general behavior and backing stores for persistent volumes available to the cluster. If you're using Kubernetes on Amazon Web Services, Google Compute Engine, or Microsoft's Azure, the public offerings all have storage classes predefined and available for use. You can see the default storage classes and how they are defined in the documentation at `https://kubernetes.io/docs/concepts/storage/storage-classes/`. If you are using Minikube locally to try things out, it also comes with a default storage class defined, which uses the volume type of `HostPast`.

Defining a `PersistentVolumeClaim` to use with your code in a deployment is very much like defining the configuration volume or cache with `EmptyDir`, with the exception that you will need to make a `persistentVolumeClaim` resource before you reference it in your pod specification.

An example `persistentVolumeClaim` that we might use for our Redis storage might be:

```
apiVersion: v1
kind: PersistentVolumeClaim
metadata:
```

```
      name: redis-pv-claim
      labels:
         app: redis-master
    spec:
      accessModes:
         - ReadWriteOnce
      resources:
         requests:
            storage: 1Gi
```

This will create a 1 GB volume available for our container to use. We can add this onto the Redis container to give it persistent storage by referencing this `persistentVolumeClaim` by name:

```
apiVersion: apps/v1beta1
kind: Deployment
metadata:
  name: redis-master
spec:
  replicas: 1
  template:
    metadata:
      labels:
          app: redis
          role: master
          tier: backend
    spec:
      containers:
      - name: redis-master
        image: redis:4
        ports:
        - containerPort: 6379
        volumeMounts:
        - name: redis-persistent-storage
          mountPath: /data
      volumes:
      - name: redis-persistent-storage
        persistentVolumeClaim:
          claimName: redis-pv-claim
```

The `mountPath` of `/data` was chosen to match how the Redis container was built. If we look at the documentation for that container (from `https://hub.docker.com/_/redis/`), we can see that the built-in configuration expects all data to be used from the `/data` path, so we can override that path with our own `persistentVolumeClaim` in order to back that space with something that will live beyond the life cycle of the deployment.

If you deployed these changes to Minikube, you can see the resulting resources reflected within the cluster:

```
kubectl get persistentvolumeclaims

NAME                STATUS    VOLUME
CAPACITY   ACCESS MODES    STORAGECLASS    AGE
redis-pv-claim    Bound      pvc-f745c6f1-e7d8-11e7-89d4-b29f363a60d7    1Gi
RWO               standard    3d

kubectl get persistentvolumes

NAME                                            CAPACITY   ACCESS MODES
RECLAIM POLICY   STATUS    CLAIM                          STORAGECLASS    REASON
AGE
pvc-f745c6f1-e7d8-11e7-89d4-b29f363a60d7    1Gi        RWO             Delete
Bound      default/redis-pv-claim    standard              3d
```

We can also open an interactive Terminal into the Redis instance to see how it was set up:

```
kubectl exec -it redis-master-6f944f6c8b-gm2cb -- /bin/sh

# df -h
Filesystem       Size  Used Avail Use% Mounted on
overlay           16G  1.8G   13G  12% /
tmpfs           1001M     0 1001M   0% /dev
tmpfs           1001M     0 1001M   0% /sys/fs/cgroup
/dev/vda1         16G  1.8G   13G  12% /data
shm               64M     0   64M   0% /dev/shm
tmpfs           1001M   12K 1001M   1%
/run/secrets/kubernetes.io/serviceaccount
tmpfs           1001M     0 1001M   0% /sys/firmware
```

Stateful Sets

Following dynamic provisioning, as you think about persistence systems – whether they are classic databases, key-value data stores, memory caches, or document-based datastores – it is common to want to have some manner of redundancy and failover. ReplicaSets and deployments go a fairly significant way to supporting some of that capability, especially with persistent volumes, but it would be greatly beneficial to these systems to have them more fully integrated with Kubernetes, so that we can leverage Kubernetes to handle the life cycle and coordination of these systems. A starting point for this effort is Stateful Sets, which act similarly to a deployment and ReplicaSet in that they manage a group of pods.

Stateful Sets differ from the other systems as they also support each pod having a stable, unique identity and specific ordered scaling, both up and down. Stateful Sets are relatively new in Kubernetes, first appearing in Kubernetes 1.5, and moving into beta in version 1.9. Stateful Sets also work closely with a specific service we touched upon earlier, a Headless Service, which needs to be created prior to the Stateful Set, and is responsible for the network identify of the pods.

As a reminder, a Headless Service is a service that does not have a specific cluster IP, and instead provides a unique service identity to all the pods associated with it as individual endpoints. This means that any system consuming the service will need to know that the service has identity-specific endpoints, and needs to be able to communicate with the one it wants. When a Stateful Set is created along with a headless service to match it, the pods will get an identity based on the name of the Stateful Set and then an ordinal number. For example, if we created a Stateful Set called datastore and requested three replicas, then the pods would be created as `datastore-0`, `datastore-1`, and `datastore-2`. Stateful Sets also have a `serviceName` field that gets included in the domain name of the service. To complete this example, if we set the `serviceName` to `db`, the associated DNS entries created for the pods would be:

- `datastore-0.db.[namespace].svc.cluster.local`
- `datastore-1.db.[namespace].svc.cluster.local`
- `datastore-2.db.[namespace].svc.cluster.local`

As the number of replicas is changed, a Stateful Set will also explicitly and carefully add and remove pods. It terminates the pods sequentially from the highest number first, and will not terminate a higher-numbered pod until lower-numbered pods are reporting `Ready` and `Running`. As of Kubernetes 1.7, Stateful Sets introduced the ability to vary this with an optional field, `podManagementPolicy`. The default, `OrderedReady`, operates as described, with the alternative, `Parallel`, which does not operate sequentially nor require lower-numbered pods to be `Running` or `Ready` prior to terminating a pod.

Rolling updates, akin to a deployment, are also slightly different on Stateful Sets. It is defined by the `updateStrategy` optional field, and if not explicitly set, uses the `OnDelete` setting. With this setting, Kubernetes will not delete older pods, even after a spec update, requiring you to manually delete those pods. When you do, the system will automatically recreate the pods, according to the updated spec. The other value is `RollingUpdate`, which acts more akin to a deployment in terminating and recreating the pods automatically, but following the ordering explicitly, and verifying that the pods are *ready and running* prior to continuing to update the next pod. `RollingUpdate` also has an additional (optional) field, `partition`, which if specified with a number, will have the `RollingUpdate` operate automatically on only a subset of the pods. For example, if partition was set to 3 and you had 6 replicas, then only pods 3, 4, and 5 would be updated automatically as the spec was updated. Pods 0, 1, and 2 would be left alone, and even if they were manually deleted, they will be recreated at the previous version. The partition capability can be useful to stage an update or to perform a phased rollout.

A Node.js example using Stateful Set

The code within the application doesn't have any need for the Stateful Set mechanics, but let's use it as an easy-to-understand update to show how you might use a Stateful Set and how to watch it operate.

The code for this update is available on GitHub with the project at: `https://github.com/kubernetes-for-developers/kfd-nodejs` on the branch 0.4.0. The project's code wasn't changed, except that the deployment specification was changed to a Stateful Set. You can use the following commands to get the code for this version:

```
git clone https://github.com/kubernetes-for-developers/kfd-nodejs -b 0.4.0

cd kfd-nodejs
```

The service definition changed, removing the `Nodeport` type and setting `clusterIP` to `None`. The new definition for `nodejs-service` now reads:

```
kind: Service
apiVersion: v1
metadata:
    name: nodejs-service
spec:
  ports:
  - port: 3000
    name: web
  clusterIP: None
```

```
    selector:
        app: nodejs
```

This sets up a headless service to use with the Stateful Set. The change from deployment to Stateful Set is equally simple, replacing type Deployment with type StatefulSet and adding values for serviceName, replicas, and setting a selector. I went ahead and added a datastore mount with a persistent volume claim as well, to show how that can integrate with your existing specification. The existing ConfigMap, livenessProbe, and readinessProbe settings were all maintained. The resulting StatefulSet specification now reads:

```
apiVersion: apps/v1beta1
kind: StatefulSet
metadata:
  name: nodejs
spec:
  serviceName: "nodejs"
  replicas: 5
  selector:
    matchLabels:
        app: nodejs
  template:
    metadata:
      labels:
          app: nodejs
    spec:
      containers:
      - name: nodejs
        image: quay.io/kubernetes-for-developers/nodejs:0.3.0
        imagePullPolicy: Always
        ports:
        - containerPort: 3000
          name: web
        envFrom:
        - configMapRef:
            name: nodejs-config
        volumeMounts:
            - name: config
              mountPath: /etc/nodejs-config
              readOnly: true
            - name: datastore
              mountPath: /opt/data
        livenessProbe:
          httpGet:
            path: /probes/alive
            port: 3000
```

```
            initialDelaySeconds: 1
            periodSeconds: 5
          readinessProbe:
            httpGet:
              path: /probes/ready
              port: 3000
            initialDelaySeconds: 5
            periodSeconds: 5
      volumes:
        - name: config
          configMap:
            name: nodejs-config
  updateStrategy:
    type: RollingUpdate
  volumeClaimTemplates:
  - metadata:
      name: datastore
    spec:
      accessModes: [ "ReadWriteOnce" ]
      resources:
        requests:
          storage: 1Gi
```

Since we updated the code in the last chapter to use Redis with its readiness probes, we will want to make sure we have Redis up and running for this Stateful Set to advance. You can deploy the updated Redis service definition set with this command:

```
kubectl apply -f deploy/redis.yaml
```

Now, we can take advantage of the watch option (-w) with kubectl get to watch how Kubernetes sets up the Stateful Set and carefully progresses. Open an additional terminal window and run this command:

```
kubectl get pods -w -l app=nodejs
```

At first, you shouldn't see any output, but updates will appear as Kubernetes advances through the Stateful Set.

In your original Terminal window, deploy the specification we've updated to be a StatefulSet with this command:

```
kubectl apply -f deploy/nodejs.yaml
```

You should see a response that the service, configmap, and statefulset objects were all created:

```
service "nodejs-service" unchanged
```

```
configmap "nodejs-config" unchanged
statefulset "nodejs" created
```

In the window where you're watching the pods, you should see output start to appear as the first container comes online. A line will appear in the output, every time the watch triggers that there's an update to one of the pods matching the descriptor we set (`-l app=nodejs`):

NAME	READY	STATUS	RESTARTS	AGE	
nodejs-0	0/1	Pending	0	2h	
nodejs-0	0/1	Pending	0	2h	
nodejs-0	0/1	ContainerCreating	0		2h
nodejs-0	0/1	Running	0	2h	
nodejs-0	1/1	Running	0	2h	
nodejs-1	0/1	Pending	0	2h	
nodejs-1	0/1	Pending	0	2h	
nodejs-1	0/1	ContainerCreating	0		2h
nodejs-1	0/1	Running	0	2h	
nodejs-1	1/1	Running	0	2h	
nodejs-2	0/1	Pending	0	2h	
nodejs-2	0/1	Pending	0	2h	
nodejs-2	0/1	ContainerCreating	0		2h
nodejs-2	0/1	Running	0	2h	
nodejs-2	1/1	Running	0	2h	
nodejs-3	0/1	Pending	0	2h	
nodejs-3	0/1	Pending	0	2h	

The definition we set has five replicas, so five pods will be generated in all. You can see the status of that rollout with this command:

```
kubectl get sts nodejs
```

NAME	DESIRED	CURRENT	AGE
nodejs	5	5	2h

In the preceding command, `sts` is a shortcut for `statefulset`. You can also get a more detailed view on the current state in a human-readable form with this command:

```
kubectl describe sts nodejs
```

```
●  ●  ●                    1. heckj@greyberry: ~/src/kfd-nodejs (bash)
heckj @~ ?src ?kfd-nodejs ?0.4.0 ?$ kubectl describe sts nodejs
Name:              nodejs
Namespace:         default
CreationTimestamp: Wed, 27 Dec 2017 16:17:45 -0800
Selector:          app=nodejs
Labels:            app=nodejs
Annotations:       kubectl.kubernetes.io/last-applied-configuration={"apiVersion":"apps/v1beta1","kind":"StatefulSet","metadata":{"an
notations":{},"name":"nodejs","namespace":"default"},"spec":{"replicas":5,"selector":{...
Replicas:          5 desired | 4 total
Pods Status:       4 Running / 0 Waiting / 0 Succeeded / 0 Failed
Pod Template:
  Labels:   app=nodejs
  Containers:
   nodejs:
    Image:       quay.io/kubernetes-for-developers/nodejs:0.3.0
    Port:        3000/TCP
    Liveness:    http-get http://:3000/probes/alive delay=1s timeout=1s period=5s #success=1 #failure=3
    Readiness:   http-get http://:3000/probes/ready delay=5s timeout=1s period=5s #success=1 #failure=3
    Environment Variables from:
     nodejs-config  ConfigMap  Optional: false
    Environment:   <none>
    Mounts:
      /etc/nodejs-config from config (ro)
      /opt/data from datastore (rw)
  Volumes:
   config:
    Type:       ConfigMap (a volume populated by a ConfigMap)
    Name:       nodejs-config
    Optional:   false
Volume Claims:
  Name:          datastore
  StorageClass:
  Labels:        <none>
  Annotations:   <none>
  Capacity:      1Gi
  Access Modes:  [ReadWriteOnce]
Events:
  Type    Reason           Age   From          Message
  ----    ------           ----  ----          -------
  Normal  SuccessfulCreate 2m    statefulset   create Claim datastore-nodejs-0 Pod nodejs-0 in StatefulSet nodejs success
  Normal  SuccessfulCreate 2m    statefulset   create Pod nodejs-0 in StatefulSet nodejs successful
  Normal  SuccessfulCreate 28s   statefulset   create Claim datastore-nodejs-1 Pod nodejs-1 in StatefulSet nodejs success
  Normal  SuccessfulCreate 28s   statefulset   create Pod nodejs-1 in StatefulSet nodejs successful
  Normal  SuccessfulCreate 19s   statefulset   create Claim datastore-nodejs-2 Pod nodejs-2 in StatefulSet nodejs success
  Normal  SuccessfulCreate 19s   statefulset   create Pod nodejs-2 in StatefulSet nodejs successful
  Normal  SuccessfulCreate 9s    statefulset   create Claim datastore-nodejs-3 Pod nodejs-3 in StatefulSet nodejs success
  Normal  SuccessfulCreate 9s    statefulset   create Pod nodejs-3 in StatefulSet nodejs successful
heckj @~ ?src ?kfd-nodejs ?0.4.0 ?$
```

If you edit the specification, change the replicas to two, and then apply the changes, you will see the pods get torn down in the reverse order to how they were set up—highest ordinal number first. The following command:

```
kubectl apply -f deploy/nodejs.yml
```

Should report back:

```
service "nodejs-service" unchanged
configmap "nodejs-config" unchanged
statefulset "nodejs" configured
```

And in the window where you're watching the pods, you will see `nodejs-4` start terminating, and it will continue until `nodejs-3` and then `nodejs-2` terminates.

If you were to run a temporary `pod` to look at DNS:

```
kubectl run -i --tty --image busybox dns-test --restart=Never --rm /bin/sh
```

You can use the `nslookup` command to verify the DNS values for the `pods`:

```
/ # nslookup nodejs-1.nodejs-service
Server:  10.96.0.10
Address 1:  10.96.0.10 kube-dns.kube-system.svc.cluster.local

Name:  nodejs-1.nodejs-service
Address 1:  172.17.0.6 nodejs-1.nodejs-service.default.svc.cluster.local

/ # nslookup nodejs-0.nodejs-service
Server:  10.96.0.10
Address 1:  10.96.0.10 kube-dns.kube-system.svc.cluster.local

Name:  nodejs-0.nodejs-service
Address 1:  172.17.0.4 nodejs-0.nodejs-service.default.svc.cluster.local
```

Custom Resource Definition

Stateful Sets don't automatically match all the persistent stores that are available, and some of them have even more complex logic requirements for managing the life cycle of the application. As Kubernetes looked at how to support extending its controllers to support more complex logic, the project started with the idea of Operators, external code that could be included in the Kubernetes project, and has evolved as of Kubernetes 1.8 to make this more explicit with `CustomResourceDefinitions`. A custom resource extends the Kubernetes API, and allows for custom API objects to be created and matched with a custom controller that you can also load into Kubernetes to handle the life cycle of those objects.

 Custom Resource Definitions go beyond the scope of what we will cover in this book, although you should be aware that they exist. You can get more details about Custom Resource Definitions and how to extend Kubernetes at the project's documentation site: `https://kubernetes.io/docs/concepts/api-extension/custom-resources/`.

There are a number of Operators available via open source projects that utilize Custom Resource Definitions to manage specific applications within Kubernetes. The CoreOS team supports operators and custom resources for managing Prometheus and etcd. There is also an open source storage resource and associated technology called Rook, which functions using Custom Resource Definitions.

The broad set of how to best run persistent stores with Kubernetes is still evolving, as of this writing. There are numerous examples of how you can run a database or NoSQL data store of your choice in Kubernetes that also supports redundancy and failover. Most of these systems were created with a variety of mechanisms to support managing them, and few of them have much support for automated scaling and redundancy. There are a number of techniques supporting a wide variety of data stores that are available as examples. Some of the more complex systems use Operators and these Custom Resource Definitions; others use sets of pods and containers with simpler Replica Sets to achieve their goals.

Summary

In this chapter, we reviewed jobs and CronJobs, which Kubernetes provides to support batch and scheduled batch processing, respectively. We also looked through a Python example of how to set up a Celery worker queue with RabbitMQ and configure the two deployments to work together. We then looked at how Kubernetes can provide persistence with volumes, `PersistentVolume`, and its concept of `PersistentVolumeClaims` for automatically creating volumes for deployments as needed. Kubernetes also supports Stateful Sets for a variation of deployment that requires stable identity and persistent volumes, and we looked at a simple Node.js example converting our previous example of a deployment into a Stateful Set. We finished the chapter with a look at Custom Resource Definitions, used to extend Kubernetes.

In the next chapter, we start to look at how to leverage Kubernetes to get information about all these structures. We review how to capture and view metrics, leveraging Kubernetes and additional open source projects, as well as examples of collating logs from the horizontally-scaled systems that Kubernetes encourages.

Monitoring and Metrics

In the previous chapters, we investigated the declarative structures used in Kubernetes objects and resources. With the end goal of having Kubernetes help run software for us, in this chapter we will look at how we can get more information, when we're running our applications at a greater scale, and some open source tools that we can use for that purpose. Kubernetes is already gathering and using some information about how utilized the nodes of the cluster are, and there is a growing capability within Kubernetes to start to collect application-specific metrics, and even use those metrics as a control point for managing the software.

In this chapter, will we dig into these aspects of basic observability and walk through how you can set them up for your local development use, and how to leverage them to gather, aggregate, and expose details of how your software is running, when you scale it up. Topics within this chapter will include:

- Built-in metrics with Kubernetes
- A Kubernetes concept—Quality of Service
- Capturing metrics with Prometheus
- Installing and using Grafana
- Using Prometheus to view application metrics

Built-in metrics with Kubernetes

Kubernetes comes built in with some basic instrumentation to know how much CPU and memory are consumed on each node in the cluster. Exactly what is captured and how it is captured has been evolving rapidly in recent Kubernetes releases (1.5 through 1.9). Many Kubernetes installations will be capturing information about what resources the underlying containers are using with a program called cAdvisor. This code was created by Google to collect, aggregate, and expose the metrics of how containers are operating, as a critical step of being able to know where best to place new containers, based on what resources a node has and where resources are available.

Every node within a Kubernetes cluster will have cAdvisor running and collecting information, and this, in turn, is captured and used by *kubelet*, which is the local agent on every node that is responsible for starting, stopping, and managing the various resources needed to run containers.

cAdvisor exposes a simple web-based UI that you can use to look at the details for any node, manually. If you can access port `4194` of the node, that is the default location that exposes the cAdvisor details. Depending on your cluster setup, this may not be easy to get access to. In the case of using Minikube, it is easily and directly available.

If you have Minikube installed and running, you can use this command:

```
minikube ip
```

To get the IP address of the virtual machine local to your development machine that is running your single-node Kubernetes cluster, you can access cAdvisor running, thereby opening a browser and navigating to that IP address at port `4194`. For example, on macOS running Minikube, you could use this command:

```
open http://$(minikube ip):4194/
```

And you'll see the simple UI, showing a page that looks something like this:

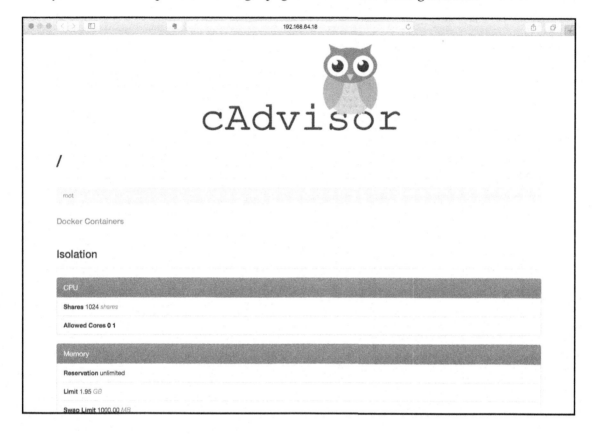

Scroll down a bit, and you will see a number of gauges and a table of information:

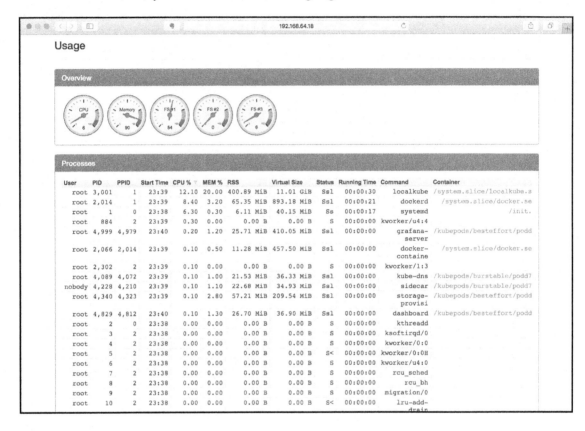

Beneath that is a set of simple graphs showing CPU, memory, network, and filesystem usage. These graphs and tables will update and automatically refresh as you watch them, and represent the basic information that Kubernetes is capturing about your cluster, as it operates.

Kubernetes also makes metrics about itself—its API server and relevant components, available through its own API. You can see these metrics directly using the `curl` command after making the API available through `kubectl` proxy:

```
kubectl proxy
```

And in a separate Terminal window:

```
curl http://127.0.0.1:8001/metrics
```

Many installations of Kubernetes have used a program called Heapster to collect metrics from Kubernetes and from each node's instance of cAdvisor, and store them in a time-series database such as InfluxDB. As of Kubernetes 1.9, the open source project is shifting a bit further away from Heapster towards a pluggable solution, with a common alternative solution being Prometheus, which is frequently used for short-term metrics capture.

If you are using Minikube, you can easily add Heapster to your local environment with a `minikube` add-on. Like the dashboard, this will run software for Kubernetes on its own infrastructure, in this case, Heapster, InfluxDB, and Grafana.

This will enable the add-on within Minikube, you can use this command:

```
minikube addons enable heapster
heapster was successfully enabled
```

In the background, Minikube will start up and configure Heapster, InfluxDB, and Grafana, creating it as a service. You can use this command:

```
minikube addons open heapster
```

This will open a browser window to Grafana. The command will wait while the containers are being set up, but when the service endpoint is available, it will open a browser window:

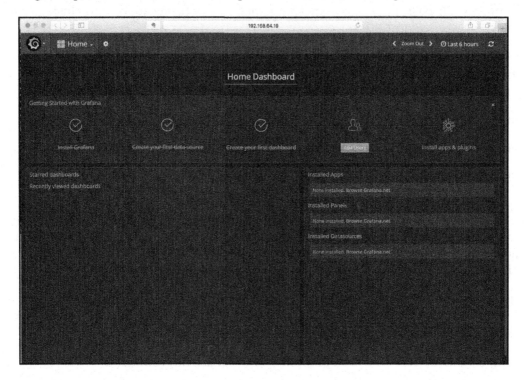

Grafana is a single-page application used to display graphs and build dashboards from common data sources. In the version that is created by the Minikube Heapster add-on, Grafana is configured with two dashboards: **Cluster** and **Pods**. If you select the pull-down menu labeled **Home** in the default view, you can choose the other dashboards to view.

It will take a minute or two before Heapster, InfluxDB, and Grafana have all coordinated to collect and capture some of the basic metrics of the environment, but fairly shortly, you can go to these other dashboards to see information about what's running. For example, I deployed all the sample applications from the prior chapters in this book and went to the **Cluster** dashboard, and after 10 minutes or so, the view looked like this:

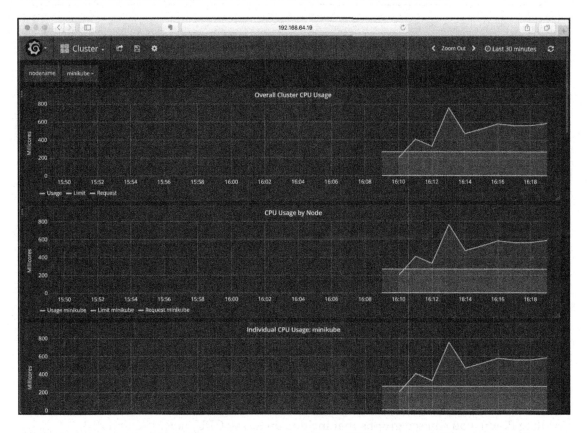

Scroll down through this dashboard, and you will see CPU, memory, filesystem, and network usage by node, as well as overall cluster views for this. You may notice the CPU graphs have three lines being tracked—usage, limit, and request—which match the resources actually in use, the amount requested, and any limits set on the pods and containers.

If you switch to the **Pods** dashboard, you will see that the dashboard has selections for all of the pods currently running in your cluster, and provides a detailed view of each one. In the example shown here, I selected the pod from our `flask` example application that I deployed:

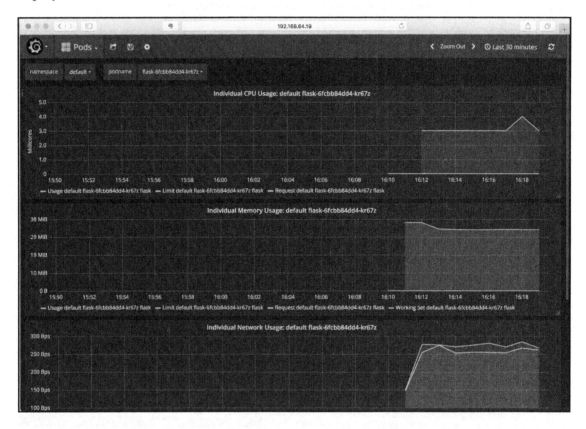

Scrolling down, you can see graphs that include memory, CPU, network, and disk utilization. The collection of Heapster, Grafana, and InfluxDB will automatically record new pods as you create them, and you can select between namespaces and pod names in the **Pods** dashboard.

Kubernetes concept – Quality of Service

When a pod is created in Kubernetes, it is also assigned a Quality of Service class, based on the data provided about the pod when it was requested. This is used by the scheduler to provide some upfront assurances during the scheduling process, and later in the management of the pods themselves. The three classes supported are:

- Guaranteed
- Burstable
- BestEffort

Which class is assigned to your pod is based on what resource limits and requests you report with the containers within your pod for CPU and memory utilization. In the previous examples, none of the containers were assigned a requests or limit, so all of those pods were classified as BestEffort when they were run.

Resource requests and limits are defined on each container within a pod. If we add a request to a container, we are asking for Kubernetes to make sure that the cluster has sufficient resources to run our pod (memory, CPU, or both) and it will validate that availability as a part of the scheduling. If we add a limit, we are requesting Kubernetes to watch the pod and react if the container exceeds the limits we set. For limits, if the container tries to exceed a CPU limit, the container will simply be throttled to the defined CPU limit. If a memory limit is exceeded, the container is frequently terminated and you will likely see the error message OOM killed in the reason description for those terminated containers.

If a request is set, the pods are generally set to the Quality of Service class of Burstable, with the exception of when a limit is also set, and that limit has the same value as the request, in which case the service class of Guaranteed is assigned. As a part of scheduling, if a pod is deemed to be in the Guaranteed service class, Kubernetes will reserve resources within the cluster and if overloaded, it will bias towards expiring and evicting BestEffort containers first, and then Burstable. A cluster will generally need to expect to lose resource capacity (for example, one or more nodes fail). In these cases, a Guaranteed class pod will have the most longevity in the face of such failures once it has been scheduled into a cluster.

We can update our flask example pod so that it will operate with a Guaranteed Quality of Service, by adding a request and limit for both CPU and memory:

```
spec:
  containers:
  - name: flask
    image: quay.io/kubernetes-for-developers/flask:0.4.0
```

```
resources:
  limits:
    memory: "100Mi"
    cpu: "500m"
  requests:
    memory: "100Mi"
    cpu: "500m"
```

This places a request and limit of the same value for both CPU and memory—in this case, 100 MB of memory and roughly half a core of CPU utilization.

It is generally considered a best practice to at least define requests, and ideally limits as well, for all containers and pods that you want to run in a production mode.

Choosing requests and limits for your containers

If you are uncertain of what values to use to set a request and/or limit for a container, the best means of determining those values is to watch them. With Heapster, or Prometheus, and Grafana, you can see how many resources are being consumed by each pod.

There is a three-step process that you can use with your code to see what it's taking:

1. Run your code and review how many resources are consumed while idle
2. Add load to your code and verify the resource consumption under load
3. Having set constraints, run another load test for an sustained period of time to see that your code fits within the defined boundaries

The first step (reviewing while idle) will give you good numbers to start with. Leverage Grafana, or utilize cAdvisor available at your cluster node, and simply deploy the pod in question. In the preceding examples, where we did that with the `flask` example from earlier in this book, you can see an that idle flask application was consuming roughly 3 millicores (.003% of a core) and roughly 35 MB of RAM. This makes a base of what to expect for a request for both CPU and memory.

The second step is often best done by running an **increasing load test** (also known as a **ramp load test**) to review how your pod reacts under load. Generally, you will see your load ramp up linearly with the requests, and then make a bend, or knee, where it starts to become bottlenecked. You can review the same Grafana or cAdvisor panels to show utilization during that load.

If you wanted to generate a simple bit of load, you could generate some specific load points with tools such as Apache benchmark (https://httpd.apache.org/docs/2.4/programs/ ab.html). For example, to run an interactive container with this tool that could work against the Flask application, you could use the following command:

```
kubectl run -it --rm --restart=Never \
--image=quay.io/kubernetes-for-developers/ab quicktest -- sh
```

This image has both `curl` and `ab` installed, so you can verify that you can talk to the Flask-service that we created in our earlier example with this command:

```
curl -v http://flask-service.default:5000/
```

This should return some verbose output, showing the connection and basic request as follows:

```
* Trying 10.104.90.234...
* TCP_NODELAY set
* Connected to flask-service.default (10.104.90.234) port 5000 (#0)
> GET / HTTP/1.1
> Host: flask-service.default:5000
> User-Agent: curl/7.57.0
> Accept: */*
>
* HTTP 1.0, assume close after body
< HTTP/1.0 200 OK
< Content-Type: text/html; charset=utf-8
< Content-Length: 10
< Server: Werkzeug/0.13 Python/3.6.3
< Date: Mon, 08 Jan 2018 02:22:26 GMT
<
* Closing connection 0
```

Once you have verified that everything is operating as you expect, you can run some load with `ab`:

```
ab -c 100 -n 5000 http://flask-service.default:5000/

This is ApacheBench, Version 2.3 <$Revision: 1807734 $>
Copyright 1996 Adam Twiss, Zeus Technology Ltd, http://www.zeustech.net/
Licensed to The Apache Software Foundation, http://www.apache.org/

Benchmarking flask-service.default (be patient)
Completed 500 requests
Completed 1000 requests
Completed 1500 requests
Completed 2000 requests
```

```
Completed 2500 requests
Completed 3000 requests
Completed 3500 requests
Completed 4000 requests
Completed 4500 requests
Completed 5000 requests
Finished 5000 requests
Server Software: Werkzeug/0.13
Server Hostname: flask-service.default
Server Port: 5000
Document Path: /
Document Length: 10 bytes
Concurrency Level: 100
Time taken for tests: 3.454 seconds
Complete requests: 5000
Failed requests: 0
Total transferred: 810000 bytes
HTML transferred: 50000 bytes
Requests per second: 1447.75 [#/sec] (mean)
Time per request: 69.072 [ms] (mean)
Time per request: 0.691 [ms] (mean, across all concurrent requests)
Transfer rate: 229.04 [Kbytes/sec] received

Connection Times (ms)
 min mean[+/-sd] median max
Connect: 0 0 0.3 0 3
Processing: 4 68 7.4 67 90
Waiting: 4 68 7.4 67 90
Total: 7 68 7.2 67 90

Percentage of the requests served within a certain time (ms)
 50% 67
 66% 69
 75% 71
 80% 72
 90% 77
 95% 82
 98% 86
 99% 89
 100% 90 (longest request)
```

You will see a corresponding jump in resource usage in cAdvisor, or after a minute or so, Grafana with Heapster. To get useful values in Heapster and Grafana, you will want to run extended load tests since that data is being aggregated—you will want to run your load test ideally for several minutes, as one minute of granularity is the basic level that Grafana aggregates to with Heapster.

cAdvisor will update more quickly, and if you're viewing the interactive graphs, you will see them update as the load test progresses:

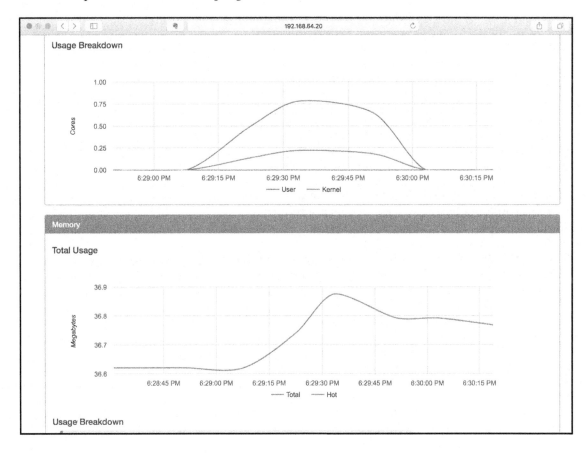

In this case, you see our memory usage stayed fairly consistent at around 36 MB, and our CPU peaked (as you might expect for this application) during the load test.

If we then applied the preceding request and limit examples, and updated the flask deployment, then you would see the load flatten off when the CPU hit the roughly 1/2 core CPU limit.

The third step in this process is primarily to validate your assessments for CPU and memory needs over a longer-running load test. Typically, you would run an extended load (a minimum of several minutes long) with your requests and limits set to validate that the container could serve the traffic expected. The most common flaw in this assessment is seeing memory slowly climb while an extended load test is being performed, resulting in the container being OOM killed (terminated for exceeding its memory constraints).

The 100 MiB of RAM that we had in the example is reserving significantly more memory than this container needs, so we could easily reduce it down to 40 MiB and do the final validation step.

When setting requests and limits, you want to choose values that most efficiently characterize your needs, but don't waste reserved resources. To run a more extended load test, type:

```
ab -c 100 -n 50000 http://flask-service.default:5000/
```

The resulting Grafana output is as follows:

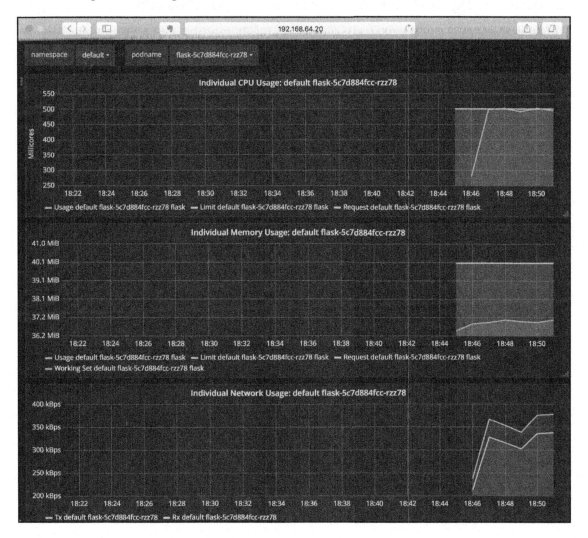

Capturing metrics with Prometheus

Prometheus is a prominent open source tool used for monitoring, and quite a bit of symbiotic work is happening between it and the Kubernetes community. Kubernetes application metrics are exposed in the Prometheus format. This format includes the data types of *counter*, *gauge*, *histogram*, and *summary*, as well as a means of specifying labels to be associated with specific metrics. As Prometheus and Kubernetes have both evolved, the metrics format from Prometheus appears to be emerging as a de facto standard within the project and across its various components.

More information about this format is available online at the Prometheus project's documentation:

- `https://prometheus.io/docs/concepts/data_model/`
- `https://prometheus.io/docs/concepts/metric_types/`
- `https://prometheus.io/docs/instrumenting/exposition_formats/`

Beyond the metrics format, Prometheus offers quite a variety of capabilities as its own open source project, and is used outside Kubernetes. The architecture of this project gives a reasonable sense of its primary components:

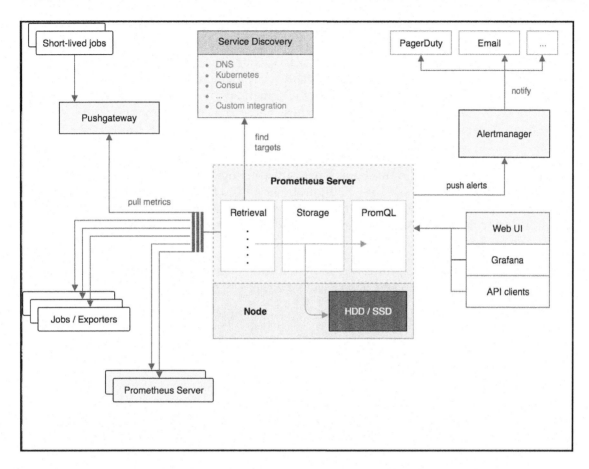

The Prometheus server itself is what we will examine in this chapter. At its core, it periodically sweeps through a number of remote locations, collecting data from those locations, storing it in a short-term time-series database, and providing a means to query that database. Extensions to Prometheus allow the system to export these time-series metrics to other systems for longer-term storage. In addition, Prometheus includes an alert manager that can be configured to send alerts, or more generally invoke actions, based on the information captured and derived from the time-series metrics.

Prometheus is not intended to be a long-term storage for metrics, and can work with a variety of other systems to capture and manage the data on a longer term. Common Prometheus installations maintain data for 6 to 24 hours, configurable per installation.

The most minimal installation of Prometheus would include the Prometheus server itself and configuration for the service. But to fully leverage Prometheus, the installation is frequently more expansive and complex, with a separate deployment each for the Alertmanager and Prometheus server, optionally a deployment for the push gateway (to allow other systems to actively send metrics to Prometheus), and a DaemonSet to capture data from every node within the cluster to expose and export that information into Prometheus, leveraging cAdvisor.

More complex installations of software can be done by managing a set of YAML files, as we have been exploring earlier in this book. There are other options for how to manage and install sets of deployments, services, configurations, and so forth. Rather than documenting all the pieces, we will leverage one of the more common tools for this sort of work, Helm, which is closely tied to the Kubernetes project and is commonly referred to as *the package manager for Kubernetes*.

> You can find significantly more information about Helm from the project's documentation site at `https://helm.sh`.

Installing Helm

Helm is a two-part system: a command-line tool and software that runs within your Kubernetes cluster that the command-line tool interacts with. Typically, what you need locally is the command-line tool, and that in turn will be used to install the components it needs into your cluster.

The documentation for installing the Helm command-line tool is available at the project's website: `https://github.com/kubernetes/helm/blob/master/docs/install.md`.

If you are using macOS locally, it is available via Homebrew and can be installed with:

```
brew install kubernetes-helm
```

Or if you're working from a Linux host, the Helm project offers a script you can use to install Helm:

```
curl https://raw.githubusercontent.com/kubernetes/helm/master/scripts/get >
get_helm.sh
chmod 700 get_helm.sh
./get_helm.sh
```

Once Helm is installed, you use it to install the component (called Tiller) that runs within your cluster, using the command `helm init`. You should see output like this:

```
$HELM_HOME has been configured at /Users/heckj/.helm.

Tiller (the Helm server-side component) has been installed into your
Kubernetes Cluster.
Happy Helming!
```

In addition to setting up some local configuration files for its use, this made a deployment on your cluster within the `kube-system` namespace for its cluster-side component, **Tiller**. You can view that deployment, if you want to see it in more detail:

```
kubectl describe deployment tiller-deploy -n kube-system
```

At this point, you have Helm installed, and you can verify the version of your installation (both command line and what's on the cluster) with the command Helm version. This operates very much like `kubectl` version, reporting both its version and the version of the system it's communicating with:

```
helm version

Client: &amp;version.Version{SemVer:"v2.7.2",
GitCommit:"8478fb4fc723885b155c924d1c8c410b7a9444e6", GitTreeState:"clean"}
Server: &amp;version.Version{SemVer:"v2.7.2",
GitCommit:"8478fb4fc723885b155c924d1c8c410b7a9444e6", GitTreeState:"clean"}
```

Now, we can move on to the reason we set up Helm: to install Prometheus.

Installing Prometheus using Helm

Helm uses a set of configuration files to describe what it needs to install, in what order, and with what parameters. These configurations are called charts, and are maintained in GitHub, where the default Helm repository is maintained.

You can view the repository that Helm is using with the command `helm repo list`:

```
helm repo list

NAME URL
stable https://kubernetes-charts.storage.googleapis.com
local http://127.0.0.1:8879/charts
```

This default is a wrapper around a GitHub repository, and you can view the contents of the repository at `https://github.com/kubernetes/charts`. Another way to see all the charts that are available for use is the command `helm search`.

It is a good idea to make sure you have the latest cache of the repository available. You can update your cache to the latest, mirroring the charts in GitHub, with the command `helm repo update`.

The resulting update should report success with output similar to:

```
help repo update

Hang tight while we grab the latest from your chart repositories...
...Skip local chart repository
...Successfully got an update from the "stable" chart repository
Update Complete.  Happy Helming!
```

We are going to use the stable/Prometheus chart (hosted at `https://github.com/kubernetes/charts/tree/master/stable/prometheus`). We can use Helm to pull that chart locally, to look at it in more detail:

```
helm fetch --untar stable/prometheus
```

This command downloads the chart from the default repository and unpacks it locally in a directory called Prometheus. Take a look in the directory, and you should see several files and a directory called `templates`:

```
.helmignore
Chart.yaml
README.md
templates
values.yaml
```

This is the common pattern for charts, where `Chart.yaml` describes the software that will be installed by the chart. `values.yaml` is a collection of default configuration values that are used throughout all the various Kubernetes resources that will be created, and the templates directory contains the collection of templated files that will get rendered out to install all the Kubernetes resources needed for this software in your cluster. Typically, the `README.md` will include a description of all the values within the `values.yaml`, what they're used for, and suggestions for installation.

We can now install prometheus, and we will do so by taking advantage of a couple of Helm's options, setting a release name and using a namespace:

```
helm install prometheus -n monitor --namespace monitoring
```

This installs the chart included in the prometheus directory, installs all the components included into the namespace, monitoring, and prefixes all the objects with a release name of monitor. If we had not specified either of those values, Helm would have used the default namespace, and generated a random release name to uniquely identify the installation.

When this is invoked, you will see quite a bit of output describing what was created and its state at the start of the process, followed by a section of notes that provides information about how to access the software you just installed:

```
NAME: monitor
LAST DEPLOYED: Sun Jan 14 15:00:40 2018
NAMESPACE: monitoring
STATUS: DEPLOYED
RESOURCES:
==> v1/ConfigMap
NAME DATA AGE
monitor-prometheus-alertmanager 1 1s
monitor-prometheus-server 3 1s

==> v1/PersistentVolumeClaim
NAME STATUS VOLUME CAPACITY ACCESS MODES STORAGECLASS AGE
monitor-prometheus-alertmanager Bound pvc-be6b3367-f97e-11e7-92ab-
e697d60b4f2f 2Gi RWO standard 1s
monitor-prometheus-server Bound pvc-be6b8693-f97e-11e7-92ab-e697d60b4f2f
8Gi RWO standard 1s

==> v1/Service
NAME TYPE CLUSTER-IP EXTERNAL-IP PORT(S) AGE
monitor-prometheus-alertmanager ClusterIP 10.100.246.164 <none> 80/TCP 1s
monitor-prometheus-kube-state-metrics ClusterIP None <none> 80/TCP 1s
monitor-prometheus-node-exporter ClusterIP None <none> 9100/TCP 1s
monitor-prometheus-pushgateway ClusterIP 10.97.187.101 <none> 9091/TCP 1s
monitor-prometheus-server ClusterIP 10.110.247.151 <none> 80/TCP 1s

==> v1beta1/DaemonSet
NAME DESIRED CURRENT READY UP-TO-DATE AVAILABLE NODE SELECTOR AGE
monitor-prometheus-node-exporter 1 1 0 1 0 <none> 1s

==> v1beta1/Deployment
NAME DESIRED CURRENT UP-TO-DATE AVAILABLE AGE
```

```
monitor-prometheus-alertmanager 1 1 1 0 1s
monitor-prometheus-kube-state-metrics 1 1 1 0 1s
monitor-prometheus-pushgateway 1 1 1 0 1s
monitor-prometheus-server 1 1 1 0 1s

==> v1/Pod(related)
NAME READY STATUS RESTARTS AGE
monitor-prometheus-node-exporter-bc9jp 0/1 ContainerCreating 0 1s
monitor-prometheus-alertmanager-6c59f855d-bsp7t 0/2 ContainerCreating 0 1s
monitor-prometheus-kube-state-metrics-57747bc8b6-l7pzw 0/1
ContainerCreating 0 1s
monitor-prometheus-pushgateway-5b99967d9c-zd7gc 0/1 ContainerCreating 0 1s
monitor-prometheus-server-7895457f9f-jdvch 0/2 Pending 0 1s

NOTES:
The prometheus server can be accessed via port 80 on the following DNS name
from within your cluster:
monitor-prometheus-server.monitoring.svc.cluster.local

Get the prometheus server URL by running these commands in the same shell:
 export POD_NAME=$(kubectl get pods --namespace monitoring -l
"app=prometheus,component=server" -o jsonpath="{.items[0].metadata.name}")
 kubectl --namespace monitoring port-forward $POD_NAME 9090

The prometheus alertmanager can be accessed via port 80 on the following
DNS name from within your cluster:
monitor-prometheus-alertmanager.monitoring.svc.cluster.local

Get the Alertmanager URL by running these commands in the same shell:
 export POD_NAME=$(kubectl get pods --namespace monitoring -l
"app=prometheus,component=alertmanager" -o
jsonpath="{.items[0].metadata.name}")
 kubectl --namespace monitoring port-forward $POD_NAME 9093

The prometheus PushGateway can be accessed via port 9091 on the following
DNS name from within your cluster:
monitor-prometheus-pushgateway.monitoring.svc.cluster.local

Get the PushGateway URL by running these commands in the same shell:
 export POD_NAME=$(kubectl get pods --namespace monitoring -l
"app=prometheus,component=pushgateway" -o
jsonpath="{.items[0].metadata.name}")
 kubectl --namespace monitoring port-forward $POD_NAME 9093

For more information on running prometheus, visit:
https://prometheus.io/
```

`helm list` will show you the current releases that you have installed:

```
NAME REVISION UPDATED STATUS CHART NAMESPACE
monitor 1 Sun Jan 14 15:00:40 2018 DEPLOYED prometheus-4.6.15 monitoring
```

And you can use the `helm status` command, along with the name of the release, to get the current state of all the Kubernetes resources created by the chart:

```
helm status monitor
```

The notes section is included in the templates and rendered again on every status call, and is generally written to include notes on how to access the software.

> You can install a chart without having explicitly retrieved it first. Helm will use any local charts first, but fall back to searching through its available repositories, so we could have installed this same chart with just this command:
>
> `helm install stable/prometheus -n monitor --namespace monitoring`

You can also have Helm mix together `values.yaml` and its templates, to render out all the objects it will create and simply display them, which can be useful to see how all the pieces will come together. The command to do this is `helm template`, and to render the YAML that was used to create the Kubernetes resources, the command would be:

```
helm template prometheus -n monitor --namespace monitoring
```

The `helm template` command does require the chart to be available on the local filesystem, so while `helm install` can work from a remote repository, you will need to use `helm fetch` to have the chart locally, in order to take advantage of the `helm template` command.

Viewing metrics with Prometheus

Using the details available in the notes, you can set up a port-forward, as we have done earlier in this book and access Prometheus directly. The information that was displayed from the notes is shown here:

```
export POD_NAME=$(kubectl get pods --namespace monitoring -l
"app=prometheus,component=server" -o jsonpath="{.items[0].metadata.name}")

kubectl --namespace monitoring port-forward $POD_NAME 9090
```

This will allow you to directly access the Prometheus server with a browser. Run these commands in a terminal, and then open a browser and navigate to `http://localhost:9090/`.

You can view the current state of what Prometheus is monitoring by looking at the list of targets at `http://localhost:9090/targets`:

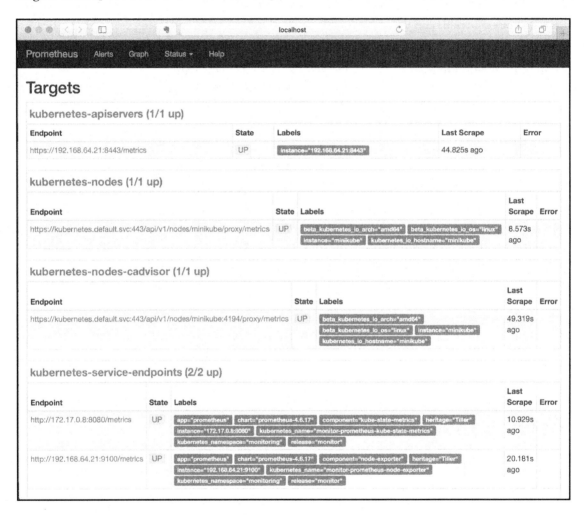

Switch to the Prometheus query/browser at `http://localhost:9090/graph` to be able to view the metrics that have been collected by Prometheus. There are a large number of metrics that are collected, and we are specifically interested in the ones that match the information we saw earlier with cAdvisor and Heapster. In Kubernetes clusters of version 1.7 and later, these metrics moved and are specifically collected by the `kubernetes-nodes-cadvisor` job that we see in the targets in the screenshot.

In the query browser, you can start typing metric names and it will attempt to autocomplete, or you can use the pull-down menu to see the list of all possible metrics. Type in the metric name, `container_memory_usage_bytes`, and hit *Enter* to see a list of those metrics in table form.

The general form of good metrics will have some identifiers of what the metric is and usually end with a unit identifier, in this case, bytes. Looking at the table, you can see the metrics that are collected along with a fairly dense set of key-value pairs for each metric.

These key-value pairs are labels on the metrics, and function similarly to the way labels and selectors do, within Kubernetes in general.

An example metric, reformatted to make it easier to read, is shown here:

```
container_memory_usage_bytes{
  beta_kubernetes_io_arch="amd64",
  beta_kubernetes_io_os="linux",
  container_name="POD",
  id="/kubepods/podf887aff9-f981-11e7-92ab-
e697d60b4f2f/25fa74ef205599036eaeafa7e0a07462865f822cf364031966ff56a9931e16
1d",
  image="gcr.io/google_containers/pause-amd64:3.0",
  instance="minikube",
  job="kubernetes-nodes-cadvisor",
  kubernetes_io_hostname="minikube",
  name="k8s_POD_flask-5c7d884fcc-217g9_default_f887aff9-f981-11e7-92ab-
e697d60b4f2f_0",
  namespace="default",
  pod_name="flask-5c7d884fcc-217g9"
} 249856
```

In the query, we can filter just the metrics we are interested in by including matches in the query to those labels. For example, all of the metrics that are associated with specific containers will have an `image` tag, so we can filter to just those metrics with:

```
container_memory_usage_bytes{image!=""}
```

You may have noticed that the namespaces and pod names are also included, and we can match on those as well. For example, to just view the metrics related to the default namespace where we have been deploying our sample applications, we could add `namespace="default"`:

```
container_memory_usage_bytes{image!="",namespace="default"}
```

This is starting to get down to a more reasonable number of metrics. While the table will show you the most recent value, the history of these values is what we're interested in seeing. If you select the **Graph** button on the current query, it will attempt to render out a single graph of the metrics that you have selected, for example:

Since the metrics also include `container_name` to match the deployment, you can tune this down to a single container. For example, to see the memory usage associated with our `flask` deployment:

```
container_memory_usage_bytes{image!="",namespace="default",container_name="
flask"}
```

If we scale up the number of replicas in our `flask` deployment, it will create new metrics for each container, so in order to view not just single containers but also sets at a time, we can take advantage of aggregating operators in the Prometheus query language. Some of the most useful operators include `sum`, `count`, `count_values`, and `topk`.

We can also use these same aggregation operators to group metrics together where the aggregated set has different tag values within it. For example, after increasing the replicas on the `flask` deployment to three, we can view the total memory usage of the deployment with:

```
sum(container_memory_usage_bytes{image!="",
namespace="default",container_name="flask"})
```

And then break it out into each container again by the pod name:

```
sum(container_memory_usage_bytes{image!="",
namespace="default",container_name="flask"}) by (name)
```

The graph function can give you a nice visual overview, including stacking the values, as follows:

With the graphs getting more complex, you may want to start to collect the queries you find most interesting, as well as put together dashboards of these graphs to be able to use them. This leads us to another open source project, Grafana, which can be easily hosted on Kubernetes, providing the dashboards and graphs.

Installing Grafana

Grafana isn't by itself a complex installation, but configuring it can be. Grafana can plug into a number of different backend systems and provide dashboarding and graphing for them. In our example, we would like to have it provide dashboards from Prometheus. We will set up an installation and then configure it through its user interface.

We can use Helm again to install Grafana, and since we have put Prometheus in the namespace monitoring, we will do the same with Grafana. We could do `helm fetch` and install to look at the charts. In this case, we will just install them directly:

```
helm install stable/grafana -n viz --namespace monitoring
```

In the resulting output, you will see a secret, ConfigMap, and deployment among the resources created, and in the notes, something like:

```
NOTES:
1. Get your 'admin' user password by running:

kubectl get secret --namespace monitoring viz-grafana -o
jsonpath="{.data.grafana-admin-password}" | base64 --decode ; echo

2. The Grafana server can be accessed via port 80 on the following DNS name
from within your cluster:

viz-grafana.monitoring.svc.cluster.local

Get the Grafana URL to visit by running these commands in the same shell:

export POD_NAME=$(kubectl get pods --namespace monitoring -l "app=viz-
grafana,component=grafana" -o jsonpath="{.items[0].metadata.name}")
  kubectl --namespace monitoring port-forward $POD_NAME 3000

3. Login with the password from step 1 and the username: admin
```

The notes first include information about retrieving the secret. This highlights a feature that you will see used in several charts: where it requires a confidential password, it will generate a unique one and save it as a secret. This secret is directly available to people with access to the namespace and `kubectl`.

Use the provided command to retrieve the password for your Grafana interface:

```
kubectl get secret --namespace monitoring viz-grafana -o
jsonpath="{.data.grafana-admin-password}" | base64 --decode ; echo
```

And then open a Terminal and run these commands to get access to the dashboard:

```
export POD_NAME=$(kubectl get pods --namespace monitoring -l "app=viz-
grafana,component=grafana" -o jsonpath="{.items[0].metadata.name}")

kubectl --namespace monitoring port-forward $POD_NAME 3000
```

Then, open a browser window and navigate to `https://localhost:3000/`, which should show you the Grafana login window:

Now, log in with the username `admin`; the password is the secret you retrieved earlier. This will bring you to a **Home** dashboard in Grafana, where you can configure data sources and assemble graphs into dashboards:

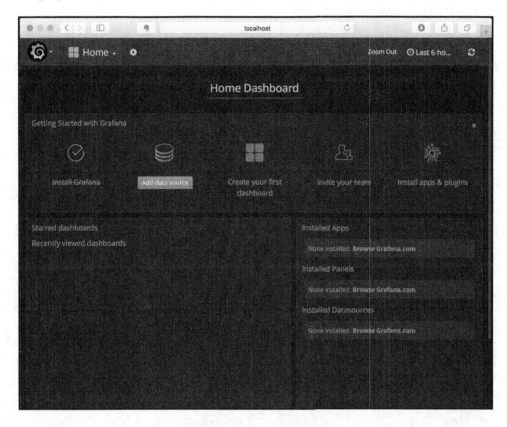

Click on **Add data source** and you will see a window with two tabs: **Config** allows you to set the location to a data source, and **Dashboards** allows you to import dashboard configurations.

Under **Config,** set the type of the data source to **Prometheus**, and where it says **Name**, you can enter `prometheus`. Naming the data source after the type is a bit redundant, and if you had multiple Prometheus instances on your cluster, you would want to name them separately and specifically for their purpose. Add in the DNS name of our Prometheus instance to the URL so that Grafana can access it:
`http://monitor-prometheus-server.monitoring.svc.cluster.local`. This same name was listed in the notes when we installed Prometheus using Helm.

Click on the **Dashboards** tab and import Prometheus stats and Grafana metrics, which will provide built-in dashboards for Prometheus and Grafana itself. Click back to the **Config** tab, scroll down, and click on the **Add** button to set up the Prometheus data source. You should see **Data source is working** when you add it:

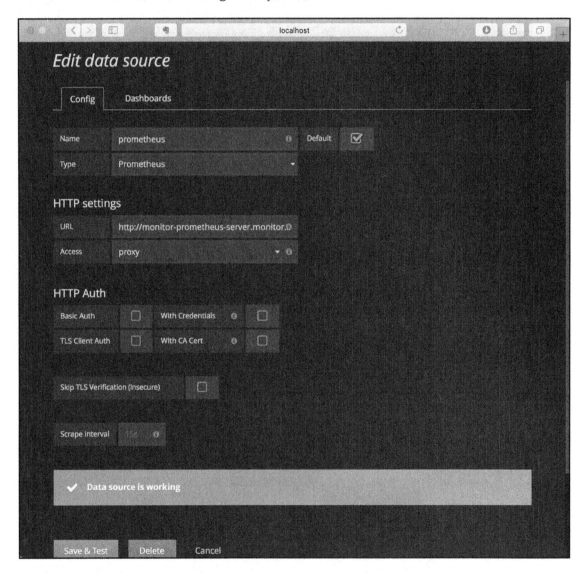

Now, you can navigate to the built-in dashboards and see some of the information. The top of the web page user interface consists of pull-downs, the top left leading to overall Grafana configuration and the next listing the dashboards you have set up, which generally starts with a **Home** dashboard. Select the **Prometheus Stats** dashboard that we just imported, and you should see some initial information about Prometheus:

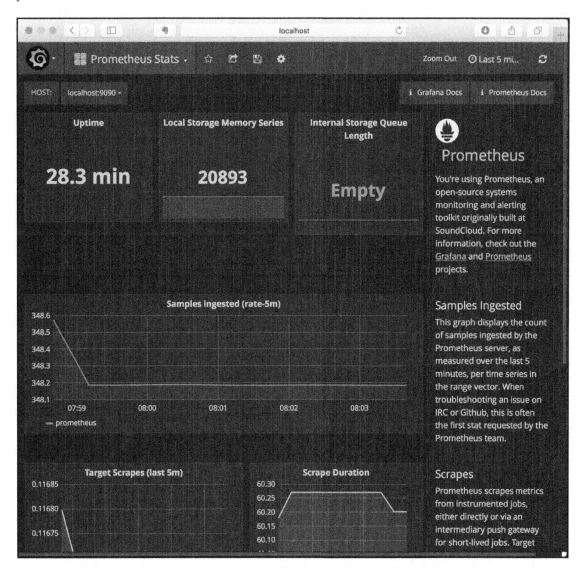

The Grafana project maintains a collection of dashboards that you can search through and either use directly, or use for inspiration to modify and create your own. You can search through the dashboards that have been shared—for example, limit it to dashboards sourced from Prometheus and related to Kubernetes. You'll see a variety of dashboards to browse through, some including screenshots, at `https://grafana.com/dashboards?dataSource=` `prometheusamp;search=kubernetes`.

You can import these into your instance of Grafana using the dashboard number. For example, dashboards **1621** and **162** are common dashboards for monitoring the health of the overall cluster:

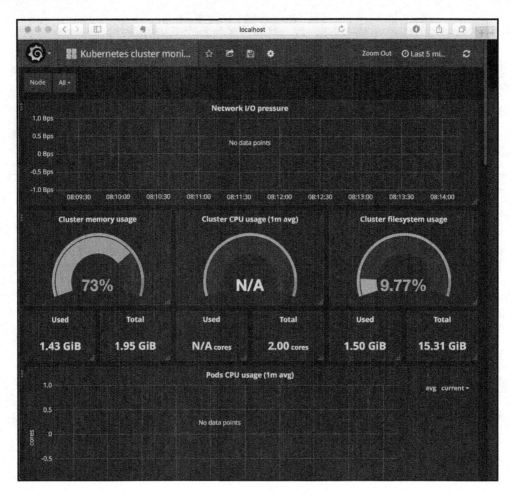

The best value of these dashboards is to show you how to configure your own graphs and make your own dashboards. Within every dashboard, you may select the graphs and choose **Edit** to see the queries used and display choices made, and tweak them to your values. Every dashboard can also be shared back to the Grafana hosting site, or you can view the JSON that is the configuration and save it locally.

The work going on with the Prometheus operator is working towards making it easier to bring up Prometheus and Grafana together, pre-configured and running to monitor your cluster and the applications within your cluster. If you are interested in trying it out, see the project README that is hosted by CoreOS at `https://github.com/coreos/prometheus-operator/tree/master/helm`, which can also be installed with Helm.

Now that you have Grafana and Prometheus installed, you may use them to follow a similar process to determine the CPU and memory utilization of your own software, while running load tests. One of the benefits of running Prometheus locally is the ability it provides to collect metrics about your application.

Using Prometheus to view application metrics

While you could add a job within Prometheus to include the configuration to scrape Prometheus metrics from a specific endpoint, the installation we did earlier includes a configuration that will update what it is looking at dynamically, based on annotations on pods. One of the benefits of Prometheus is that it has support for automatically detecting changes in your cluster, based on annotations, and it can look up the endpoints for the pods that back a service.

Since we deployed Prometheus using Helm, you can find the relevant configuration embedded within the `values.yaml` file. Look for the Prometheus job `kubernetes-service-endpoints`, and you will find both the configuration and some documentation of how it can be used. If you don't have the files locally, you can view this configuration at `https://github.com/kubernetes/charts/blob/master/stable/prometheus/values.yaml#L747-L776`.

This configuration looks for services within the cluster that have an annotation `prometheus.io/scrape`. If this is set to `true`, then Prometheus will automatically attempt to add that endpoint to the list of targets it is watching. By default, it will attempt to access the metrics at the URI `/metrics` and use the same port as the service. You can use additional annotations to change those defaults, for example, `prometheus.io/path = "/alternatemetrics"` will attempt to read the metrics from the path `/alternatemetrics`.

By using the service as the means of organizing metric gathering, we have a mechanism that will automatically scale with the number of pods. Whereas in other environments you might have to reconfigure the monitoring every time you add or remove instances, Prometheus and Kubernetes working together seamlessly capture this data.

This capability allows us to easily expose custom metrics from our application and have them picked up by Prometheus. There are several ways this can be used, but the most obvious is simply getting better visibility on how your application is doing. With Prometheus collecting the metrics and Grafana installed as a dashboard tool, you could also use the combination to create your own application dashboards.

The Prometheus project supports client libraries in a wide variety of languages that make it easier to collect and expose metrics in its format. We will use some of these libraries to show you how to instrument our Python and Node.js examples. Before you dive in to directly using these libraries yourself, it is very worthwhile reading the documentation that the Prometheus project provides on how to write metric exporters, and their expected conventions for metric names. You can find this documentation at the project website: `https://prometheus.io/docs/instrumenting/writing_exporters/`.

Flask metrics with Prometheus

You can find the library to expose metrics from Python at `https://github.com/prometheus/client_python` and can install it using `pip` with this command:

```
pip install prometheus_client
```

Depending on your setup, you may need to use **sudo pip install prometheus_client** to install the client with `pip`.

For our `flask` example, you can download the full sample code from `https://github.com/kubernetes-for-developers/kfd-flask` from branch 0.5.0. The commands to get this updated sample are:

```
git clone https://github.com/kubernetes-for-developers/kfd-flask -b 0.5.0
```

If you look within `exampleapp.py`, you can see the code where we use two metrics, a histogram and a counter, and use the flask framework to add in callbacks at the beginning of a request, and the end of a request, and capture that time difference:

```
FLASK_REQUEST_LATENCY = Histogram('flask_request_latency_seconds', 'Flask
Request Latency',
  ['method', 'endpoint'])
FLASK_REQUEST_COUNT = Counter('flask_request_count', 'Flask Request Count',
  ['method', 'endpoint', 'http_status'])

def before_request():
    request.start_time = time.time()

def after_request(response):
    request_latency = time.time() - request.start_time
    FLASK_REQUEST_LATENCY.labels(request.method,
request.path).observe(request_latency)
    FLASK_REQUEST_COUNT.labels(request.method, request.path,
response.status_code).inc()
    return response
```

The library also includes a helper application to make it very easy to generate the metrics to be scraped by Prometheus:

```
@app.route('/metrics')
def metrics():
    return make_response(generate_latest())
```

This code has been made into a container image, `quay.io/kubernetes-for-developers/flask:0.5.0`. With those additions in place, we only need to add the annotation to `flask-service`:

```
kind: Service
apiVersion: v1
metadata:
  name: flask-service
  annotations:
      prometheus.io/scrape: "true"
spec:
  type: NodePort
  ports:
```

```
      - port: 5000
      selector:
          app: flask
```

Once deployed with `kubectl apply -f deploy/` from the example's directory, the service will be backed by a single pod, and Prometheus will begin to pick it up as a target. If you use the `kubectl proxy` command, you can see the specific metric response that this generates. In our case, the pods name is `flask-6596b895b-nqqqz`, so the metrics can be easily queried at `http://localhost:8001/api/v1/proxy/namespaces/default/pods/flask-6596b895b-nqqqz/metrics`.

A sample of those metrics is as follows:

```
flask_request_latency_seconds_bucket{endpoint="/",le="0.005",method="GET"}
13.0
flask_request_latency_seconds_bucket{endpoint="/",le="0.01",method="GET"}
13.0
flask_request_latency_seconds_bucket{endpoint="/",le="0.025",method="GET"}
13.0
flask_request_latency_seconds_bucket{endpoint="/",le="0.05",method="GET"}
13.0
flask_request_latency_seconds_bucket{endpoint="/",le="0.075",method="GET"}
13.0
flask_request_latency_seconds_bucket{endpoint="/",le="0.1",method="GET"}
13.0
flask_request_latency_seconds_bucket{endpoint="/",le="0.25",method="GET"}
13.0
flask_request_latency_seconds_bucket{endpoint="/",le="0.5",method="GET"}
13.0
flask_request_latency_seconds_bucket{endpoint="/",le="0.75",method="GET"}
13.0
flask_request_latency_seconds_bucket{endpoint="/",le="1.0",method="GET"}
13.0
flask_request_latency_seconds_bucket{endpoint="/",le="2.5",method="GET"}
13.0
flask_request_latency_seconds_bucket{endpoint="/",le="5.0",method="GET"}
13.0
flask_request_latency_seconds_bucket{endpoint="/",le="7.5",method="GET"}
13.0
flask_request_latency_seconds_bucket{endpoint="/",le="10.0",method="GET"}
13.0
flask_request_latency_seconds_bucket{endpoint="/",le="+Inf",method="GET"}
13.0 flask_request_latency_seconds_count{endpoint="/",method="GET"} 13.0
flask_request_latency_seconds_sum{endpoint="/",method="GET"}
0.0012879371643066406
# HELP flask_request_count Flask Request Count
```

```
# TYPE flask_request_count counter
flask_request_count{endpoint="/alive",http_status="200",method="GET"} 645.0
flask_request_count{endpoint="/ready",http_status="200",method="GET"} 644.0
flask_request_count{endpoint="/metrics",http_status="200",method="GET"}
65.0 flask_request_count{endpoint="/",http_status="200",method="GET"} 13.0
```

You can see the metrics named `flask_request_latency_seconds` and `flask_request_count` in this sample, and you can query for those same metrics in the Prometheus browser interface.

Node.js metrics with Prometheus

JavaScript has similar client libraries to Python. In fact, it is even easier to instrument Node.js express applications with the use of `express-prom-bundle`, which in turn uses `prom-client`. You can install this library for your use with this command:

npm install express-prom-bundle --save

You can then use it in your code. The following will set up a middleware for express:

```
const promBundle = require("express-prom-bundle");
const metricsMiddleware = promBundle({includeMethod: true});
```

And then, you simply include the middleware, as you're setting up this application:

```
app.use(metricsMiddleware)
```

The example code at `https://github.com/kubernetes-for-developers/kfd-nodejs` has these updates, and you can check out this code from branch 0.5.0 with the command:

git clone https://github.com/kubernetes-for-developers/kfd-nodejs -b 0.5.0

Like the Python code, the Node.js example includes updating the service with the annotation `prometheus.io/scrape: "true"`:

```
kind: Service
apiVersion: v1
metadata:
 name: nodejs-service
 annotations:
   prometheus.io/scrape: "true"
spec:
 ports:
 - port: 3000
   name: web
```

```
clusterIP: None
selector:
  app: nodejs
```

Service signals in Prometheus

You can tell the health and status of your service with three key metrics. It has become relatively common for service dashboards to instrument and build on these metrics as a baseline for understanding how your service is running.

These key metrics for a web-based service are:

- Error rate
- Response time
- Throughput

Error rate can be gathered by using the labels within the `http_request_duration_seconds_count` metric, which is included from `express-prom-bundle`. The query we can use in Prometheus. We can match on the format of the response code and count the increase in the number of 500 responses versus all responses.

The Prometheus query could be:

```
sum(increase(http_request_duration_seconds_count{status_code=~"^5..$"}[5m])
) / sum(increase(http_request_duration_seconds_count[5m]))
```

With little load on our own example services and probably no errors, this query isn't likely to return any data points, but you can use it as an example to explore building your own error response queries.

Response time is complex to measure and understand, especially with busy services. The reason that we typically include a histogram metric for the time it takes to process the request is to be able to view the distribution of those requests over time. Using a histogram, we can aggregate the requests across a window, and then look at the rate of those requests. In our preceding Python example, the `flask_request_latency_seconds` is a histogram, and each request gets label with where it was in the histogram bucket, the HTTP method used, and the URI endpoint. We can aggregate the rates of those requests using those labels, and look at the median, 95th, and 99th percentile with the following Prometheus queries:

Median:

```
histogram_quantile(0.5, sum(rate(flask_request_latency_seconds_bucket[5m]))
by (le, method, endpoint))
```

95th percentile:

```
histogram_quantile(0.95,
sum(rate(flask_request_latency_seconds_bucket[5m])) by (le, method,
endpoint))
```

99th percentile:

```
histogram_quantile(0.99,
sum(rate(flask_request_latency_seconds_bucket[5m])) by (le, method,
endpoint))
```

Throughput is about measuring the total number of requests over a given timeframe, and can be derived directly from `flask_request_latency_seconds_count` and viewed against endpoint and method:

```
sum(rate(flask_request_latency_seconds_count[5m])) by (method, endpoint)
```

Summary

In this chapter, we introduced Prometheus and showed how to install it, used it to capture metrics from your Kubernetes cluster, and showed how to install and use Grafana to provide dashboards, using the metrics captured and temporarily stored in Prometheus. We then looked at how you can expose custom metrics from your own code and leverage Prometheus to capture them, along with a few examples of metrics you might be interested in tracking, such as error rate, response time, and throughput.

In the next chapter, we continue to look into observability for our applications with tools to help us capture logs and traces.

8
Logging and Tracing

When we first started with containers and Kubernetes, we showed how we could get the log output from any of our individual containers using the `kubectl log` command. As we scale the number of containers from which we want to get information, the ability to easily find the relevant logs becomes increasingly difficult. In the previous chapter, we looked at how to aggregate and collect metrics, and in this chapter we extend that same concept, looking at how to aggregate logging and getting a better understanding of how containers work together with distributed tracing.

Topics for this chapter include:

- A Kubernetes concept—DaemonSet
- Installing Elasticsearch, Fluentd, and Kibana
- Viewing logs using Kibana
- Distributed tracing with Jeager
- An example of adding tracing to your application

A Kubernetes concept – DaemonSet

A Kubernetes resource that we have now used (through Helm) is DaemonSet. This resource is a wrapper around pods very similar to ReplicaSet, but with the purpose of running a pod on every node in a cluster. When we installed Prometheus using Helm, it created a DaemonSet to run node-collector on each node within the Kubernetes cluster.

There are two common patterns for running software in a support role with your application: the first is using the side-car pattern, and the second is using a DaemonSet. A side-car is when you include a container within your pod whose sole purpose is to run alongside the primary application and provide some supporting, but external, role. An example of a useful side-car might be a cache, or a proxy service of some form. Running a side-car application obviously increases the resources needed for a pod, and if the number of pods is relatively low or they are sparse compared to the size of a cluster, this would be the most efficient way to provide that supporting software.

When the support software you are running will be potentially replicated many times on a single node, and the service it is providing is fairly generic (such as log aggregation or metric collection), then it can be significantly more efficient to run a single pod on each node in a cluster. That is exactly where DaemonSet comes in.

Our earlier example of using a DaemonSet was running an instance of node-collector on every node within the cluster. The purpose of the node-collector DaemonSet is to collect statistics and metrics about the operation of every node. Kubernetes also uses DaemonSet to run its own services, such as kube-proxy, which operate on every node in the cluster. If you are using an overlay network to connect your Kubernetes cluster, such as Weave or Flannel, it is also frequently run using a DaemonSet. Another common use case is the one we'll explore more in this chapter, collecting and forwarding logging.

The required fields for a DaemonSet specification are similar to a deployment or job; in addition to the `apiVersion`, `kind`, and `metadata`, the DaemonSet also needs a spec, which includes a template that is used to create the pods on each node. In addition, the template can have a `nodeSelector` to match a set or subset of the nodes available.

Take a look at the YAML that Helm created when it installed `prometheus`. You can get a sense of how the data for the DaemonSet is laid out. The following output is from the command:

```
helm template prometheus -n monitor --namespace monitoring
```

The DaemonSet specification that Helm generated is as follows:

```
apiVersion: extensions/v1beta1
kind: DaemonSet
metadata:
  labels:
    app: prometheus
    chart: prometheus-4.6.17
    component: "node-exporter"
    heritage: Tiller
    release: monitor
```

```
    name: monitor-prometheus-node-exporter
spec:
  updateStrategy:
    type: OnDelete
  template:
    metadata:
      labels:
        app: prometheus
        component: "node-exporter"
        release: monitor
    spec:
      serviceAccountName: "default"
      containers:
      - name: prometheus-node-exporter
        image: "prom/node-exporter:v0.15.0"
        imagePullPolicy: "IfNotPresent"
        args:
          - --path.procfs=/host/proc
          - --path.sysfs=/host/sys
        ports:
          - name: metrics
            containerPort: 9100
            hostPort: 9100
        resources:
          {}

        volumeMounts:
          - name: proc
            mountPath: /host/proc
            readOnly: true
          - name: sys
            mountPath: /host/sys
            readOnly: true
      hostNetwork: true
      hostPID: true
      volumes:
        - name: proc
          hostPath:
            path: /proc
        - name: sys
          hostPath:
            path: /sys
```

This DaemonSet runs a single container with a pod on each node, the image `prom/node-exporter:0.15`, which collects metrics from the volume mount points (`/proc` and `/sys` are very Linux-specific), and exposes them on port `9100` for `prometheus` to scrape with an HTTP request.

Installing and using Elasticsearch, Fluentd, and Kibana

Fluentd is software that's frequently used to collect and aggregate logging. Hosted at `https://www.fluentd.org`, like prometheus it is open source software that is managed under the umbrella of the **Cloud Native Computing Foundation** (**CNCF**). When it comes to talking about aggregating logs, the problem has existed long before containers, and ELK was a frequent acronym used to represent a solution, the combination of Elasticsearch, Logstash, and Kibana. When using containers, the number of log sources expands, making the problem of collecting all the logs even larger, and Fluentd evolved to support the same space as Logstash, focusing on structured logging with a JSON format, routing it, and supporting plugins to process the logs. Fluentd was written in Ruby and C, intending to be faster and more efficient than LogStash, and the same pattern is continuing with Fluent Bit (`http://fluentbit.io`), which has an even smaller memory footprint. You may even see references to EFK, which stands for the combination of Elasticsearch, Fluentd, and Kibana.

Within the Kubernetes community, one of the more common solutions for capturing and aggregating logs is Fluentd, and it is even built into recent versions of Minikube as one of the add-ons that you can use.

If you are using Minikube, you can experiment with EFK very easily by enabling the Minikube add-on. While Fluentd and Kibana are fairly small in terms of resource needs, Elasticsearch has higher resource requirements, even for a small demonstration instance. The default VM that Minikube uses to create a single-node Kubernetes cluster has 2 GB of memory allocated to it, which is insufficient for running EFK and any additional workloads, as ElasticSearch by itself wants to utilize 2 GB of memory while it is initializing and starting up.

Fortunately, you can ask Minikube to start up and allocate more memory to the VM that it creates. To see how Elasticsearch, Kibana, and Fluentd work together, you should start Minikube with at least 5 GB of RAM allocated, which you can do with the following command:

```
minikube start --memory 5120
```

You can then see what add-ons are enabled and disabled for Minikube with the Minikube add-ons command. For example:

```
minikube addons list

- addon-manager: enabled
- coredns: enabled
```

```
- dashboard: enabled
- default-storageclass: enabled
- efk: disabled
- freshpod: disabled
- heapster: disabled
- ingress: disabled
- kube-dns: disabled
- registry: disabled
- registry-creds: disabled
- storage-provisioner: enabled
```

And enabling EFK is simply done using this command:

```
minikube addons enable efk

efk was successfully enabled
```

`enabled` does not mean instantly running. FluentD and Kibana will start fairly quickly, but ElasticSearch does take significantly longer. Being an add-on implies that software within Kubernetes will manage the containers within the kube-system namespace, so getting information about the current state of these services won't be as simple as `kubectl get pods`. You will need to either reference `-n kube-system` or use the option `--all-namespaces`:

```
kubectl get all --all-namespaces

NAMESPACE NAME DESIRED CURRENT UP-TO-DATE AVAILABLE AGE
kube-system deploy/coredns 1 1 1 1 5h
kube-system deploy/kubernetes-dashboard 1 1 1 1 5h

NAMESPACE NAME DESIRED CURRENT READY AGE
kube-system rs/coredns-599474b9f4 1 1 1 5h
kube-system rs/kubernetes-dashboard-77d8b98585 1 1 1 5h

NAMESPACE NAME DESIRED CURRENT UP-TO-DATE AVAILABLE AGE
kube-system deploy/coredns 1 1 1 1 5h
kube-system deploy/kubernetes-dashboard 1 1 1 1 5h

NAMESPACE NAME DESIRED CURRENT READY AGE
kube-system rs/coredns-599474b9f4 1 1 1 5h
kube-system rs/kubernetes-dashboard-77d8b98585 1 1 1 5h

NAMESPACE NAME READY STATUS RESTARTS AGE
kube-system po/coredns-599474b9f4-6fp8z 1/1 Running 0 5h
kube-system po/elasticsearch-logging-4zbpd 0/1 PodInitializing 0 3s
kube-system po/fluentd-es-hcngp 1/1 Running 0 3s
kube-system po/kibana-logging-stlzf 1/1 Running 0 3s
kube-system po/kube-addon-manager-minikube 1/1 Running 0 5h
```

```
kube-system po/kubernetes-dashboard-77d8b98585-qvwlv 1/1 Running 0 5h
kube-system po/storage-provisioner 1/1 Running 0 5h

NAMESPACE NAME DESIRED CURRENT READY AGE
kube-system rc/elasticsearch-logging 1 1 0 3s
kube-system rc/fluentd-es 1 1 1 3s
kube-system rc/kibana-logging 1 1 1 3s

NAMESPACE NAME TYPE CLUSTER-IP EXTERNAL-IP PORT(S) AGE
default svc/kubernetes ClusterIP 10.96.0.1 <none> 443/TCP 5h
kube-system svc/elasticsearch-logging ClusterIP 10.109.100.36 <none>
9200/TCP 3s
kube-system svc/kibana-logging NodePort 10.99.88.146 <none> 5601:30003/TCP
3s
kube-system svc/kube-dns ClusterIP 10.96.0.10 <none> 53/UDP,53/TCP,9153/TCP
5h
kube-system svc/kubernetes-dashboard NodePort 10.98.230.226 <none>
80:30000/TCP 5h
```

You can see the Minikube add-on manager loads up EFK as three ReplicaSets, each running a single pod, and fronted with a service that is exposed from the virtual machine as a NodePort. With Minikube, you can also see the list of services using this command:

```
minikube service list
```

```
|--------------|-----------------------|-------------------------------|
| NAMESPACE    | NAME                  | URL                           |
|--------------|-----------------------|-------------------------------|
| default      | kubernetes            | No node port                  |
| kube-system  | elasticsearch-logging | No node port                  |
| kube-system  | kibana-logging        | http://192.168.64.32:30003    |
| kube-system  | kube-dns              | No node port                  |
| kube-system  | kubernetes-dashboard  | http://192.168.64.32:30000    |
|--------------|-----------------------|-------------------------------|
```

Log aggregation with EFK

Fluentd starts as the source for collecting logs from all the containers. It uses the same underlying sources that the command `kubectl logs` uses. Within the cluster, every container that is operating is generating logs that are handled in some fashion by the container runtime, the most common of which is Docker, which maintains log files for every container on each of the hosts.

The Minikube add-on that sets up Fluentd configures it with a `ConfigMap`, which references where to load these log files, and includes additional rules to annotate the log data with information from Kubernetes. As Fluentd runs, it keeps track of these log files, reading in the data as it is updated from each container, parsing the log file output into data structures in JSON format, and adding the Kubernetes-specific information. The same configuration also details what to do with the output, and in the case of the Minikube add-on, it specifies an endpoint, which is the `elasticsearch-logging` service, where it sends this structured JSON data.

Elasticsearch is a popular open source data and search index, with corporate support from `Elastic.co`. Although it requires quite a bit of resources to run, it scales up extremely well and has a very flexible structure for adding a variety of data sources and providing a search interface for that data. You can get more details about how ElasticSearch works at `https://github.com/elastic/elasticsearch`, the GitHub repository.

Kibana is the final part of this trio, and provides the web-based user interface for searching the content that is stored in Elasticsearch. Also maintained by `Elastic.co`, it provides some dashboard capabilities and an interactive query interface for Elasticsearch. You can find more information on Kibana at `https://www.elastic.co/products/kibana`.

While using Minikube, everything in your cluster is on a single node, so there are limits and differences to using the same kind of framework in a larger cluster. If you are using a remote cluster with several nodes, you may want to look at something like Helm to install Elasticsearch, Fluentd, and Kibana. Many service providers who are supporting Kubernetes also have something set up to aggregate, store, and provide a searchable index of your containers logs. Google Stackdriver, Datadog, and Azure are examples that provide a similar mechanism and service, specific to their hosted solutions.

Viewing logs using Kibana

For this book, we will explore how to use Kibana, taking advantage of it as an add-on to Minikube. After you have enabled it, and when the pods are fully available and reporting as Ready, you can access Kibana with this command:

```
minikube service kibana-logging -n kube-system
```

This will bring up a web page that is backed by the `kibana-logging` service. When it is first accessed, the web page will ask you to specify a default index, which is used by Elasticsearch to build its search indices:

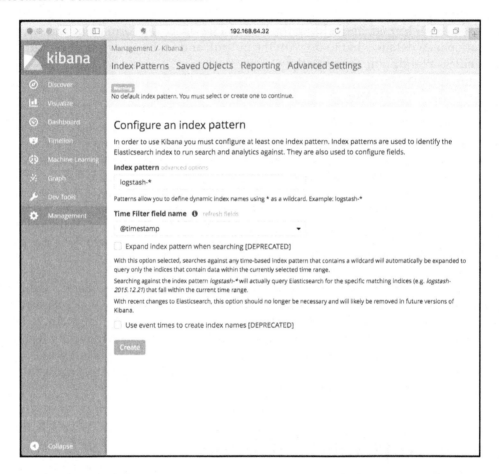

Click on **Create**, taking the defaults that are provided. The default index pattern of `logstash-*` doesn't mean it has to come from `logstash` as a source, and the data that has already been sent to ElasticSearch from Fluentd will all be directly accessible.

One you have defined a default index, the next page that is displayed will show you all the fields that have been added into Elasticsearch as Fluentd has taken the data from the container logs and Kubernetes metadata:

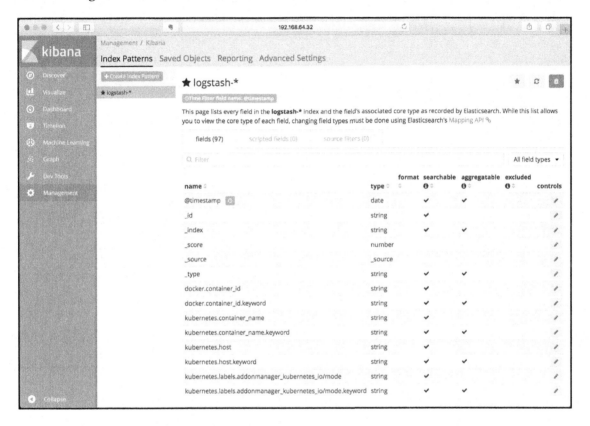

You can browse through this list to see what is being captured by field name, which will give you a little sense of what is available to browse and search.

To see the logs that are flowing from the system, the **Discover** button on the top left of the web page will take you to a view that is built from these indices we just created, and by default, will reflect all of the logs that are happening that Fluentd is collecting:

The logging that you are seeing is primarily coming from the Kubernetes infrastructure itself. To get a better picture of how to use the logging, spin up the earlier examples we created, and we will scale those up to multiple instances to see the output.

We will grab the two-tier example app of Flask and Redis from `https://github.com/kubernetes-for-developers/kfd-flask`:

```
git clone https://github.com/kubernetes-for-developers/kfd-flask -b 0.5.0

kubectl apply -f kfd-flask/deploy/
```

This will deploy our earlier Python and Redis examples, with a single instance of each. Once these pods are active, go back and refresh the browser with Kibana active in it, and it should update to show you the latest logging. You can set the time period that Kibana is summarizing at the top of the window, and set it to auto-refresh on a regular basis, if you desire.

Finally, let's scale up our Flask deployment to have multiple instances, which will make learning how to use Kibana a bit easier:

```
kubectl scale deploy/flask --replicas=3
```

Filtering by app

The key to using Kibana effectively is to filter to just the data you are interested in seeing. The default discovery view is set to give you a sense of how large the logs are from specific sources, and we can use filtering to narrow down to what we want to see.

As you view the data, scroll down on the left side through the list of fields, and each of these can be used as a filter. If you tap on one, **Kubernetes.labels.app** for example, Kibana will give you a summary of what different values this field has collected for the timespan that you are viewing.

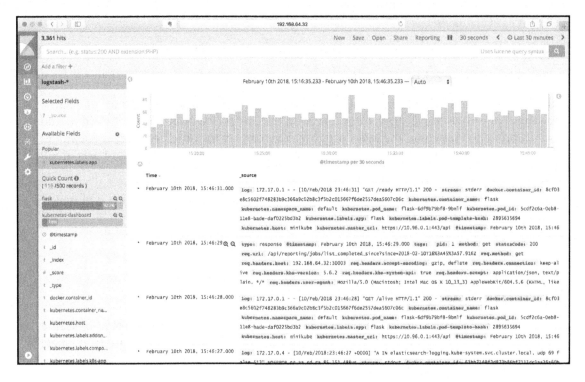

In the preceding example, you can see that the two `app` labels that are within the timespan are `flask` and `kubernetes-dashboard`. We can limit it to the Flask application by clicking the magnifying glass icon with a plus in it. The result constrains to only log items that include those values:

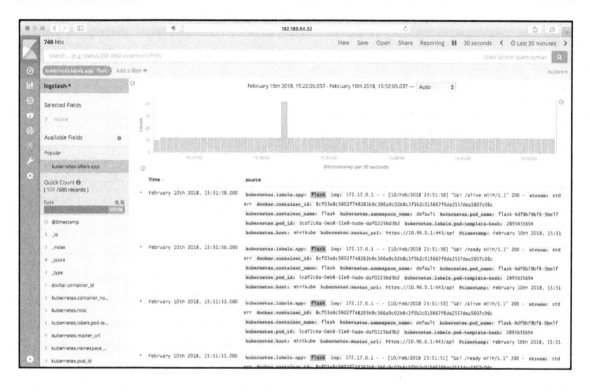

The icon with a magnifying glass with a minus symbol is used to set an exclusion filter. Since we used the `kubectl scale` command earlier to create multiple instances, you can scroll down to `kubernetes.pod_name` in the list of fields and see the pods that are listed and reporting as matching the first filter:

You can now refine the filter to only include one, or exclude one of those pods, to see all the remaining logs. As you add filters, they will appear at the top of the screen, and by clicking on that reference you can remove, pin, or temporarily disable the filter.

Lucene query language

You can also use the Lucene query language, which is what ElasticSearch uses by default, to refine your searches to data within the fields, make more complex filters, or otherwise track down the data with more precision. The Lucene query language goes beyond what we will cover in this book, but you can get an excellent overview in the Kibana documentation at `https://www.elastic.co/guide/en/kibana/current/lucene-query.html`.

Lucene's search language is oriented around searching unstructured text data, so basic searching for a word is as simple as entering a word. Multiple words are treated as individual searches, so if you are searching for a specific phrase, put the phrase in quotes. The search parser will also understand explicit OR and AND for simple Boolean searches.

The default on the query syntax is to search all fields, and you may specify a field to search. To do so, name the field, followed by a colon, and then the search terms. For example, to search for `error` in the field `log`, you can use this search query:

```
log:error
```

This search query also supports wildcard searches, using the character ? to represent any single unknown character, and * to represent zero or more characters. You can also use regular expressions in your query, by wrapping your query with / characters, for example:

```
log:/*error*/
```

This will search for `error` or `errors` in the log field.

NOTE: Because Lucene breaks down the fields, regular expressions are applied to each word in a string, and not the string as a whole. Because of this, regular expressions are best used when you want to hunt for a composed word, and not a phrase or string that includes whitespaces.

The Lucene query language also includes some advanced search options that can accommodate misspellings and slight variations, which can be immensely useful. The syntax includes support for fuzzy searches using the ~ character as a wildcard, which allows for slight variations in spelling, transposition, and so on. Phrases also support using ~ as a variation indicator, and it is used for making proximity searches, a maximum distance between two words in a phrase. To get more information on how these specific techniques work and how to use them, dig into the `ElasticSearch Query DSL documentation`.

Running Kibana in production

Kibana has a variety of other features, including setting up dashboards, making data visualizations, and even using simple machine learning to hunt for anomalies in the log data. These features are beyond the scope of this book. You can learn more about them in the Kibana user's guide at `https://www.elastic.co/guide/en/kibana/current/`.

Running more complex developer support tools, such as Elasticsearch, Fluentd, and Kibana, is a more complex task than we can cover in this book. There is some documentation around using Fluentd and Elasticsearch as an add-on, as you have seen previously with the Minikube example. EFK is its own complex application to be managed. There are several Helm charts that might suit your needs, or you may want to consider leveraging a cloud provider's solution, rather than take on the administration of these components yourself.

Distributed tracing with Jaeger

As you decompose your services into multiple containers, one of the hardest things to understand is the flow and path of requests, and how containers are interacting. As you expand and use more containers to support components within your system, knowing which containers are which and how they're contributing to the performance of a request becomes a significant challenge. For simple systems, you can often add logging and get a view through the log files. As you move into dozens, or even hundreds, of different containers making up a service, that process becomes far less tenable.

One solution to this problem is called Distributed Tracing, which is a means of tracking the path of requests between containers, much like a profiler can track requests within a single application. This involves using libraries or frameworks that support a tracing library to create and pass along the information, as well as a system external to your application to collect this information and present it in a usable form. The earliest examples of this are documented in research papers from a Google system called Dapper, and an early open source implementation inspired by Dapper was called Zipkin, made by folks working at Twitter. The same concept has been repeated several times, and in 2016, a group started to come together to collaborate on the various tracing attempts. They formed OpenTracing, which is now a part of the Cloud Native Compute Foundation, to specify the format for sharing tracing across a variety of systems and languages.

Jaeger is an implementation of the OpenTracing standards, inspired by Dapper and Zipkin, created by engineers working at Uber, and donated to the Cloud Native Compute Foundation. Full documentation for Jaeger is available at `http://jaeger.readthedocs.io/`. Released in 2017, Jaeger is in active development and use.

There are other tracing platforms, notably OpenZipkin (`https://zipkin.io`), also available, so Jaeger isn't the only option in this space.

Spans and traces

When looking at distributed tracing, there are two common terms that you will see repeatedly: span and trace. A span is the smallest unit that is tracked in distributed tracing, and represents an individual process getting a request and returning a response. As the process makes requests to other services in order to do its work, it passes information along with the request so that the service being requested can create its own span and reference the requesting one. Each of these spans is collected and exported from each process, gathered up, and can then be analyzed. A full collection of spans that are all working together is called a trace.

Adding, gathering, and transferring all this additional information is additional overhead for each of the services. While this information is valuable, it can also generate a huge amount of information, and if every service interacting always created and published every trace, the amount of data processing needed to handle the tracing system would exponentially outgrow the service itself. To provide value to tracing, tracing systems have implemented sampling so that not every request gets traced, but a reasonable volume, you still have enough information to get a good representation of the system's overall operation.

Different tracing systems handle this differently, and how much data and what data is passed between services is still very much in flux. Additionally, services that don't follow the request/response pattern – such as a background queue or fan-out processing – aren't easily represented by the current tracing systems. The data can still be captured, but presenting a consistent view of the processing can be far more complex.

When you view the details of a trace, you are often presented with a flame-graph style output, which shows a timeline view of how long each trace took and what service was processing it. For example, here is an example trace detail view from the Jaeger documentation:

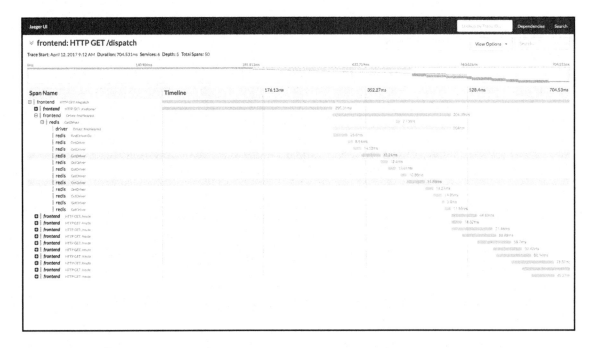

Architecture of Jaeger distributed tracing

Like (**Elasticsearch, Fluentd, and Kibana (EFK)**), Jaeger is a complex system that collects and processes quite a bit of information. It is shown here:

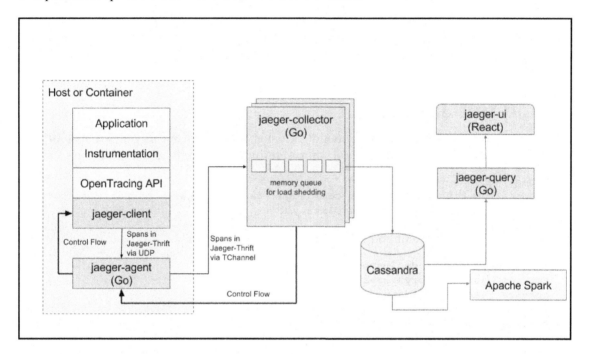

This is the architecture of how Jaeger worked at Uber as of 2017. The configuration uses the side-car pattern we mentioned earlier, with each container running a nearby container that collects the spans from the instrumentation using UDP, and then forwards those spans into a storage system based on Cassandra. Setting up a Cassandra cluster, as well as the individual collectors and the query engine, is far more than can be easily created in a local development environment.

Fortunately, Jaeger also has an all-in-one option for experimenting with and learning how to use Jaeger and what it can do. The all-in-one option has the agent, collector, query engine, and UI in a single container image that doesn't store any information persistently.

The Jaeger project has the all-on-one option, as well as Helm charts and variations that utilize Elasticsearch for persistence, documented and stored on GitHub at `https://github.com/jaegertracing/jaeger-kubernetes`. In fact, the Jaeger project tests their development of Jaeger and each of the components by leveraging Kubernetes.

Trying out Jaeger

You can try out the current version of Jaeger by using their all-in-one development setup. Since they maintain this on GitHub, you can run it directly from there with this command:

```
kubectl create -f
https://raw.githubusercontent.com/jaegertracing/jaeger-kubernetes/master/al
l-in-one/jaeger-all-in-one-template.yml
```

This will create a deployment and a number of service frontends:

```
deployment "jaeger-deployment" created
service "jaeger-query" created
service "jaeger-collector" created
service "jaeger-agent" created
service "zipkin" created
```

And when the `jaeger-deployment` pod is reporting ready, you can use the following command to access the Jaeger query interface:

```
minikube service jaeger-query
```

The resulting web page should appear:

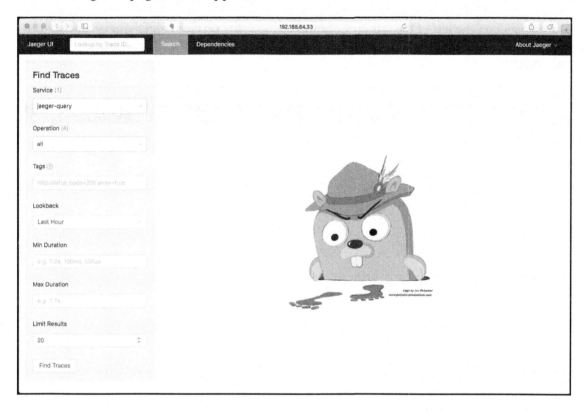

By default, the Jaeger system is reporting on its own operations, so as you use the query interface, it will also generate its own traces that you can start to investigate. The **Find Traces** panel on the left of the window should show at the service **jaeger-query**, and if you click on the **Find Traces** button at the bottom, it will search based on the default parameters:

This page shows the times of all the traces found and how long they took, allowing you to dig down into them by API endpoint (which is called operation in this user interface), limiting the time span, and providing a rough representation of how long the queries took to process.

These traces are all made up of a single span, so are quite simple. You can select one of those spans and look at the trace detail, including expanding the information that it captured and passed along with those traces. Looking at that detail fully expanded should show you something like this:

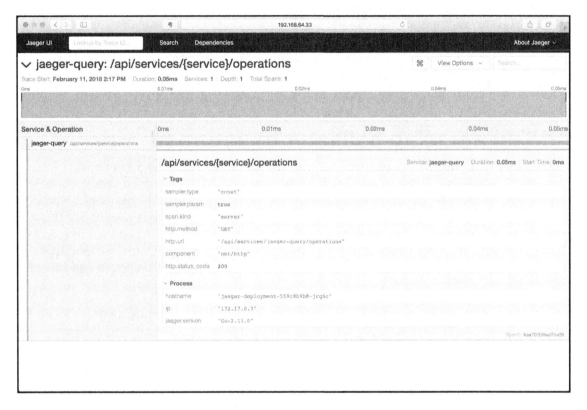

Let's look at how to add tracing to your own application.

Example – adding tracing to your application

There are several things we will need to do to enable tracing from our example applications:

- Add the libraries and code to generate traces
- Add a tracing collector side-car to your pod

Let's look at enabling the tracing side-car first, and we will use the Python Flask example that we have been building earlier in the book.

The code for this example is online at the GitHub project at `https://github.com/kubernetes-for-developers/kfd-flask`, and the branch for this addition is `0.6.0`. You can get the code for this project locally using the following commands:

```
git clone https://github.com/kubernetes-for-developers/kfd-flask -b 0.6.0
```

Adding a tracing collector to your pod

The libraries that implement open-tracing typically use a very lightweight network connection, in this case UDP, to send traces from our code. UDP does not guarantee connections, so this also means that trace information could be lost if the network became too congested. OpenTracing and Jaeger minimize that by taking advantage of one of the guarantees of Kubernetes: two containers in the same pod will be placed on the same node, sharing the same network space. If we run a process in another container in our pod that captures the UDP packets, the network connectivity will be all on the same node and have very little chance of interference.

The Jaeger project has an image that listens to a variety of ports to capture these traces and forward them to its storage and query system. The container `jaegertracing/jaeger-agent` is published to DockerHub and is maintained as a very small image size (5 MB for version 1.2). This small size and the benefit of being close to our application makes it ideal for running as a side-car: another container in our pod, supporting the main process.

We can do this by adding another container to the pod defined in our flask deployment (`deploy/flask.yaml`):

```yaml
- name: jaeger-agent
  image: jaegertracing/jaeger-agent
  ports:
  - containerPort: 5775
    protocol: UDP
  - containerPort: 5778
  - containerPort: 6831
    protocol: UDP
  - containerPort: 6832
    protocol: UDP
  command:
  - "/go/bin/agent-linux"
  - "--collector.host-port=jaeger-collector:14267"
```

This example is based off the Jaeger `deployment documentation`, which provides an example of how to use this with Docker, but not Kubernetes directly.

It is important to notice the command that we have in this container. By default, the container runs `/go/bin/agent-linux`, but without any options. In order to send data to our local installation of Jaeger, we will need to tell the collector where to send it. The destination is defined by the option `--collector.host-port`.

In this case, we installed the Jaeger all-in-one into the default namespace, and it includes a service named `jaeger-collector`, so that will be directly available to this pod. If you have an installation of Jaeger in your cluster that's more robust, you may also have it defined in a different namespace. For example, the Helm installation of Jaeger installs into a namespace, `jaeger-infra`, and in those cases the value of the `collector.host-port` option would need to change to reflect that: `jaeger-collector.jaeger-infra.svc:14267`.

There are multiple ports used by Jaeger here as well, intentionally to allow the agent to collect from a number of legacy mechanisms used by alternate languages. We will be using UDP port `6382` for the `python jaeger-tracing` client library.

Add the libraries and code to generate traces

We start by adding two libraries for the tracing to our project: `jaeger-client` and `flask_opentracing`. `flask-opentracing` adds tracing into Flask projects so that you can easily have all HTTP endpoints traced automatically. The OpenTracing project doesn't include any collectors, so we also need a library to collect and send the trace data somewhere, in this case, jaeger-client.

The example also adds the requests library, as in this example we will add an HTTP endpoint that makes a remote request, processes the responses, and returns the values—and add tracing to that sequence.

Importing the libraries and initializing the tracer is fairly straightforward:

```
import opentracing
from jaeger_client import Config
from flask_opentracing import FlaskTracer

# defaults to reporting via UDP, port 6831, to localhost
def initialize_tracer():
    config = Config(
        config={
            'sampler': {
                'type': 'const',
                'param': 1
            },
            'logging': True
        },
        service_name='flask-service'
    )
    # also sets opentracing.tracer
    return config.initialize_tracer()
```

Jeager recommends you use a method to initialize the tracer indirectly, as shown previously. The configuration in this case sets the sampler to forward all requests; when you use this in production, you want to consider that carefully as a configuration option, as tracing every request can be overwhelming in high volume services.

The tracer is initialized right after we create the Flask application:

```
app = Flask(__name__) flask_tracer = FlaskTracer(initialize_tracer, True,
app, ["url_rule"])
```

This works with Flask to instrument all `@app.routes` with tracing, each route will be labeled as an operation based on the name of the Python function. You can also trace only specific routes with a different configuration setup and add tracing annotations on the Flask routes you want to trace.

Rebuilding the Flask image and deploying it will immediately start to generate traces, and with the jaeger-agent running in a side-car, the local `jaeger dev` instance will start showing traces immediately. You should see a service named `flask-service`, based on our application name and it should have multiple operations listed within it:

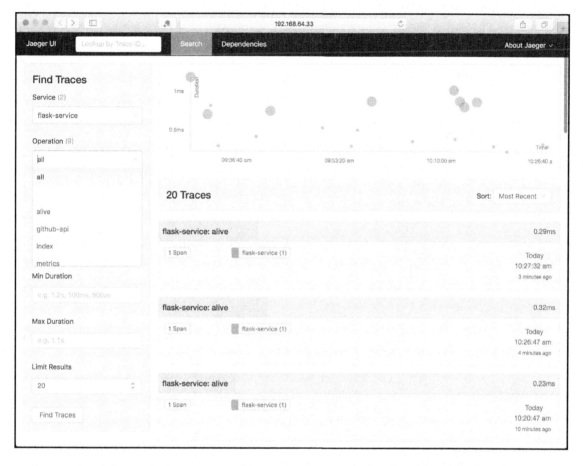

The operations **alive**, **ready**, and **metrics** are the Flask routes that have been enabled to support the liveness and readiness probes, as well as the `prometheus` metrics. With this already defined on our example pod, they are getting consistent connections, which in turn generates the traces associated with the requests.

This alone is useful, but does not yet tell you what within the method took more or less time. You can add spans into a trace around methods or sections of code that you're interested in instrumenting, using the `opentracing` library that gets installed with `flask-opentracing`. The following code snippet shows how to wrap the call to Redis that we use in our readiness probe with a trace span, so that it will show up separately:

```
@app.route('/ready')
def ready():
    parent_span = flask_tracer.get_span()
    with opentracing.tracer.start_span('redis-ping', child_of=parent_span) as
```

```
span:
    result = redis_store.ping()
    span.set_tag("redis-ping", result)
  if result:
    return "Yes"
  else:
    abort(500)
```

The keys here are getting the current tracing span that we generated for every request with `flask_tracer.get_span()`, and then using that in a `with` statement, which adds the span to a discrete bit of code that executes within that context. We can also use methods on the span, which is available within that block of code. We use the method `set_tag` to add a tag with the value of the result of the ping, so that it will be available in the specific trace output.

We will go ahead and add a `@app.route` called `/remote` to make a remote HTTP request to GitHub, and add tracing around that to see it as sub spans:

```
@app.route('/remote')
def pull_requests():
    parent_span = flask_tracer.get_span()
    github_url =
"https://api.github.com/repos/opentracing/opentracing-python/pulls"

    with opentracing.tracer.start_span('github-api', child_of=parent_span)
as span:
        span.set_tag("http.url",github_url)
        r = requests.get(github_url)
        span.set_tag("http.status_code", r.status_code)

    with opentracing.tracer.start_span('parse-json', child_of=parent_span)
as span:
        json = r.json()
        span.set_tag("pull_requests", len(json))
        pull_request_titles = map(lambda item: item['title'], json)
    return 'PRs: ' + ', '.join(pull_request_titles)
```

This example is similar to the readiness probe, except we're wrapping different sections of code in different spans and naming them explicitly: `github-api` and `parse-json`.

While adding code, you can use commands such as `kubectl delete` and `kubectl apply` to recreate the deployment with building it and pushing it to your container registry. For these examples, my pattern was to run the following commands from the project's home directory:

kubectl delete deploy/flask

```
docker build -t quay.io/kubernetes-for-developers/flask:0.6.0 .
docker push quay.io/kubernetes-for-developers/flask
kubectl apply -f deploy/
```

You will want to replace the image registry reference and Docker tag with values from your project.

And then, check the status of the deployment with:

```
kubectl get pods
```

```
NAME                                 READY STATUS RESTARTS AGE
flask-76f8c9767-56z4f                0/2   Init:0/1 0 6s
jaeger-deployment-559c8b9b8-jrq6c    1/1   Running 0 5d
redis-master-75c798658b-cxnmp        1/1   Running 0 5d
```

Once it's fully online, you'll see it reporting as Ready:

```
NAME                                 READY STATUS RESTARTS AGE
flask-76f8c9767-56z4f                2/2   Running 0 1m
jaeger-deployment-559c8b9b8-jrq6c    1/1   Running 0 5d
redis-master-75c798658b-cxnmp        1/1   Running 0 5d
```

The 2/2 shows you that two containers are running for the Flask pod, our main code and the jaeger-agent side-car.

If you are using Minikube, you can also use the service commands to make it easy to open these endpoints in a browser:

```
minikube service list
```

```
|-------------|-----------------------|------------------------------|
| NAMESPACE   | NAME                  | URL                          |
|-------------|-----------------------|------------------------------|
| default     | flask-service         | http://192.168.64.33:30676   |
| default     | jaeger-agent          | No node port                 |
| default     | jaeger-collector      | No node port                 |
| default     | jaeger-query          | http://192.168.64.33:30854   |
| default     | kubernetes            | No node port                 |
| default     | redis-service         | No node port                 |
| default     | zipkin                | No node port                 |
| kube-system | kube-dns              | No node port                 |
| kube-system | kubernetes-dashboard  | http://192.168.64.33:30000   |
| kube-system | tiller-deploy         | No node port                 |
|-------------|-----------------------|------------------------------|
```

Any service with a node port setting can be easily opened locally with commands such as:

```
minikube service flask-service
```

```
minikube service jaeger-query
```

With this code added, built, and deployed, you can see the traces in Jaeger. Direct your browser to make some requests to /remote to generate spans from the requests, and in the Jaeger query browser you should see something like the following:

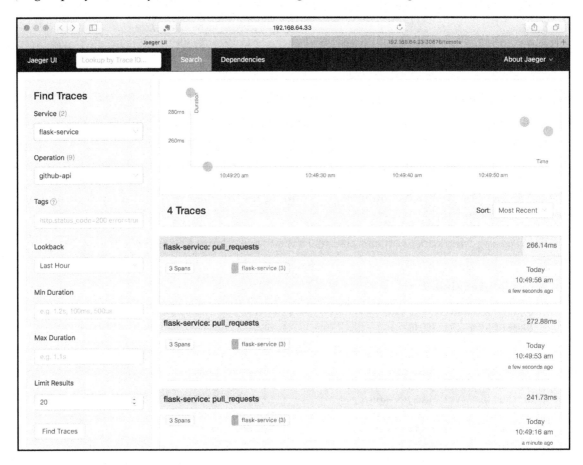

The top of the Jaeger query window will show you dots indicating the time of the query and the relative duration, and you'll see the various traces that it found listed below – four in our case. If you select a trace, you can get to the detailed view, which will include the sub-spans. Click on the spans to get more detail from each of them:

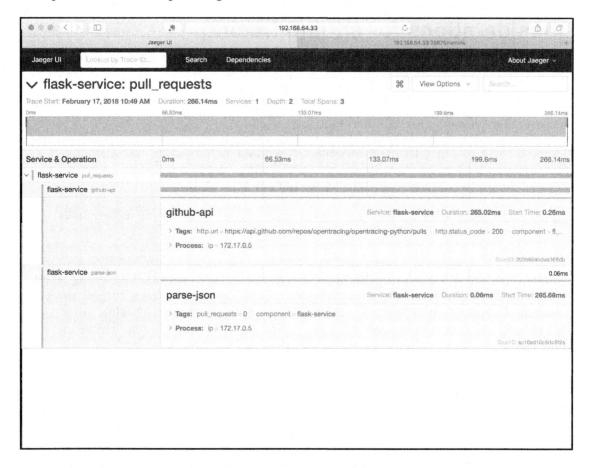

With the span detail view, any tags you set on the span within the code will be viewable, and you can see that the `github-api` call took the majority of the time (265 of 266 ms) in responding to the request to `/remote`.

Considerations for adding tracing

Tracing is an immensely powerful tool that also comes with a cost. Every trace is (although small) some overhead to process and manage. You may be excited to add tracing to every method in your application, or to build it into a library that attaches tracing and span creation to every method call. This can be done, and you will quickly find your infrastructure overwhelmed with trace information.

Tracing is also a tool that has the most benefit when tied directly to the responsibility of running the code. Be very aware that as you add tracing, you are also adding a lot of ancillary processing needed to capture, store, and query the data created by the traces.

A good way to handle the balancing act of the trade-offs is to add tracing intentionally, iteratively, and slowly – building to gain visibility as you need it.

OpenTracing as a standard is supported by a number of vendors. OpenTracing is also an evolving standard. While writing this book, there is a lot of conversation happening about how to best share and handle the span data (often called "baggage") that is carried along with requests between processes. Like tracing itself, adding data can add value, but it comes with the cost of larger requests and more processing needed to capture and handle the information.

Summary

In this chapter, we introduced logging and tracing with Fluentd and Jaeger. We showed how to deploy it and use it, capturing and aggregating data from your code when it runs at scale. We walked through how to use an Elasticsearch query to find data. We also looked at how to view Jaeger traces and how to add tracing to your code.

In the next chapter, we will look at ways of using Kubernetes to support and run integration testing, as well as using it with continuous integration.

Integration Testing

9

So far, we have reviewed how to run your code and describe your services in Kubernetes. We also looked into how to utilize additional tools to get information about how your code is running on each pod and on aggregate. This chapter builds on this to look at how to use Kubernetes to validate your code, with examples of different ways to accomplish that testing, and suggestions for how to leverage Kubernetes for validation testing.

Topics for this chapter include:

- Testing strategies using Kubernetes
- Simple validation with Bats
- Example – testing code with Python
- Example – testing code with Node.js
- Continuous integration with Kubernetes

Testing strategies using Kubernetes

There is a wide variety of kinds of tests that are used during development and validation, in software engineering. Across this taxonomy, there are some kinds of tests that utilize the strengths of Kubernetes extremely well. The terms associated with testing can be vague and confusing, so for clarity, we will briefly review the terms I'll use and the differences between these kinds of tests. There are many more variants of these themes that I haven't detailed here, but for the purpose of describing where Kubernetes is most effective, this list is sufficient:

- **Unit tests**: Unit tests are the *lowest level* of testing; this focuses on the interfaces, implementations, and modules within your application. Unit testing frequently implies isolated testing of just the component that the test focuses on. These tests are generally intended to be very fast, easily run on a developer's system directly, and often with no access to external services upon which the relevant code may depend. These tests often do not deal with state or persistence, and primarily focus on business logic and interface validation.

- **Functional tests**: Functional tests are the next step up from unit tests, implying that code the libraries are used against their underlying systems without fakes, mocks, or other layers that would otherwise pretend to act like the remote dependencies. These kinds of tests are usually applied to a subset of a service, testing and validating a full service, and using immediate dependencies (often a database or persistence store). Functional tests often imply a validation of state in persistence stores, and how that changes with the operation of your code.

- **Integration tests**: Integration tests assemble all the required parts of your software together and validate the individual components as well as the components, working together and their interactions. The state of the system is often defined or set as a key setup in integration tests, and because state is represented and validated within the system, tests have a tendency to be ordered and more linear, often using composed interactions to validate the code and how it works (and how it fails).

  There is a blurry line between functional tests and integration tests, with the former typically being focused on a subset of your overall service being validated, and the latter representing either large portions or your service or the whole system at once.

- **End-to-end tests**: Where integration tests can mean testing a portion of a system, end-to-end tests are specific to meaning testing and validating the whole of a system and all its dependencies. Frequently, end-to-end tests and integration tests are used synonymously.

- **Performance tests**: Where the previous terms focused on the scope of validation between code and any underlying dependencies it interacts with, performance tests focus on the type of validation more than the scope. These tests intend to measure the efficiency or utilization of code and services; how much CPU and memory they utilize, and how fast they respond with a given set of underlying resources. Rather than focusing on the correctness of code, they focus on validation of scale and underlying service needs. Performance tests frequently require dependent systems to be not only operational, but fully resourced to provide accurate results, and run with some measure of expectation isolation so that external resource constraints don't artificially limit the results.

- **Interactive/exploratory tests**: Interactive tests, sometimes also known as exploratory tests, are again not so much a term about scope as much as implying an intent. These kinds of tests typically require at least a portion of the system operational, and often imply the whole system is operational if not scaled to support high levels of requests. These tests focus on letting people interact with the system without any predefined or structured stream of events, and this same setup is often used for acceptance validation or refinement of other kinds of tests as a means of validating the tests themselves.

Reviewing resources needed for testing

As we walk through this taxonomy of tests, the compute resources and time needed to run the tests typically grow and become more significant. Depending on the scope of the software being developed, it is quite possible to require more resources than can be accommodated in a single machine. And where lower-level tests can often be optimized to leverage all possible resources within a computer, the serialized nature of end-to-end tests tends to be less efficient and more time consuming in the validation process.

As you establish your tests, you need to be aware of the size of the compute resources that are needed to validate your software. This can correspond to the process of determining how much memory and CPU a given pod needs, and extends to needing to be aware of all the resources for all the dependencies based on what you are testing and wanting to achieve.

Where we have been using Minikube for most of these examples, modern development and dependencies can easily exceed the amount of resources you can give to Minikube for its single-node cluster.

Using Kubernetes in your testing is most effective where you want to set up and use large portions of your environment that correspond to integration testing and testing scenarios that expect a complete system with all dependencies operational.

You can, of course, use Kubernetes in the process of development where you run tests such as unit tests, or perhaps functional tests, within Kubernetes, although you may find far more benefit from leveraging Kubernetes when you are focusing more at integration, end-to-end, and those later portions of the taxonomy outlined previously.

Because Kubernetes excels at describing a desired state for services and keeping them running, it can be very effectively used where you want to set up large portions or many services interacting together. Additionally, where you expect tests to take more time and resources, Kubernetes is a good fit, as it requires you to lock down the code into discrete, versioned containers, which can also take significant time and processing.

Patterns of using Kubernetes with testing

There are quite a number of ways to use Kubernetes for testing, and one of the first things you need to determine is where you're running the system being tested, and where you are running the tests that will validate that system.

Tests local and system-under-test in Kubernetes

The most common pattern, especially while developing tests, is to run tests from your development machine against your code running within Kubernetes. After you create the tests, the same pattern can be employed to run your tests against a Kubernetes cluster housing your code from a continuous integration service. When you are starting out with development, you may be able to run all of this on your local development machine, with Minikube. In general, this pattern is an excellent way to get started, and solves the problem of getting feedback from the tests by running the tests where you want to get the feedback—either on your own development system, or from a CI system acting on your behalf.

Tests local and system-under-test in Kubernetes namespaces

If, or perhaps when, the system you are testing exceeds what Minikube can support, the common solution is to start using a remote cluster, either managed by you, your IT team, or a cloud provider. As you start to use remote compute to do this, sharing and isolation become important, particularly with tests that are dependent on the state of the system, where the control of that state is critical to understanding if the validation is correct or not. Kubernetes has good isolation in general, and taking advantage of how namespaces work can make the setup of your code and testing it significantly easier. You can leverage namespaces by running the related pods and services all in a single namespace, and consistently referencing between them by taking advantage of the short DNS names for each service. This can be visualized as a stack, where you can deploy many of these effectively in parallel. In the earlier pattern, and in most of the examples in this book, we have used the default namespace, but all of the commands can include a namespace as an option by simply adding on `-n <namespace>` to the kubectl commands.

> Namespaces support quotas for a variety of resources, and you will want to see what is defined and validate that you have sufficient allowances set up. Especially in shared environments, using Quota to put a cap on consumption is common.

Tests in Kubernetes and system-under-test in Kubernetes namespaces

A variation of the theme is to also package and run your tests within Kubernetes—either in the same namespace, or in a separate namespace from your system under test. This is slower than running the tests locally, as it requires you to package your tests into a container, just as you do with your code. The trade-off is having a very consistent means of running those tests and interacting with the system-under-test.

If you work in a very diverse development environment where everyone has a slightly different setup, then this pattern can consolidate the testing so that everyone has the same experience. Additionally, where local tests need to access the remote Kubernetes through exposed services (such as NodePort using Minikube, or perhaps `LoadBalancer` on a provider), you can simplify that access by using the service names, either within the same namespace or using the longer service names with the namespace included.

Another challenge with running tests within Kubernetes is getting the results. While it is quite possible to collect the results and post them to a remote location, this pattern is not common. A more frequent resolution when using this pattern is to have a cluster dedicated to testing that also includes some continuous integration infrastructure, either as a part of the cluster, or alongside and with dedicated access to the cluster, that then runs the tests and captures the results as a part of the test automation. We will look at continuous integration in more depth later in this chapter.

Simple validation with Bats

A fairly common desire is to simply get everything deployed and make a few queries to validate that the resulting system is operational. As you do these operations, they are frequently captured in either Makefiles or shell scripts as simple programs to validate a baseline of functionality. Several years ago, a system called Bats, which stands for Bash Automated Testing System, was developed to make it slightly more convenient to run tests using shell scripts.

There are several examples of using Bats to test systems deployed in Kubernetes. The tests are generally straightforward and easy to read, and it is easy to extend and use. You can find more information on Bats at its GitHub home `https://github.com/sstephenson/bats`. You may see Bats used in some Kubernetes-related projects as well, for simple validation.

Bitnami has set up an example GitHub repository to use as a starting point that uses Bats and Minikube, and was designed to also work with external CI systems such as Travis.CI. You can find the example at `https://github.com/bitnami/kubernetes-travis`.

If you leverage Bats, you will want to have helper scripts to set up your deployments and wait until the relevant deployments are reporting ready, or fail the tests at setup. In the Bitnami example, the scripts `cluster_common.bash` and `libtest.bash` have these helper functions. If you want to use this path, you can start with the files from their repository and update and extend them to match your needs.

The integration tests start by loading the libraries and creating a local cluster, followed by deploying the system under test:

```
# __main__ () {
. scripts/cluster_common.bash
. scripts/libtest.bash
# Create the 'minikube' or 'dind' cluster
create_k8s_cluster ${TEST_CONTEXT}
# Deploy our stack
bats tests/deploy-stack.bats
```

`deploy-stacks.bats` can be represented as a Bats test, and in the Bitnami example it validates that Kubernetes tools are all defined locally and then encapsulates the deployment itself as a test:

This is from the example at `https://github.com/bitnami/kubernetes-travis/blob/master/tests/deploy-stack.bats`:

```
# Bit of sanity
@test "Verify needed kubernetes tools installed" {
 verify_k8s_tools
}
@test "Deploy stack" {
# Deploy the stack we want to test
./scripts/deploy.sh delete >& /dev/null || true
./scripts/deploy.sh create
    k8s_wait_for_pod_running --namespace=kube-system -lname=traefik-ingress-
lb
    k8s_wait_for_pod_running -lapp=my-nginx
}
```

The script `deploy.sh` is set up to either delete or create and load manifests just as we have been doing earlier in this book, by using the `kubectl create`, `kubectl delete`, or `kubectl apply` commands.

Once that is complete, the integration test continues with getting access to the cluster. In the Bitnami example, they are using Kubernetes Ingress to consistently access the cluster, and have scripts set up to capture and return the IP address and URL path for accessing the underlying system through `Ingress`. You could also utilize `kubectl port-forward` or `kubectl proxy`, as we showed earlier in the book:

```
# Set env vars for our test suite
# INGRESS_IP: depend on the deployed cluster (dind or minikube)
INGRESS_IP=$(get_ingress_ip ${TEST_CONTEXT})
# URL_PATH: Dynamically find it from 1st ingress rule
URL_PATH=$(kubectl get ing -
ojsonpath='{.items[0].spec.rules[0].http.paths[0].path}')
# Verify no empty vars:
: ${INGRESS_IP:?} ${URL_PATH:?}
```

Once that is set, then the integration tests are invoked again using Bats, and the exit code from that whole process is captured and used to reflect whether the tests succeeded or failed:

```
# With the stack ready, now run the tests thru bats:
export SVC_URL="http://my-nginx.default.svc${URL_PATH:?}"
export ING_URL="${INGRESS_IP:?}${URL_PATH:?}"
```

```
bats tests/integration-tests.bats
exit_code=$?

[[ ${exit_code} == 0 ]] && echo "TESTS: PASS" || echo "TESTS: FAIL"
exit ${exit_code}
# }
```

While this is easy to get started with, programming in bash quickly becomes its own speciality, and while basic bash usage is frequent and easily understood, some of the more complex helpers within that example can take some digging to fully understand.

 If you are having trouble with a shell script, then a common debugging solution is to add `set -x` near the top of the script. Within bash, this turns on a command echo, so that all the commands within the script are echoed to standard out so that you can see what is happening.

A good pattern to follow is to write tests in a language that you are familiar with. You can frequently leverage the testing frameworks of those languages to help you. You still may want to use shell scripts like the Bitnami example to set up and deploy your code to your cluster, and use the logic and structure of a language you are more comfortable with for the tests.

Example – integration testing with Python

In the case of Python, the example code here uses PyTest as a test framework. The example code can be found on GitHub, in the 0.7.0 branch of the repository `https://github.com/kubernetes-for-developers/kfd-flask/`.

You can download the example using the following command:

```
git clone https://github.com/kubernetes-for-developers/kfd-flask/ -b 0.7.0
```

In the example, I changed the code structure to move all the Python code for the application itself under the `src` directory, following the recommended pattern from PyTest. If you have not used PyTest before, reviewing their best practices at `https://docs.pytest.org/en/latest/goodpractices.html` is very worthwhile.

If you view the code or download it, you will also notice a new file, `test-dependencies.txt`, which defines a number of dependencies specific to testing. Python does not have a manifest where they separate out dependencies for production from ones used during development or testing, so I separated the dependencies out myself:

```
pytest
pytest-dependency
kubernetes
requests
```

The actual integration tests are housed under the directory `e2e_tests`, primarily as a pattern that would let you have a local directory for any unit or functional tests you wanted to create during normal development.

The pattern that I'm using in this example is leveraging our code in Kubernetes and accessing it external to the cluster, leveraging Minikube. The same pattern can work nicely with a cluster hosted in AWS, Google, or Azure if your environment requires more resources than you have available on your local development machine.

The `README` file in `e2e_tests` shows an example of how to run the tests. I take advantage of `pip` and `virtualenv` to set up a local environment, install the dependencies, and then use PyTest to run the tests directly:

```
virtualenv .venv
source .venv/bin/activate
pip3 install -r test-requirements.txt
pytest -v
```

If you run through these tests, you should see output akin to the following:

```
======= test session starts =======
platform darwin -- Python 3.6.4, pytest-3.4.2, py-1.5.2, pluggy-0.6.0 --
/Users/heckj/src/kfd-flask/e2e_tests/.venv/bin/python3.6
cachedir: .pytest_cache
rootdir: /Users/heckj/src/kfd-flask/e2e_tests, inifile:
plugins: dependency-0.3.2
collected 7 items

tests/test_smoke.py::test_kubernetes_components_healthy PASSED [ 14%]
tests/test_smoke.py::test_deployment PASSED [ 28%]
tests/test_smoke.py::test_list_pods PASSED [ 42%]
tests/test_smoke.py::test_deployment_ready PASSED [ 57%]
tests/test_smoke.py::test_pods_running PASSED [ 71%]
tests/test_smoke.py::test_service_response PASSED [ 85%]
tests/test_smoke.py::test_python_client_service_response PASSED [100%]

======= 7 passed in 1.27 seconds =======
```

PyTest includes a large number of plugins, including a means to export the test results in JUnit XML format. You can get such a report created by PyTest by invoking it with the `--junitxml` option:

```
pytest --junitxml=results.xml
```

The code within these tests leverages the examples we have built so far: our deployment YAML and the images we have made with the code in the repository. The tests do a simple verification that the cluster is available and healthy (and that we can communicate with it), and then uses `kubectl` to deploy our code. It then waits until the code is deployed, with a max timeout defined, before continuing on to interact with the service and get a simple response.

This example is primarily aimed at showing you how you can interact with a remote Kubernetes cluster, including using the `python-kubernetes` client library.

PyTest and pytest-dependency

PyTest is foremost a unit testing framework. Unit testing frameworks generally have different needs from integration tests, and fortunately PyTest has a means to allow a developer to specify that one test needs to run and complete before another. This is done with the `pytest-dependency` plugin. Within the code, you will see some of the test cases annotated with dependency markers. To use this plugin, you define which tests can be dependency targets, and for any test that needs to run after it, you define the tests upon which they depend:

```
@pytest.mark.dependency()
def test_kubernetes_components_healthy(kube_v1_client):
    # iterates through the core kuberneters components to verify the
cluster is reporting healthy
    ret = kube_v1_client.list_component_status()
    for item in ret.items:
        assert item.conditions[0].type == "Healthy"
        print("%s: %s" % (item.metadata.name, item.conditions[0].type))
```

The test checks to verify that the cluster is accessible and responding as healthy. This test doesn't depend on any others, so it has just the basic annotation, and tests further down will specify that this test needs to have completed before they will run, with this annotation:

```
@pytest.mark.dependency(depends=["test_kubernetes_components_healthy"])
```

This can make the test annotations quite verbose, but allows you to explicitly define the ordering of execution. By default, most unit testing frameworks do not guarantee a specific order or execution, which can be critical when you are testing a system that includes state and changes to that state—exactly what we do with integration testing.

PyTest fixtures and the python-kubernetes client

The preceding example also leverages a simple text fixture to provide us an instance of a Python Kubernetes client to interact with the cluster. The Python client can be awkward to use, since it is generated from an OpenAPI specification, and has class setups for each API endpoint, of which there are several. In particular, as sections of the Kubernetes API evolve through alpha, beta, and final release stages, these API endpoints will move, which means the client code you're using may need to change as you upgrade the version of the Kubernetes cluster with which you are interacting.

The `python-kubernetes` client does come with readily available source code and a generated index to all the methods, which I recommend having handy if you're going to use the client. The code is housed at `https://github.com/kubernetes-client/python`, and the releases are stored in branches. The release that I was using was 5.0, which is paired with Kubernetes version 1.9 and supports earlier versions. The README that includes all the documentation for the OpenAPI-generated methods is available at `https://github.com/kubernetes-client/python/blob/release-5.0/kubernetes/README.md`.

A PyTest fixture sets up the client for the other tests:

```
@pytest.fixture
def kube_v1_client():
    kubernetes.config.load_kube_config()
    v1 = kubernetes.client.CoreV1Api()
    return v1
```

In this case, the client loads the locally available `kubeconfig` for access to the cluster. Depending on your development environment, you may want to investigate alternatives to authenticating to the cluster.

While it is possible to do the deployment with the python-kubernetes client, the example shows how to use the local `kubectl` command line to interact with the cluster as well. In this case, it's significantly fewer lines than defining the full definition of what you want deployed in Python:

```
@pytest.mark.dependency(depends=["test_kubernetes_components_healthy"])
def test_deployment():
```

```
    # https://docs.python.org/3/library/subprocess.html#subprocess.run
    # using check=True will throw an exception if a non-zero exit code is
returned, saving us the need to assert
    # using timeout=10 will throw an exception if the process doesn't
return within 10 seconds
    # Enables the deployment
    process_result = subprocess.run('kubectl apply -f ../deploy/',
check=True, shell=True, timeout=10)
```

If you want to leverage other tools to deploy your code, this kind of mechanism can be invaluable, and is always a useful fallback in writing integration tests. Also note that this test depends on the test we mentioned earlier, forcing it to run after the cluster health validation test.

Be aware that debugging these commands when the system fails can be more difficult, because so much is happening outside of the actual test with commands like these. You will want to be aware of what process is invoking the test, its permissions relative to your environment, and so forth.

Waiting for state changes

Following the deployment, we expect the deployment and services to all become active, but this does not happen instantaneously. Depending on your environment, it may happen quite quickly, or fairly slowly. The bane of integration tests is not being able to know when something has completed, and working around the issue with an invocation of sleep() to wait a little longer. In this example, we explicitly check the status rather than just waiting an arbitrary amount of time and hoping the system is ready to go:

```
@pytest.mark.dependency(depends=["test_deployment_ready"])
def test_pods_running(kube_v1_client):
    TOTAL_TIMEOUT_SECONDS = 300
    DELAY_BETWEEN_REQUESTS_SECONDS = 5
    now = time.time()
    while (time.time() < now+TOTAL_TIMEOUT_SECONDS):
        pod_list = kube_v1_client.list_namespaced_pod("default")
        print("name\tphase\tcondition\tstatus")
        for pod in pod_list.items:
            for condition in pod.status.conditions:
                print("%s\t%s\t%s\t%s" % (pod.metadata.name,
pod.status.phase, condition.type, condition.status))
                if condition.type == 'Ready' and condition.status ==
'True':
                    return
```

```
        time.sleep(DELAY_BETWEEN_REQUESTS_SECONDS)
    assert False
```

This example has a maximum timeout of 300 seconds for the deployment to become active, and includes a short delay in requesting the status of the environment before it will continue. Should the overall timeout be exceeded, the test will report a failure—and by using `pytest-dependency`, all the following tests that depend on this will not be run—short circuiting the testing process to report the failure.

Accessing the deployment

The last two tests highlight two ways of interacting with the code running within the cluster.

The first example expects something to be set up and running that provides access to the cluster outside of the test, and simply uses the Python `requests` library to make an HTTP request directly:

```
@pytest.mark.dependency(depends=["test_deployment_ready"])
def test_service_response(kubectl_proxy):
    NAMESPACE="default"
    SERVICE_NAME="flask-service"
    URI = "http://localhost:8001/api/v1/namespaces/%s/services/%s/proxy/" %
(NAMESPACE, SERVICE_NAME)
    print("requesting %s" % (URI))
    r = requests.get(URI)
    assert r.status_code == 200
```

It's an incredibly basic test and is fairly fragile. It uses a PyTest fixture defined earlier in the code to set up an invocation of `kubectl proxy` to provide access to the cluster:

```
@pytest.fixture(scope="module")
def kubectl_proxy():
    # establish proxy for kubectl communications
    #
https://docs.python.org/3/library/subprocess.html#subprocess-replacements
    proxy = subprocess.Popen("kubectl proxy &", stdout=subprocess.PIPE,
shell=True)
    yield
    # terminate the proxy
    proxy.kill()
```

While this generally works, it's harder to track down issues when things fail, and the fixture mechanism wasn't entirely reliable in setting up (and tearing down) the proxy invocation in a forked shell command.

The second example uses the python-kubernetes client to access the service through a series of methods that allow you to easily invoke HTTP requests through the proxy that is included with Kubernetes. The client configuration takes care of the authentication to the cluster, and you access the code through the proxy by leveraging the client directly rather than using an external proxy to provide access:

```
@pytest.mark.dependency(depends=["test_deployment_ready"])
def test_python_client_service_response(kube_v1_client):
    from pprint import pprint
    from kubernetes.client.rest import ApiException
    NAMESPACE="default"
    SERVICE_NAME="flask-service"
    try:
        api_response =
kube_v1_client.proxy_get_namespaced_service(SERVICE_NAME, NAMESPACE)
        pprint(api_response)
        api_response =
kube_v1_client.proxy_get_namespaced_service_with_path(SERVICE_NAME,
NAMESPACE, "/metrics")
        pprint(api_response)
    except ApiException as e:
        print("Exception when calling
CoreV1Api->proxy_get_namespaced_service: %s\n" % e)
```

This mechanism is great if you don't need to fiddle with headers or otherwise get complicated with your HTTP requests, which is more accessible when using a general Python client such as `requests`. There are a whole series of methods that support a variety of HTTP/REST style calls all prefixed with `proxy`:

- `proxy_get`
- `proxy_delete`
- `proxy_head`
- `proxy_options`
- `proxy_patch`
- `proxy_put`

Each of these is mapped to the following endpoints:

- `namespaced_pod`
- `namespaced_pod_with_path`
- `namespaced_service`
- `namespaced_service_with_path`

This gives you some flexibility in standard REST commands to send to either a pod directly, or to a service endpoint. The `with_path` option allows you to define the specific URI with which you're interacting on the pod or service.

Example – integration testing with Node.js

The Node.js example uses mocha, chai, supertest, and the JavaScript kubernetes client in much the same fashion as the Python example. The example code can be found on GitHub, in the 0.7.0 branch of the repository at `https://github.com/kubernetes-for-developers/kfd-nodejs/`.

You can download the example using the following command:

```
git clone https://github.com/kubernetes-for-developers/kfd-nodejs/ -b 0.7.0
```

I took advantage of Node.js's mechanism to have development dependencies separate from production dependencies, and added most of these dependencies into `package.json`. I also went ahead and set up a simple unit test directly in a `test` directory, and a separate integration test in an `e2e-tests` directory. I also set up the commands so that you can run these tests through `npm`:

```
npm test
```

For the unit tests, the code runs locally and takes advantage of `supertest` to access everything within a JavaScript runtime on your local machine. This doesn't account for any remote services or systems (such as interacting with endpoints that depend on Redis):

```
> kfd-nodejs@0.0.0 test /Users/heckj/src/kfd-nodejs
> mocha --exit

express app
GET / 200 283.466 ms - 170
  ✓ should respond at the root (302ms)
GET /probes/alive 200 0.930 ms - 3
  ✓ should respond at the liveness probe point
```

```
2 passing (323ms)
```

Within the e2e_tests directory, there is an analog of the Python tests, which validates the cluster is operational, sets up the deployment, and then accesses that code. This can be invoked with the following command:

npm run integration

Invoking the tests would show you something akin to the following:

```
> kfd-nodejs@0.0.0 integration /Users/heckj/src/kfd-nodejs
> mocha e2e_tests --exit

kubernetes
 cluster
 ✓ should have a healthy cluster
 ✓ should deploy the manifests (273ms)
 should repeat until the pods are ready
 - delay 5 seconds...
 ✓ check to see that all pods are reporting ready (5016ms)
 should interact with the deployed services
 ✓ should access by pod...

4 passing (5s)
```

Node.js tests and dependencies with mocha and chai

The test code itself is at e2e_tests/integration_test.js, and I leverage mocha and chai to lay out the tests in a BDD-style structure. A convenient side effect of the BDD structure with mocha and chai is that tests can be wrapped by describe and it, which structure how the tests get run. Anything within a describe block doesn't have a guaranteed ordering, but you can nest describe blocks to get the structure you want.

Validating the cluster health

The JavaScript Kubernetes client is generated in much the same fashion as the Python client, from the OpenAPI definition and mapped to the releases of Kubernetes. You can find the client at `https://github.com/kubernetes-client/javascript`, although this repository doesn't have the same level of generated documentation as the Python client. Instead, the developers have gone to some length to reflect the types in TypeScript with the client, which results in editors and IDEs being able to do some level of automatic code completion as you are writing your tests:

```
const k8s = require('@kubernetes/client-node');
var chai = require('chai')
  , expect = chai.expect
  , should = chai.should();

var k8sApi = k8s.Config.defaultClient();

describe('kubernetes', function() {
  describe('cluster', function() {
    it('should have a healthy cluster', function() {
        return k8sApi.listComponentStatus()
        .then((res) => {
          // console.log(util.inspect(res.body));
          res.body.items.forEach(function(component) {
          // console.log(util.inspect(value));
          expect(component.conditions[0].type).to.equal("Healthy");
          expect(component.conditions[0].status).to.equal("True");
        })
      }, (err) => {
          expect(err).to.be.null;
      });
    }) // it
```

The nesting of the code can make indenting and tracking at the right level quite tricky, so the test code leverages promises where it can to simplify the callback structures. The preceding example uses a Kubernetes client that automatically grabs credentials from the environment in which it's run, a feature of several of these clients, so be aware of it if you wish to arrange specific access.

Where the Python client had a method, `list_component_status`, the JavaScript pattern scrunches the names together with CamelCase formatting, so the same call here is `listComponentStatus`. The result is then passed in a promise, and we iterate through the various elements to verify that the cluster components are all reporting healthy.

The example leaves in some commented out code that inspects the objects that were returned. With little external documentation, I found it convenient to see what was returned while developing the tests, and the common trick is to use the `util.inspect` function and log the results to STDOUT:

```
const util = require('util');
console.log(util.inspect(res.body));
```

Deploying with kubectl

Following the Python example, I used `kubectl` on the command line to deploy the code, invoking it from the integration test:

```
it('should deploy the manifests', function() {
  var manifest_directory =
path.normalize(path.join(path.dirname(__filename), '..', '/deploy'))
  const exec = util.promisify(require('child_process').exec);
  return exec('kubectl apply -f '+manifest_directory)
  .then((res) => {
    // console.log(util.inspect(res));
    expect(res.stdout).to.not.be.null;
    expect(res.stderr).to.be.empty;
  }, (err) => {
    expect(err).to.be.null;
  })
})
```

This particular bit of code is dependent on where you have this test case and its relative directory to the deploy directory where the manifests are stored, and like the preceding example it uses promises to chain the validation of the execution of the invocation.

Waiting for the pods to become available

The process of waiting and retrying was significantly more tricky with Node.js, promises, and callbacks. In this case, I leveraged a capability of the mocha test library to allow a test to be retried and manipulate the overall timeout for a section of the test structure to get the same end result:

```
describe('should repeat until the pods are ready', function() {
  // Mocha supports a retry mechanism limited by number of retries...
  this.retries(30);
  // an a default timeout of 20,000ms that we can increase
  this.timeout(300000);

it('check to see that all pods are reporting ready', function() {
    return new Promise(function(resolve, reject) {
        console.log(' - delay 5 seconds...')
        setTimeout(() => resolve(1), 5000);
    }).then(function(result) {
        return k8sApi.listNamespacedPod('default')
        .then((res) => {
          res.body.items.forEach(function(pod) {
            var readyCondition = _.filter(pod.status.conditions, { 'type':
'Ready' })
              //console.log("checking: "+pod.metadata.name+" ready:
"+readyCondition[0].status);
            expect(readyCondition[0].status).to.equal('True')
        }) // pod forEach
    })
  })
}) // it

}) // describe pods available
```

By returning promises in the tests, every one of the tests is already asynchronous with a preset timeout that mocha provides of 20 seconds. Within each `describe`, you can tweak how mocha runs the tests—in this case, setting the overall timeout to five minutes and asserting that the test can be retried up to 30 times. To slow down the checking iterations, I also included a timeout promise that simply introduces a five-second delay before invoking the check of the cluster to get the pod health.

Interacting with the deployment

The code to interact with the deployment is simpler than the Python example, utilizing the Kubernetes client and the proxy:

```
describe('should interact with the deployed services', function() {
  // path to access the port through the kubectl proxy:
  //
http://localhost:8001/api/v1/namespaces/default/services/nodejs-service:web
/proxy/
  it('should access by pod...', function() {
    return k8sApi.proxyGETNamespacedServiceWithPath("nodejs-service:web",
```

```
    "default", "/")
      .then(function(res) {
         // console.log(util.inspect(res,{depth:1}));
         expect(res.body).to.not.be.null;
      });
   })
}) // interact with the deployed services
```

In this branch, I changed the code running from a stateful set to a deployment, as getting proxy access to the headless endpoints proved complicated. The stateful sets can be easily accessed from within the cluster via DNS, but mapping to external didn't appear to be easily supported in the current client code.

Like the Python code, there's a matrix of calls to make REST style requests through the client:

- `proxyGET`
- `proxyDELETE`
- `proxyHEAD`
- `proxyOPTIONS`
- `proxyPATCH`
- `proxyPUT`

And each is mapped to endpoints:

- `namespacedPod`
- `namespacedPodWithPath`
- `namespacedService`
- `namespacedServiceWithPath`

This gives you some flexibility in standard REST commands to send to either a pod directly or to a service endpoint. Like the Python code, the `withPath` option allows you to define the specific URI with which you're interacting on the pod or service.

If you're writing these tests in an editor such as Visual Studio Code, code completion will help provide some of the details that are otherwise missing from the documentation. The following is an example of code completion showing the `method` options:

And when you choose a method, the TypeScript annotations are also available to show you what options the JavaScript methods expect:

Continuous integration with Kubernetes

Once you have integration tests, getting something operational to validate those tests is very important. If you don't run the tests, they're effectively useless—so having a means of consistently invoking the tests while you're doing development is important. It is fairly common to see continuous integration do a lot of the automated lifting for development.

There are a number of options available to development teams to help you with continuous integration, or even its more advanced cousin, continuous deployment. The following tools are an overview of what was available at the time of writing, and in use by developers working with their code in containers and/or in Kubernetes:

- **Travis.CI**: Travis.CI (`https://travis-ci.org/`) is a hosted continuous integration service, and it is quite popular as the company offers free service with an easy means of plugging into GitHub for public and open source repositories. Quite a number of open source projects leverage Travis.CI to do basic testing validation.

- **Drone.IO**: Drone.IO (`https://drone.io/`) is a hosted or local option for continuous integration that is also open source software itself, hosted at `https://github.com/drone/drone`. Drone has an extensive plugin library, including a plugin for Helm (`https://github.com/ipedrazas/drone-helm`), which has made it attractive to some development teams who are using Helm to deploy their software.

- **Gitlab**: Gitlab (`https://about.gitlab.com/`) is an opensource source control solution that includes continuous integration. Like Drone, it can be leveraged in your local environment, or you can use the hosted version. Where the previous options were agnostic to the source control mechanism, Gitlab CI is tightly bound to Gitlab, effectively making it useful only if you're also willing to use Gitlab.

- **Jenkins**: Jenkins (`https://jenkins.io/`) is the grandaddy of the CI solutions, originally known as Hudson, and it is used extensively in a wide variety of environments. A hosted version of Jenkins is available through some providers, but it is primarily a opensource solution that you're expected to deploy and manage yourself. It has an amazing (perhaps overwhelming) number of plugins and options available to it, and notably a Kubernetes plugin (`https://github.com/jenkinsci/kubernetes-plugin`) that will let a Jenkins instance run its tests within a Kubernetes cluster.

- **Concourse**: Concourse (`https://concourse-ci.org/`), like Jenkins, is an open source project rather than a hosted solution, built in the CloudFoundry project and focusing on pipelines for deployment as a first-class concept (it's relatively new to some older projects such as Jenkins). Like Drone, it is set up to be a continuous delivery pipeline and an integral part of your development process.

Example – using Minikube with Travis.CI

The example earlier that showed using Bats to run a test was created by the team at Bitnami, and they also leveraged that same example repository for building and deploying code into an instance of Minikube hosted and run on Travis.CI. Their example repository is online at `https://github.com/bitnami/kubernetes-travis`, and it installs Minikube as well as additional tooling to build and deploy into a small Kubernetes instance.

Travis.CI is configured through a `.travis.yml` file, and the documentation for how to configure it and what options are available is hosted online at `https://docs.travis-ci.com`. Travis.CI, by default, will attempt to understand what language is being used, and orient its build scripts to the language, focusing primarily on running builds for every pull request and merge into a repository.

The Node.js example added a sample `.travis.yml` that sets up and runs the current integration test:

```
language: node_js
node_js:
 - lts/*
cache:
 directories:

 - "node_modules"
sudo: required
services:
 - docker
env:
- CHANGE_MINIKUBE_NONE_USER=true

before_script:
- curl -Lo kubectl
https://storage.googleapis.com/kubernetes-release/release/v1.9.0/bin/linux/
amd64/kubectl && chmod +x kubectl && sudo mv kubectl /usr/local/bin/
- curl -Lo minikube
https://storage.googleapis.com/minikube/releases/latest/minikube-linux-amd6
4 && chmod +x minikube && sudo mv minikube /usr/local/bin/
- sudo minikube start --vm-driver=none --kubernetes-version=v1.9.0
- minikube update-context
- JSONPATH='{range .items[*]}{@.metadata.name}:{range
@.status.conditions[*]}{@.type}={@.status};{end}{end}'; until kubectl get
nodes -o jsonpath="$JSONPATH" 2>&1 | grep -q "Ready=True"; do sleep 1; done

script:
- npm run integration
```

The key `language`, which is set to `nodejs` in our example, defines a large part of how Travis will run. We define which versions of Node.js are used (`lts/*`) and by default the system would use `npm`, running `npm test` to validate our build. That would run our unit tests, but wouldn't invoke our integration tests.

You can extend what happens before the testing, and what is used by the tests, by manipulating the values under the keys `before_script` and `script`. In the preceding example, we preload `minikube` and `kubectl` by downloading them from their released locations, and the preceding example then starts Minikube and waits until the command `kubectl get nodes` returns with a positive result.

By adding `npm run integration` under the key script, we override the default Node.js behavior and instead run our integration test. When the example was developed, updates were pushed to the 0.7.0 branch, which was open as a pull request to the main repository. The results of those updates were published into the hosted solution, available at `https://travis-ci.org/kubernetes-for-developers/kfd-nodejs`. For example, the following is a build page showing a successful build:

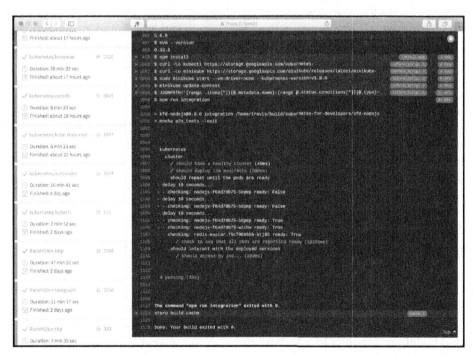

Next steps

This example build does not do the entire process from source to container to deployment. Instead, it relies on a pre-built image with a tag that is set in the deployment manifests, managed in source control. Travis.CI does include the capability of building an image using Docker, and has documentation on how to leverage Docker to test a single container by itself at `https://docs.travis-ci.com/user/docker/`.

Travis also has the capability of storing credentials to build and push Docker images into an image repository, and recently added the capability of building in stages so that you can pipeline in a container build and then utilize it in your integration tests.

You need to update the Kubernetes declarations to use the image in question, and this example doesn't show that process. The common pattern for enabling this sort of functionality involves templating the manifests that we have stored in the deploy directory in our examples, and rendering them out with specific variables passed in.

Helm (`https://docs.helm.sh/`) is one way to accomplish this need: instead of having a `deploy` directory with the manifests, we might have a `charts` directory, and write up the manifests as templates. Helm uses a `values` file, which can be created as needed, to provide the variables that are used to render out the templates, and after creating a Docker image with a tag, that same tag value could be added to the `values` file and used for deployment.

Another option is a newer project called ksonnet (`https://ksonnet.io`), which builds on an opensource library, `http://jsonnet.org/`, to make a composable template-style language available that builds on prototypes for Kubernetes. ksonnet is relatively new and is still getting established. Using Helm, you utilize Go templates and need to have some familiarity with that format while creating the chart. ksonnet has its own style of writing the templates, and you can find a tutorial and examples at the project's site: `https://ksonnet.io/tour/welcome`.

Example – using Jenkins and the Kubernetes plugin

While not a hosted solution, Jenkins is one of the most frequently used continuous integration tools available. It is very simple to get an instance of Jenkins operational on a Kubernetes cluster, and thanks to a Kubernetes-specific plugin, it can also do all of its builds within a Kubernetes cluster.

One of the quickest ways to install Jenkins in this fashion is to use Helm. The default Helm repository includes a maintained chart for running Jenkins, along with the configuration to use the Jenkins Kubernetes plugin. The chart that we will use is available on GitHub at `https://github.com/kubernetes/charts/tree/master/stable/jenkins`. You can also get more details on the Jenkins Kubernetes plugin that gets installed with that chart at `https://wiki.jenkins.io/display/JENKINS/Kubernetes+Plugin`.

Installing Jenkins using Helm

In this example, I'm going to walk through how you can set up and install Jenkins into a Minikube cluster on your local machine in order to experiment with it. You can use a very similar process to install into any Kubernetes cluster, but you will need to make some modifications depending on your target cluster.

If you don't have Helm already installed on your laptop, you can install it by following the instructions at the project's website: `https://docs.helm.sh/using_helm/#installing-helm`. Once you have the command-line client on your local system, you can bootstrap the rest.

The first step will be to install Helm onto your cluster and update the repositories. This is accomplished by running two commands:

```
helm init
```

The output will be very minimal, showing something akin to the following:

```
$HELM_HOME has been configured at /Users/heckj/.helm.

Tiller (the Helm server-side component) has been installed into your
Kubernetes Cluster.

Please note: by default, Tiller is deployed with an insecure 'allow
unauthenticated users' policy.
For more information on securing your installation see:
https://docs.helm.sh/using_helm/#securing-your-helm-installation
Happy Helming!
```

Tiller, as it mentions, is the server-side component of Helm, and it is responsible for coordinating the installations invoked from the `helm` command-line tool. By default, `helm init` will install Tiller into the `kube-system` namespace, so you can see it in your cluster using the following command:

```
kubectl get pods -n kube-system
```

```
NAME READY STATUS RESTARTS AGE
coredns-599474b9f4-gh99f 1/1 Running 0 3m
kube-addon-manager-minikube 1/1 Running 0 3m
kubernetes-dashboard-77d8b98585-f4qh9 1/1 Running 0 3m
storage-provisioner 1/1 Running 0 3m
tiller-deploy-865dd6c794-5b9g5 1/1 Running 0 3m
```

Once it's in the state `Running`, it is a good idea to get the latest repository index loaded. It comes with a number of charts already installed, but the charts do get updated fairly regularly, and this will ensure that you have the latest charts:

```
helm repo update
```

The update process is usually pretty fast, returning something like the following:

```
Hang tight while we grab the latest from your chart repositories...
...Skip local chart repository
...Successfully got an update from the "stable" chart repository
Update Complete. ❋ Happy Helming!❋
```

The `"stable" chart repository` that it's mentioning is the one hosted on GitHub at the Kubernetes project: `https://github.com/kubernetes/charts`. Within that repository, there is a `stable` directory that includes all the charts. If you use the command `helm search`, it will display a list of charts and the relevant versions, which matches with the GitHub repository.

Using the `helm search jenkins` command will show you the target we'll be using:

```
NAME CHART VERSION APP VERSION DESCRIPTION
stable/jenkins 0.14.1 2.73 Open source continuous integration server. It
s...
```

Note that charts have a chart version as well as a reported *app version*. Many charts wrap existing opensource projects, and the charts are maintained separately from the systems they deploy. Charts within the `stable` repository at the Kubernetes project strive to be examples of how to build charts as well as to be useful to the community at large. In this case, the chart version is `0.14.1`, and it is reported to be deploying Jenkins version `2.73`.

You can get more details on the specific chart using the `helm inspect` command, for example:

```
helm inspect stable/jenkins
```

This will show you a large amount of output, starting with the following:

```
appVersion: "2.73"
description: Open source continuous integration server. It supports
multiple SCM tools
  including CVS, Subversion and Git. It can execute Apache Ant and Apache
Maven-based
  projects as well as arbitrary scripts.
home: https://jenkins.io/
icon: https://wiki.jenkins-ci.org/download/attachments/2916393/logo.png
maintainers:
- email: lachlan.evenson@microsoft.com
  name: lachie83
- email: viglesias@google.com
  name: viglesiasce
name: jenkins
sources:
- https://github.com/jenkinsci/jenkins
- https://github.com/jenkinsci/docker-jnlp-slave
version: 0.14.1


---
# Default values for jenkins.
# This is a YAML-formatted file.
# Declare name/value pairs to be passed into your templates.
# name: value

## Overrides for generated resource names
# See templates/_helpers.tpl
# nameOverride:
# fullnameOverride:

Master:
  Name: jenkins-master
  Image: "jenkins/jenkins"
  ImageTag: "lts"
  ImagePullPolicy: "Always"
# ImagePullSecret: jenkins
  Component: "jenkins-master"
  UseSecurity: true
```

The very top is the information that goes into the chart repository index and what is used to provide the results from the `helm search` commands, and the section after that is the configuration options that the chart supports.

Most charts strive to have and use good defaults, but expect that you might provide overridden values where appropriate. In the case of deploying Jenkins into Minikube, we will want to do just that, as the default `values.yaml` that the chart uses expects to use a `LoadBalancer`, which Minikube doesn't support.

You can see the full details of `values.yaml` in the extended output of `helm inspect`. Before you install anything with Helm, it is a good idea to see what it is doing on your behalf, and what values it offers for configuration.

We will create a small `yaml` file to override just one of the defaults: `Master.ServiceType`. If you scan through the output of the `helm inspect` command, you will see a reference to changing this to install on Minikube.

Create a `jenkins.yaml` file with the following content:

```
Master:
  ServiceType: NodePort
```

Now, we can see what Helm will create when we ask it to install, using the options `--dry-run` and `--debug` to get detailed output:

```
helm install stable/jenkins --name j \
-f jenkins.yaml --dry-run --debug
```

Running this command will dump a lot of information to your Terminal screen, the rendered manifests of everything that Helm would install on your behalf. You can see the deployments, secrets, configmaps, and services.

You can start the installation process by running that exact same command, minus the `--dry-run` and `--debug` options:

```
helm install stable/jenkins --name j -f jenkins.yaml
```

This will provide you with a list of all the Kubernetes objects that it has created, and then some notes:

```
NAME: j
LAST DEPLOYED: Sun Mar 11 20:33:34 2018
NAMESPACE: default
STATUS: DEPLOYED
```

```
RESOURCES:
==> v1/Pod(related)
NAME READY STATUS RESTARTS AGE
j-jenkins-6ff797cc8d-qlhbk 0/1 Init:0/1 0 0s
==> v1/Secret
NAME TYPE DATA AGE
j-jenkins Opaque 2 0s
==> v1/ConfigMap
NAME DATA AGE
j-jenkins 3 0s
j-jenkins-tests 1 0s
==> v1/PersistentVolumeClaim
NAME STATUS VOLUME CAPACITY ACCESS MODES STORAGECLASS AGE
j-jenkins Bound pvc-24a90c2c-25a6-11e8-9548-0800272e7159 8Gi RWO standard
0s
==> v1/Service
NAME TYPE CLUSTER-IP EXTERNAL-IP PORT(S) AGE
j-jenkins-agent ClusterIP 10.107.112.29 <none> 50000/TCP 0s
j-jenkins NodePort 10.106.245.61 <none> 8080:30061/TCP 0s
==> v1beta1/Deployment
NAME DESIRED CURRENT UP-TO-DATE AVAILABLE AGE
j-jenkins 1 1 1 0 0s


NOTES:
1. Get your 'admin' user password by running:
 printf $(kubectl get secret --namespace default j-jenkins -o
jsonpath="{.data.jenkins-admin-password}" | base64 --decode);echo
2. Get the Jenkins URL to visit by running these commands in the same
shell:
 export NODE_PORT=$(kubectl get --namespace default -o
jsonpath="{.spec.ports[0].nodePort}" services j-jenkins)
 export NODE_IP=$(kubectl get nodes --namespace default -o
jsonpath="{.items[0].status.addresses[0].address}")
 echo http://$NODE_IP:$NODE_PORT/login

3. Login with the password from step 1 and the username: admin

For more information on running Jenkins on Kubernetes, visit:
https://cloud.google.com/solutions/jenkins-on-container-engine
```

The notes that are generated are rendered as a template and generally provide instructions for how to access the service. You can always get this same information repeated to you using the `helm status` command.

When we invoked Helm, we named this `release j` to keep it short and simple. To get information about the current state of this release, use the following command:

```
helm status j
```

This is a fairly large installation and it will take a while to install. You can watch the events that roll out from this installation using a command such as `kubectl get events -w`. This will update events as the deployment progresses, with output looking something like the following:

```
2018-03-11 20:08:23 -0700 PDT 2018-03-11 20:08:23 -0700 PDT 1
minikube.151b0d76e3a375e1 Node Normal NodeReady kubelet, minikube Node
minikube status is now: NodeReady

2018-03-11 20:38:28 -0700 PDT 2018-03-11 20:38:28 -0700 PDT 1 j-
jenkins-6ff797cc8d-qlhbk.151b0f1b339a1485 Pod spec.containers{j-jenkins}
Normal Pulling kubelet, minikube pulling image "jenkins/jenkins:lts"

2018-03-11 20:38:29 -0700 PDT 2018-03-11 20:38:29 -0700 PDT 1 j-
jenkins-6ff797cc8d-qlhbk.151b0f1b7a153b09 Pod spec.containers{j-jenkins}
Normal Pulled kubelet, minikube Successfully pulled image
"jenkins/jenkins:lts"

2018-03-11 20:38:29 -0700 PDT 2018-03-11 20:38:29 -0700 PDT 1 j-
jenkins-6ff797cc8d-qlhbk.151b0f1b7d270e5e Pod spec.containers{j-jenkins}
Normal Created kubelet, minikube Created container

2018-03-11 20:38:30 -0700 PDT 2018-03-11 20:38:30 -0700 PDT 1 j-
jenkins-6ff797cc8d-qlhbk.151b0f1b8359a5e4 Pod spec.containers{j-jenkins}
Normal Started kubelet, minikube Started container
```

Once the deployment is fully available, you can start to access it using the instructions in the notes.

Accessing Jenkins

The chart and images together make some secrets as the deployment is progressing to hold things such as the password to access Jenkins. The notes include a command to use to get this password from Kubernetes and display it on your Terminal:

```
printf $(kubectl get secret --namespace default j-jenkins -o
jsonpath="{.data.jenkins-admin-password}" | base64 --decode);echo
```

Run that command and copy the output, as we'll need it to log in to your instance of Jenkins. The next commands tell you how to get a URL to access Jenkins. You can use those commands to get the information and open a browser to access Jenkins. If you deployed this to Minikube, you can also use Minikube to open a browser window for the relevant service:

```
minikube service j-jenkins
```

The first page will provide you with a request for credentials. Use admin as the username and the password that you read in the preceding command:

Then, logging in should provide you with administrative access to Jenkins:

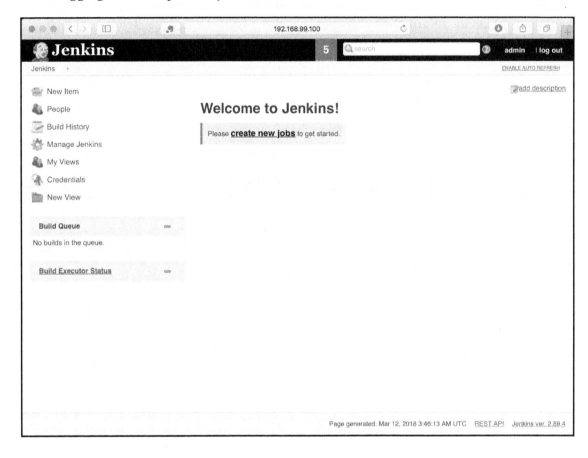

Updating Jenkins

When you connect, and in the preceding example, you may see a menu item in red with a number. This is how Jenkins alerts you to things that you should consider immediately updating. I highly recommend that you click on the number and review what it's presenting:

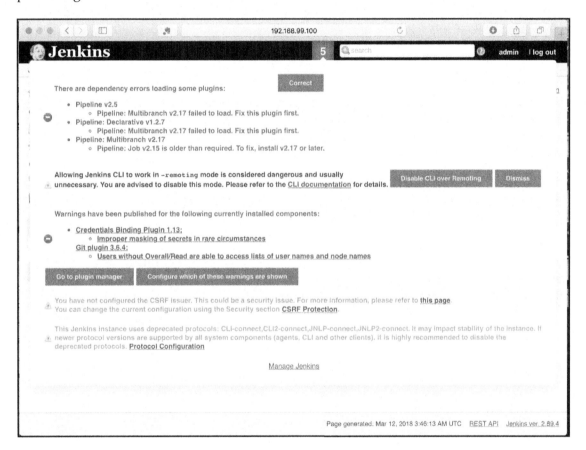

While the charts and base images are maintained, updates or considerations that can't be determined in advance can become available. Plugins to Jenkins, in particular, can get updated, and Jenkins reviews the existing plugins for possible updates. You can click on the buttons on this page to run the updates, restart Jenkins, or learn more about its suggestions.

The Jenkins chart includes a `persistent-volume-claim` where plugin updates are stored, so unless you disabled it, you can safely load updates to the Jenkins plugins and tell it to restart itself to have those plugin updates take effect.

Example pipeline

One of the benefits to this install is that jobs you create can run pipelines that completely build and run within the Kubernetes cluster. Pipelines can be defined as something you build using the tooling within Jenkins, you can enter them directly, or you can load them from source control.

The example code for the Python/Flask application has a basic Jenkinsfile to show you how this can work. The Jenkinsfile was added to the 0.7.0 branch, and you can view it online at `https://github.com/kubernetes-for-developers/kfd-flask/blob/0.7.0/Jenkinsfile`.

The pipeline is set up to be used from source control, build a Docker image, and interact with Kubernetes. The example does not push the image to a repository or deploy the image, following the same pattern as the previous Travis.CI example.

To enable this example in your instance of Jenkins, you will want to navigate to the front page of Jenkins and select **New Item**. From there, select **Multibranch Pipeline** and name the job `kfd-flask-pipeline`:

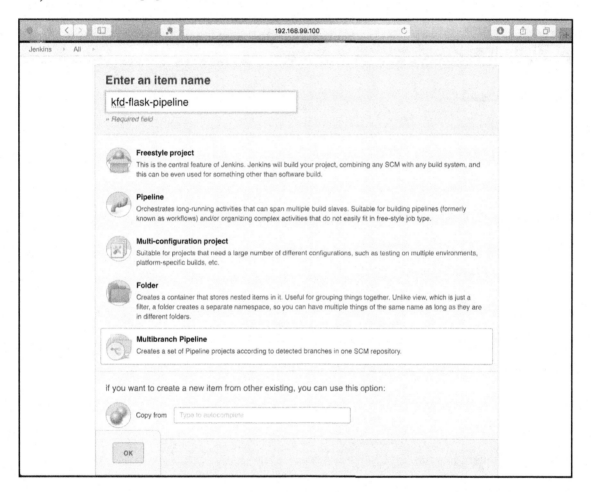

Once created, the critical item to enter is the location of content from source control. You can enter `https://github.com/kubernetes-for-developers/kfd-flask` to use this example:

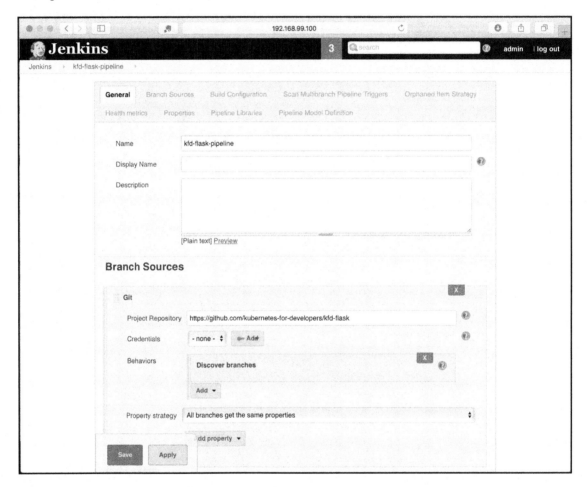

Save the configuration, and it should build the example, reaching out to GitHub, getting the pipeline, and then configuring it and running it.

Loading the various images can take quite a bit of time, and once it is complete the results will be available in Jenkins:

In the pipeline example, it checks out from source control, builds a new Docker image with a tag name based on the branch and `git commit`, and then later interacts with Kubernetes to show you the list of current pods active in the cluster in which its running.

Jenkins has the same needs as our Travis.CI example, such as changing the manifests to run a complete sequence, and this is something you can solve by using Helm or perhaps ksonnet to build onto the preceding example.

Next steps with pipelines

The full extent of what you can do with Jenkins pipelines is beyond what we can cover here, but the full documentation for both pipelines and the Kubernetes plugin additions is available online:

- `https://jenkins.io/doc/book/pipeline/syntax/` provides documentation on the pipeline syntax, how to write pipelines, and what options are built in by default.
- `https://github.com/jenkinsci/kubernetes-plugin` offers details on what the Jenkins Kubernetes plugin does and how it operates, as well as including examples of how to use it with some sample pipelines at its GitHub repo: `https://github.com/jenkinsci/kubernetes-plugin/tree/master/examples`.
- The general Jenkins documentation is very extensive, available at `https://jenkins.io/doc/`, along with more details about how to create and use a Jenkinsfile at `https://jenkins.io/doc/book/pipeline/jenkinsfile/`. A significant benefit to using a Jenkinsfile is that the declaration for what your pipelines should do can be stored alongside your code in source control.
- `https://jenkins.io/doc/pipeline/steps/credentials-binding/` details one way to expose secrets and credentials so that you can use them within pipelines, for example, to push image updates to DockerHub, Quay, or your own private image repository.

Summary

In this chapter, we delved into how to use Kubernetes when testing your code. We looked at the patterns you might explore with integration testing. We pointed at a simple example of using shell scripts to run integration tests within Kubernetes, and then dove more deeply into examples using Python and Node.js that run integration tests using Kubernetes. Finally, we wrapped up the chapter with an overview of options that are readily available for continuous integration that can use a cluster, and explored two options: using Travis.CI as a hosted solution and how to use Jenkins on your own Kubernetes cluster.

In the next chapter, we will look at how we can pull together multiple pieces that we have explored and show how to benchmark your code running on Kubernetes.

10
Troubleshooting Common Problems and Next Steps

The previous chapters have explored how to use Kubernetes in your development process. In this chapter, we wrap up the examples by looking at some of the common errors you might encounter. We look at how to understand them, and techniques for diagnosing the issues as well as how to resolve them. This chapter also reviews some of the emerging projects that are forming to assist developers with using Kubernetes.

Topics for this chapter include:

- Common errors and how to resolve them
- Emerging projects for developers
- Interacting with the Kubernetes project

Common errors and how to resolve them

Throughout the book, we have provided examples that illustrate how to work with Kubernetes. In developing these examples, we hit all the same issues you are likely to encounter, some of them confusing—and it isn't always clear how to determine what the problem is and how to resolve it so that the system works. This section will go through a number of the errors that you might see, discuss how to diagnose them, and provide you with some techniques to help you understand if you see these same issues yourself.

Error validating data

When you are writing your own manifests for Kubernetes and using them directly, it is very easy to make simple mistakes that result in the error message : `error validating ....`

These are fortunately very easy to understand, if terribly inconvenient. To illustrate this example, I created a slightly broken deployment manifest:

```
  1 apiVersion: apps/v1beta1
  2 kind: Deployment
  3 metadata:
  4   name: flask
  5   labels:
  6     run: flask
  7 spec:
  8   template:
  9     metadata:
 10       labels:
 11         app: flask
 12     spec:
 13       containers:
 14       - named: flask
 15         image: quay.io/kubernetes-for-developers/flask:0.2.0
 16         ports:
 17         - containerPort: 5000
```

```
"test.yml" 17L, 312C                           14,13          All
```

When running `kubectl apply` with this manifest, you will receive an error:

```
error: error validating "test.yml": error validating data:
[ValidationError(Deployment.spec.template.spec.containers[0]): unknown
field "named" in io.k8s.api.core.v1.Container,
ValidationError(Deployment.spec.template.spec.containers[0]): missing
required field "name" in io.k8s.api.core.v1.Container]; if you choose to
ignore these errors, turn validation off with --validate=false
```

In this case, I made a subtle typo, misnaming a required field, `name`, which is highlighted by the message `missing required field` in the error.

If you include an extra field that the system does know about, you will also receive an error, but a slightly different one:

```
error: error validating "test.yml": error validating data:
ValidationError(Deployment.spec.template.spec.containers[0]): unknown field
"color" in io.k8s.api.core.v1.Container; if you choose to ignore these
errors, turn validation off with --validate=false
```

In this case, the key to understanding the message is the `unknown field` section. These messages also reference a path through the data structure to exactly where the error is occurring. In the preceding example, this is `Deployment` (the object defined in the `kind` key) and within that `spec` -> `template` -> `spec` -> `container`. The error message also defines exactly what object the Kubernetes API was attempting to validate against: `io.k8s.api.core.v1.Container`. If you are confused about what it required, you can use this information to look up the documentation at the Kubernetes website. These objects are versioned (note the `v1` in the object name), and in this case you can find the full definition in the reference documentation for Kubernetes.

The reference documentation is released per version of Kubernetes, and for version 1.9 that documentation resides at `https://kubernetes.io/docs/reference/generated/kubernetes-api/v1.9/`. The documentation includes some example details as well as the definitions within a three-column view:

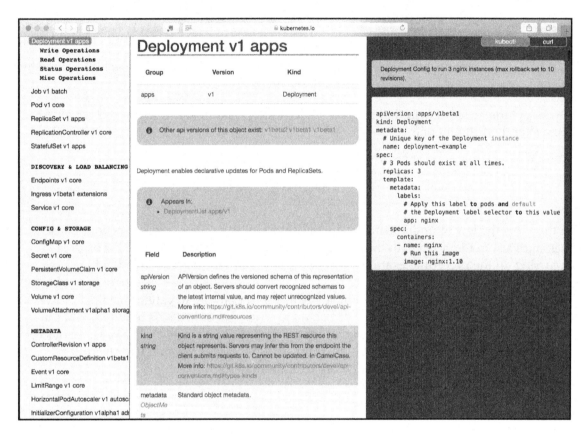

Navigating the documentation

The documentation follows the same pattern that we've seen from the Kubernetes objects themselves: they're composed of smaller primitives. When you are navigating the documentation, for example looking at Deployment as shown in the screenshot, you will often see a reference to the objects that are encapsulated, and to dig into the details you may need to reference some of these object areas. For example, the Deployment example encapsulates Pods, so to properly define all the attributes in the template, you may need to reference the Pod v1 core documentation.

ErrImagePull

ErrImagePull is quite possibly the most common, and is fortunately straightforward to debug and diagnose. You'll see `ErrImagePull` as the status message when this occurs, indicating that Kubernetes was not able to retrieve the image you specified in the manifest. It's most commonly seen when simply requesting pod status:

```
kubectl get pods

NAME                     READY STATUS       RESTARTS AGE
flask-659c86495-vlplb 0/1    ErrImagePull 0          4s
```

You can immediately get more detailed information about why this error occurred using the `kubectl describe` command. It's not entirely an error condition, as Kubernetes is technically in a waiting state hoping that the image will become available.

In this example, we get more detail with this command:

```
kubectl describe pod flask-659c86495-vlplb
```

This provides information like this:

```
Name: flask-659c86495-vlplb
Namespace: default
Node: minikube/192.168.99.100
Start Time: Sat, 17 Mar 2018 14:56:09 -0700
Labels: app=flask
 pod-template-hash=215742051
Annotations: <none>
Status: Pending
IP: 172.17.0.4
Controlled By: ReplicaSet/flask-659c86495
Containers:
 flask:
```

```
Container ID:
Image: quay.io/kubernetes-for-developers/flask:0.2.1
Image ID:
Port: 5000/TCP
State: Waiting
  Reason: ImagePullBackOff
Ready: False
Restart Count: 0
Environment: <none>
Mounts:
/var/run/secrets/kubernetes.io/serviceaccount from default-token-bwgcr
(ro)
Conditions:
 Type Status
 Initialized True
 Ready False
 PodScheduled True
Volumes:
 default-token-bwgcr:
 Type: Secret (a volume populated by a Secret)
 SecretName: default-token-bwgcr
 Optional: false
QoS Class: BestEffort
Node-Selectors: <none>
Tolerations: <none>
```

You can see the container is in a waiting state from this detail, and it's typically the events associated with the pod that provide the most useful information. The information is dense, so generally having a wider terminal window available when you invoke this command makes it easier to parse:

```
●  ●  ●                                            1. bash
  Ready:          False
  Restart Count:  0
  Environment:    <none>
  Mounts:
    /var/run/secrets/kubernetes.io/serviceaccount from default-token-bwgcr (ro)
Conditions:
  Type          Status
  Initialized   True
  Ready         False
  PodScheduled  True
Volumes:
  default-token-bwgcr:
    Type:        Secret (a volume populated by a Secret)
    SecretName:  default-token-bwgcr
    Optional:    false
QoS Class:       BestEffort
Node-Selectors:  <none>
Tolerations:     <none>
Events:
  Type     Reason               Age           From               Message
  ----     ------               ----          ----               -------
  Normal   Scheduled            3m            default-scheduler  Successfully assigned flask-659c86495-vlplb to minikube
  Normal   SuccessfulMountVolume 3m           kubelet, minikube  MountVolume.SetUp succeeded for volume "default-token-bwgcr"
  Normal   Pulling              2m (x4 over 3m) kubelet, minikube  pulling image "quay.io/kubernetes-for-developers/flask:0.2.1"
  Warning  Failed               2m (x4 over 3m) kubelet, minikube  Failed to pull image "quay.io/kubernetes-for-developers/flask:0.2.1": rpc error:
  code = Unknown desc = Error response from daemon: manifest for quay.io/kubernetes-for-developers/flask:0.2.1 not found
  Warning  Failed               2m (x4 over 3m) kubelet, minikube  Error: ErrImagePull
  Normal   BackOff              1m (x6 over 3m) kubelet, minikube  Back-off pulling image "quay.io/kubernetes-for-developers/flask:0.2.1"
  Warning  Failed               1m (x6 over 3m) kubelet, minikube  Error: ImagePullBackOff
heck] greyberry   :]$
```

You can see the process steps that Kubernetes has taken:

1. Kubernetes scheduled the pod
2. The node where the pod was scheduled attempted to retrieve the requested image
3. It reported a warning that the image wasn't found, set the status to `ErrImagePull`, and started retrying with a back-off

The first thing to do is verify that the image you have requested is indeed the one you intended to request. In this case, I made an intentional typo to request an image that doesn't exist.

Another common problem can be that the image does exist, but isn't allowed to be pulled for some reason. For example, when you first create a container and push it to `quay.io`, it keeps that container build private until you explicitly go to the website and make it available publicly.

This same error message can appear if you are pulling from a private repository, but the credentials used are invalid (or have become invalid in the process of updating them).

One of the best debugging techniques to verify access, at least to public images, is to attempt to retrieve the image yourself. If you have Docker installed locally, this is as simple as invoking a Docker `pull` command. In this case, we could verify the image:

```
docker pull quay.io/kubernetes-for-developers/flask:0.2.1
```

The error response is fairly direct from the Docker command line:

```
Error response from daemon: manifest for quay.io/kubernetes-for-
developers/flask:0.2.1 not found
```

CrashLoopBackOff

You may find your pod reporting a status of `CrashLoopBackOff`, another incredibly common error state.

This is an error condition that happens only after a container is invoked, so it can be delayed in appearing. You will typically see it when invoking `kubectl get pods`:

```
NAME                             READY STATUS             RESTARTS AGE
flask-6587cb9b66-zzw8v           1/2   CrashLoopBackOff   2        1m
redis-master-75c798658b-4x9h5    1/1   Running            0        1m
```

This explicitly means that one of the containers in the pod has exited unexpectedly, and perhaps with a non-zero error code. The first course of action in understanding what happened is to utilize the `kubectl describe` command to get more detail. In this case:

```
kubectl describe pod flask-6587cb9b66-zzw8v
```

Scan through the resulting content, looking at the status for each of the containers within the pod:

```
● ⬚ ●                                    1. bash
Containers:
  jaeger-agent:
    Container ID:   docker://11e1dd617d27aab2abf91ddbcaf5082040c48cb313e8ce6a9724b22d3333edaf
    Image:          jaegertracing/jaeger-agent
    Image ID:       docker-pullable://jaegertracing/jaeger-agent@sha256:254243861e9411f8d2730cdda1c4206ef2bb181346ea26a84572f
1addb4f73ed
    Ports:          5775/UDP, 5778/TCP, 6831/UDP, 6832/UDP
    Command:
      /go/bin/agent-linux
      --collector.host-port=jaeger-collector:14267
    State:          Running
      Started:      Sat, 17 Mar 2018 15:21:53 -0700
    Ready:          True
    Restart Count:  0
    Environment:    <none>
    Mounts:
      /var/run/secrets/kubernetes.io/serviceaccount from default-token-bwgcr (ro)
  flask:
    Container ID:   docker://bdcabd96b3427da27a87793bd5f899b1deb8356bf697f4f7c8c4fb3c6406a85b
    Image:          quay.io/kubernetes-for-developers/flask:latest
    Image ID:       docker-pullable://quay.io/kubernetes-for-developers/flask@sha256:75497576c35b9c1534e06fafafe01ba5bcae352
1d7068305c52ddb60bcfd09db
    Port:           5000/TCP
    State:          Waiting
      Reason:       CrashLoopBackOff
    Last State:     Terminated
      Reason:       Error
      Exit Code:    2
      Started:      Sat, 17 Mar 2018 15:25:06 -0700
      Finished:     Sat, 17 Mar 2018 15:25:07 -0700
    Ready:          False
    Restart Count:  5
    Limits:
      cpu:          500m
      memory:       40Mi
    Requests:
      cpu:          500m
      memory:       40Mi
    Liveness:       http-get http://:5000/alive delay=1s timeout=1s period=15s #success=1 #failure=3
    Readiness:      http-get http://:5000/ready delay=5s timeout=1s period=15s #success=1 #failure=3
    Environment Variables from:
      flask-config  ConfigMap  Optional: false
```

In the preceding example, you can see the Jaeger collector container is in the `Running` state, and `Ready` is reporting `True`. The flask container, however, is in a state of `Terminated`, with the reason only `Error` and an exit code of `2`.

The step that often provides at least some information about why the container exited is leveraging the `kubectl logs` command, to see what we reported in `STDOUT` and `STDERR`.

If you invoke `kubectl logs` and the pod name, you may also see this error:

```
kubectl logs flask-6587cb9b66-zzw8v

Error from server (BadRequest): a container name must be specified for pod
flask-6587cb9b66-zzw8v, choose one of: [jaeger-agent flask] or one of the
init containers: [init-myservice]
```

This is simply asking you to be more specific in identifying the container. In this example, we are using a pod that has an init container as well as two containers: the main and a Jaeger collector side-car. Simply appending the container to the end of the command, or using the `-c` option with the container name, will do what you want:

```
kubectl logs flask-6587cb9b66-zzw8v -c flask

python3: can't open file '/opt/exampleapp/exampleapp': [Errno 2] No such
file or directory
```

What gets returned, and how useful it is, will depend on how you created the container and what container runtime your Kubernetes cluster is using.

> As a reminder, `kubectl logs` also has the `-p` flag, which is exceptionally useful in retrieving the logs from the previous run of the container.

If, for some reason, you aren't entirely sure what's been set in the container, we can use some of the Docker commands to retrieve and then inspect the container image directly and locally, which can often shed light on what the issue may be.

As a reminder, pull the image:

```
docker pull quay.io/kubernetes-for-developers/flask:latest
```

Then, inspect it:

```
docker inspect quay.io/kubernetes-for-developers/flask:latest
```

Scrolling down to the content, you can see what the container will attempt to run and how it's set up:

```
                    "quay.io/kubernetes-for-developers/flask:latest"
            ],
            "RepoDigests": [
                    "quay.io/kubernetes-for-developers/flask@sha256:75497576c35b9c1534e06fafafe01ba5bcae3521d7068305c52ddb60bcfd09db"
            ],
            "Parent": "sha256:700482bef430fb1c2229b58a956e14dd7a1881e0f68ba2bbd62adf86bd555969",
            "Comment": "",
            "Created": "2018-03-17T22:20:38.367580073Z",
            "Container": "cbf8d40b6fe7a7f2e97ce4a34ade6de02523d30593a76160412c93e97b557415",
            "ContainerConfig": {
                    "Hostname": "cbf8d40b6fe7",
                    "Domainname": "",
                    "User": "",
                    "AttachStdin": false,
                    "AttachStdout": false,
                    "AttachStderr": false,
                    "Tty": false,
                    "OpenStdin": false,
                    "StdinOnce": false,
                    "Env": [
                            "PATH=/usr/local/sbin:/usr/local/bin:/usr/sbin:/usr/bin:/sbin:/bin"
                    ],
                    "Cmd": [
                            "/bin/sh",
                            "-c",
                            "#(nop) ",
                            "CMD [\"/opt/exampleapp/exampleapp\"]"
                    ],
                    "ArgsEscaped": true,
                    "Image": "sha256:700482bef430fb1c2229b58a956e14dd7a1881e0f68ba2bbd62adf86bd555969",
                    "Volumes": null,
                    "WorkingDir": "",
                    "Entrypoint": [
                            "python3"
                    ],
                    "OnBuild": null,
                    "Labels": {}
            },
            "DockerVersion": "17.12.0-ce",
            "Author": "",
            "Config": {
                    "Hostname": "",
                    "Domainname": "",
                    "User": "",
                    "AttachStdin": false,
                    "AttachStdout": false,
                    "AttachStderr": false,
                    "Tty": false,
```

In this particular example, I intentionally introduced a typo into the name of the Python file getting invoked, leaving off the `.py` extension. This may not be obvious when you're looking at this output, but specifically look for `EntryPoint` and `Cmd`, and try and verify that those are expected values. In this case, the entrypoint is `python3`, and the command is what gets invoked with it: `/opt/exampleapp/exampleapp`.

Starting and inspecting the image

Since this may be unclear without actually inspecting the image, a common way to diagnose something like this is to run the image with an alternative command, such as `/bin/sh`, and use an interactive session to look around and do your validation and debugging. You can do this locally if you have Docker installed; when you do so, make sure you explicitly override the `entrypoint` and command to run a command interactively:

```
docker run -it --entrypoint=/bin/sh \
quay.io/kubernetes-for-developers/flask:latest -i
```

You can then manually invoke what the container would have run, `python3 /opt/exampleapp/exampleapp`, and do any additional debugging there.

You can do this same thing in a Kubernetes cluster, if you don't happen to have Docker installed locally. If the pod already exists, you can use `kubectl exec` as we have done earlier, but when the container has crashed this typically isn't available, as the container isn't already running to utilize.

In those cases, creating a completely new, short lived, and ephemeral deployment with `kubectl run` is a good way to continue:

```
kubectl run -i --tty interactive-pod \
--image=quay.io/kubernetes-for-developers/flask:latest \
--restart=Never --command=true /bin/sh
```

You will want to be careful to have `--command=true` in your options if you want to override the entrypoint for the container, which is otherwise set to `python3`. Without that option, the `kubectl run` command will presume you are trying to pass different arguments to be used with the default entrypoint.

You may also find that when you attempt to invoke a command like this, you get this message:

```
Error from server (AlreadyExists): pods "interactive-pod" already exists
```

When you create a bare deployment like this, the pod doesn't get deleted after the container exits (or errors). Invoking `kubectl get pods` with the `-a` option should show you the pods that exist:

```
kubectl get pods -a

NAME                          READY  STATUS           RESTARTS AGE
flask-6587cb9b66-zzw8v        1/2    CrashLoopBackOff 14       49m
interactive-pod               0/1    Completed        0        5m
redis-master-75c798658b-4x9h5 1/1    Running          0        49m
```

You can delete it in order to make another attempt at running it:

```
kubectl delete pod interactive-test
```

Adding your own setup to the container

When you are working with a container that includes code and systems you didn't create, you may find yourself wanting to set up some environment variables or otherwise establish some configuration files before whatever process in the container gets run. This is extremely common when using other prebuilt open source software, especially software that doesn't already have a well-established container that you can utilize.

A common technique for handling this situation is to add a shell script into the container and then have the entrypoint and arguments set to run that script. If you do this, make sure you include the appropriate options for invoking the script.

A common example is to invoke a script with `/bin/bash -c /some/script`. It can be easy to miss the `-c` argument, which can lead to a very confusing error message:

```
/bin/sh: can't open '/some/script'
```

This happens when the script referenced isn't set to be executable, and you didn't include the `-c` option to have the shell attempt to read and interpret the file you specified.

No endpoints available for service

One of the most subtle issues to hunt down is why isn't my service acting as I expect? A common error to see in these cases is this message:

```
no endpoints available for service
```

If you have created a deployment and a service together, and everything seems to be running, but when you access the service endpoint you see this output:

```
{
    "kind": "Status",
    "apiVersion": "v1",
    "metadata": {
    },
    "status": "Failure",
    "message": "no endpoints available for service \"flask-service\"",
    "reason": "ServiceUnavailable",
    "code": 503
}
```

In this case, I received this message when using `kubectl proxy` to access the service endpoint `flask-service` through the proxy using the URL:

```
http://localhost:8001/api/v1/proxy/namespaces/default/services/flask-servic
e
```

In these cases, use the command `kubectl describe` to get details on how the service is set up:

`kubectl describe service flask-service`

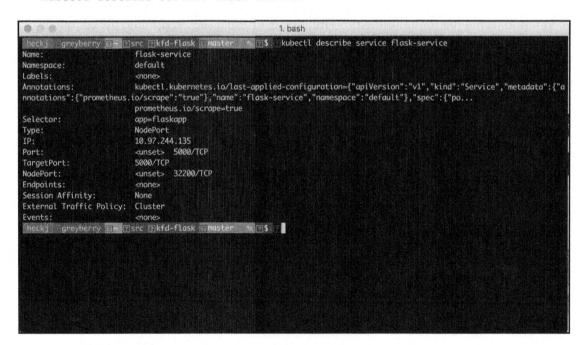

Take close note of the selector that is set for the service, and then compare it to the deployment you think it should be matching. In this case, the selector is `app=flaskapp`, and looks at the detail on our deployment:

```
kubectl describe deploy flask
```

```
                                        1. bash
[heck] greyberry     src  kfd-flask  master     $  kubectl describe deploy flask
Name:                   flask
Namespace:              default
CreationTimestamp:      Sat, 17 Mar 2018 16:26:54 -0700
Labels:                 run=flask
Annotations:            deployment.kubernetes.io/revision=1
                        kubectl.kubernetes.io/last-applied-configuration={"apiVersion":"apps/v1beta1","kind":"Deployment","me
tadata":{"annotations":{},"labels":{"run":"flask"},"name":"flask","namespace":"default"},"spec":{"t...
Selector:               app=flask
Replicas:               1 desired | 1 updated | 1 total | 1 available | 0 unavailable
StrategyType:           RollingUpdate
MinReadySeconds:        0
RollingUpdateStrategy:  25% max unavailable, 25% max surge
Pod Template:
  Labels:  app=flask
  Init Containers:
   init-myservice:
    Image:  busybox
    Port:   <none>
    Command:
      sh
      -c
      until nslookup redis-service; do echo waiting for redis-service; sleep 2; done;
    Environment:  <none>
    Mounts:       <none>
  Containers:
   jaeger-agent:
    Image:  jaegertracing/jaeger-agent
    Ports:  5775/UDP, 5778/TCP, 6831/UDP, 6832/UDP
    Command:
      /go/bin/agent-linux
      --collector.host-port=jaeger-collector:14267
    Environment:  <none>
    Mounts:       <none>
   flask:
    Image:  quay.io/kubernetes-for-developers/flask:0.7.0
    Port:   5000/TCP
    Limits:
      cpu:     500m
      memory:  40Mi
    Requests:
```

The immediate thing you should verify is that the containers are running and operational, which they are in this case. The very next thing is to look at the labels on the deployment, and in this case you see them set to `app=flask`, not `app=flaskapp` which is why nothing is responding on that service.

Another way to see what's happening to pods backing a service is to specifically request pods using a label selected with the `kubectl get` command. For example, we could have used this command:

```
kubectl get pods -l app=flaskapp -o wide
```

And because we haven't set any pods with the relevant labels, we would have received this response:

```
No resources found.
```

Labels and selectors are how a lot of elements are loosely coupled together within Kubernetes. Being loosely coupled, Kubernetes does not validate that you have correctly set the right values to bind pods to services. Not making sure the labels and selectors are correct is an easy mistake to make, and won't show up as an error other than nothing responding as you expected.

Stuck in PodInitializing

You may see a scenario where your pods appear to be hanging while initializing, especially when you are first setting up the configuration where it involves volume mounts and ConfigMaps.

The status from `kubectl get pods` will look something like this:

```
NAME                          READY STATUS    RESTARTS AGE
flask-6bc4b4c8dc-cm6gx        0/2   Init:0/1  0        7m
redis-master-75c798658b-p4t7c 1/1   Running   0        7m
```

And the status doesn't change. Trying to get logs about what is happening, such as:

```
kubectl logs flask-6bc4b4c8dc-cm6gx init-myservice
```

Results in this message:

```
Error from server (BadRequest): container "init-myservice" in pod
"flask-6bc4b4c8dc-cm6gx" is waiting to start: PodInitializing
```

The best thing to do here is to use `kubectl describe` to get the detail of what is set up on the pod and the recent events:

```
kubectl describe pod flask
```

Here you will see output showing the containers are all in a state of `Waiting`, with a reason of `PodInitializing`:

It may take a few minutes for the events that really show what happen to appear, but after a few minutes they should appear:

You see the warning `FailedMount`, and the relevant information:

```
MountVolume.SetUp failed for volume "config" : configmaps "flaskConfig" not
found
```

This takes some time to appear because Kubernetes provides for some longer timeouts when attempting to mount volumes, as well as retries. In this case, the error was a typo in the pod specification referencing a ConfigMap that doesn't exist: `flaskConfig`.

Missing resources

In many respects, this issue we just described is very similar to the labels and selectors bug, but exhibits itself quite differently. The underlying system does its best to look for volumes, ConfigMaps, secrets, and so on, and to let you create them in any order. If you make a typo, or if a ConfigMap, secret, or volume isn't referenced correctly or is just missing, then the pod will ultimately fail.

These resources are all referenced dynamically. In doing that referencing, Kubernetes provides retries and timeouts, but cannot explicitly validate the failures before actually looking for the related resources and ultimately failing. This can make debugging these issues more time consuming. When you first look for why issues are failing, not all the information may be visible (a failed volume mount, a missing ConfigMap or secret, and so forth). The best option is to keep an eye on the events from the `kubectl describe` command, and look explicitly for warnings in the events, where these issues will ultimately appear.

Some development teams are resolving this *Class A* problem by generating the manifests, using a program that they have verified themselves to create the appropriate links and making sure they are correct.

Emerging projects for developers

Looking at alternatives to help the development process that uses Kubernetes starts to expose a large number of projects in development. While writing this book, Kubernetes advanced from version 1.7 to the beta release of Kubernetes v1.10. At the same time, a large number of projects have started to establish themselves around Kubernetes, working to help smooth some of the rough edges around using Kubernetes actively in a development workflow.

Linters

In the previous section, we were talking about missing components that can't be pre-validated by Kubernetes, but which we can look for ourselves. Three projects that are related to validation are kubeval, kube-lint, and kubetest, described here:

- kubeval : `https://github.com/garethr/kubeval`

  kubeval was created by Gareth Rushgrove to validate manifests and configuration files before attempting to apply them. This tool can be extremely handy in double-checking your work when you're creating manifests from your own code or using another project. It can't check everything, but it makes an excellent first pass check.

- kube-lint : `https://github.com/viglesiasce/kube-lint`

  Created by Vic Iglesias, kube-lint is more of an early experiment or functional prototype than a growing project. It is intended to validate a set of Kubernetes manifests against a group of common rules. Many of these best practices and common patterns are forming from the Helm project, in which Vic participates extensively, and there is ongoing conversation within the Kubernetes project about possible ways to help do more validation along these lines with a `lint` command.

- kubetest : `https://github.com/garethr/kubetest`

  Also by Gareth Rushgrove, kubetest was built to run a pass of testing across Kubernetes configuration files. Rather than explicitly encapsulating best practices and rules, it is written more in the form of unit testing, allowing assertions against sets of files and letting you specify your own constraints.

Helm

We have mentioned about and used Helm in earlier chapters, using it to install software within Kubernetes so that we can take advantage of it. Available at `https://helm.sh`, Helm has been stable at version 2 for quite a while, and is actively used by a number of development teams. The charts that represent the collected best practices are available at `https://github.com/kubernetes/charts`, and are updated as the software they encapsulate, and Kubernetes, advances:

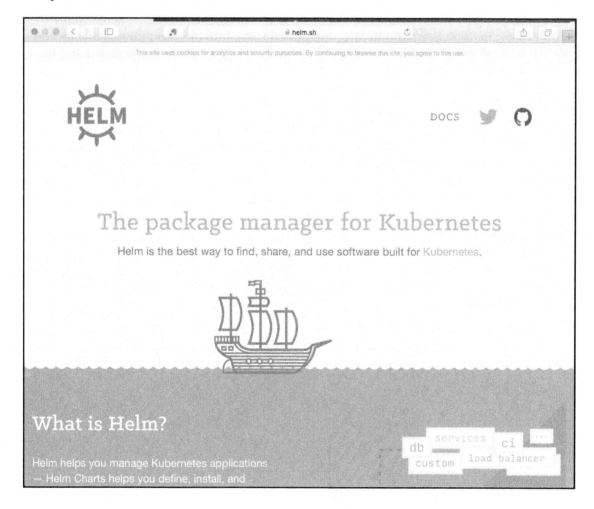

Helm version 3 is the next large step forward with Helm, breaking some of the backwards compatibility guarantees they have been keeping while in version 2. With the transition, the project team has been very clear that there will be a clear migration path and the current charts and examples will both be useful as they are, as well as updated as the project evolves. The details of the vision for Helm v3 are still forming and this project will undoubtedly be a key one in the larger Kubernetes ecosystem.

In version 2, it sets itself as a package manager for Kubernetes, primarily focusing on being a consistent way (and examples) of how to package sets of pods, deployments, services, ConfigMaps, and so on together, and deploy them as a whole within Kubernetes. Many teams created their own charts and have integrated Helm into their continuous integration pipeline, using Helm to render manifests as the underlying software was updated and to deploy as a part of that process.

One of the shortcomings of Helm may be that it is fairly complicated to create templates for your own software. The templating system that Helm uses is called sprig, and may be unfamiliar to a number of development teams. The next major revision of Helm, which is being defined as this book is being published, hopes to tackle a broad number of challenges, including making it easier for developers to write and publish charts. It is really worth keeping an eye on this project.

ksonnet

ksonnet (`https://ksonnet.io`) was also mentioned earlier as another means of templating and rendering manifests for Kubernetes. ksonnet approaches the task differently to Helm, focusing on a means of templating the manifests, and making those templates very easy to compose:

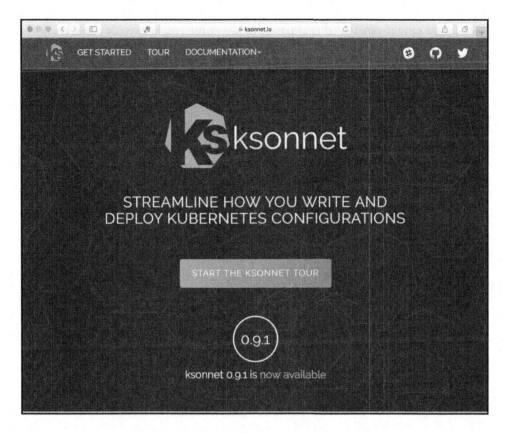

ksonnet uses the credentials of a user, and doesn't attempt to manage the state of releases that it renders, focusing instead on the templating. It is built upon a library called Jsonnet, which adds some programmatic aspects to JSON templating.

ksonnet is a fairly new project, and is starting to see some traction with other projects adopting it. They have stated that they are actively working with the Helm community as well, and hopes to enable ksonnet as an alternative way to create charts.

Brigade

Brigade, available at `https://brigade.sh`, takes a slightly different tack to solving the deploy to Kubernetes problem. Rather than focus on the templating and what sort of DSL that might be used to programmatically generate Kubernetes manifests, it leans more towards embracing scripting and programming with Kubernetes and its events as first-class citizens:

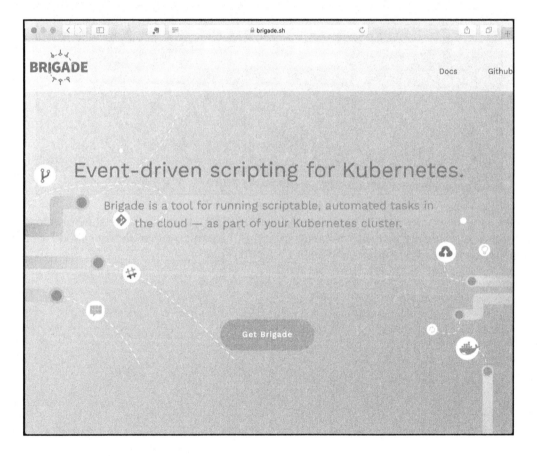

The Microsoft team from Azure built Brigade to extend on JavaScript, exposing Kubernetes objects and events as elements to be composed into workflows and pipelines. If your development team is familiar with JavaScript, then Brigade may be an especially appealing means of coordinating and interacting with Kubernetes.

skaffold

Skaffold is available at `https://github.com/GoogleCloudPlatform/skaffold` and is developed by a team from Google:

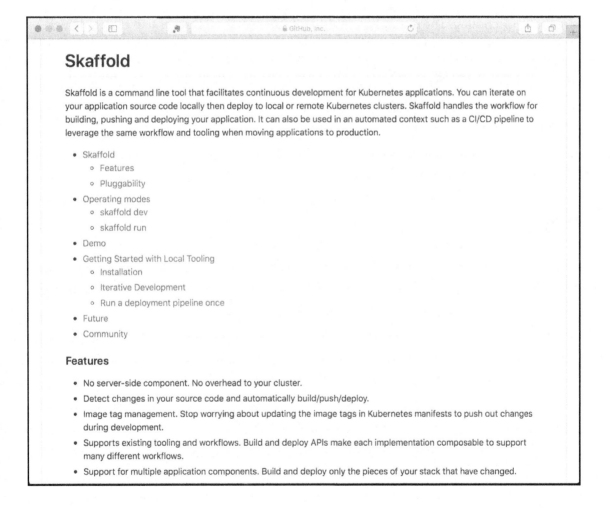

It is the most recent of these developer-focused projects, and focuses specifically on being a command-line tool to enable the process of going from code checked in to source control, through building containers to Kubernetes manifests updated and deployed. It is also set up to be a component in a larger toolchain, and has hooked to work with other projects, most notably Helm, for the deployment portion of what it does.

img

While looking at tools and projects as components, the img project, which is hosted under `genuinetools.org` and is available on GitHub at `https://github.com/genuinetools/img`, is really worth noting. The examples in this book have all used Docker to build container images, and img builds on the underlying toolkit that the team at Docker has been evolving from their product to support creating containers. Most importantly, the img project allows for the creation of Docker images without a Daemon or running with significant privileges. This makes creating containers far more amenable to being built within a Kubernetes cluster, or more generally without having to give the process extensive permissions to the system hosting it.

The genuinetools project hosts a number of other useful components, most of them focused on alternative container runtimes.

Draft

Another tool from the team at Microsoft, Draft, is available at `https://draft.sh`, and is a tool focused on trying to optimize the time going from a change in source control to being deployed within Kubernetes and to seeing those changes in action:

Draft focuses on simple commands and a local configuration file to create a local Helm chart for your application and to streamline getting it running on a Kubernetes cluster, encapsulating the repetitive process of building the container, pushing it to a container registry, and then deploying updated manifests to upgrade.

Like a few of these other tools, Draft builds on and uses Helm.

ksync

ksync, available at `https://vapor-ware.github.io/ksync/`, takes a very different tactic for a development tool. Rather than optimizing the time to build and deploy into a Kubernetes cluster, it focuses on expanding the proxy capabilities to reach into a cluster and manipulate the code within a specific container:

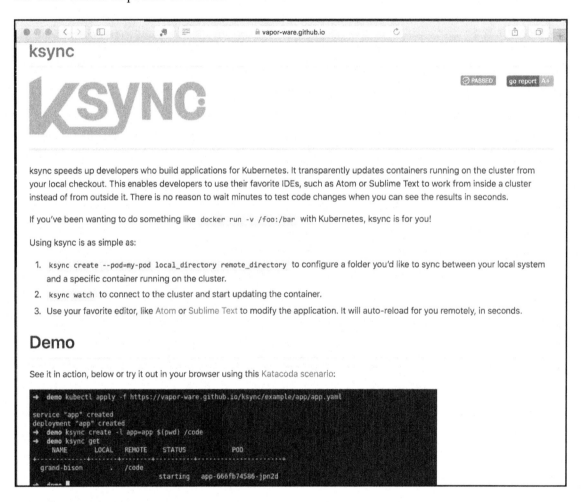

A common pattern for developing with Docker has been to mount a local directory that contains interpreted code (such as our Python and JavaScript examples in this book) and to have the container run that code, so that you can edit it on the fly and quickly restart and retry. ksync mimics this capability by running both on your local development machine and within your cluster, watching for changes locally and reflecting them into Kubernetes.

ksync focuses on the development process for software within a single pod. So while it won't help with deploying all the supporting applications, it may make the development process with a single component in Kubernetes much faster.

Telepresence

Telepresence, available at `https://www.telepresence.io`, is another project that focuses on providing the developer with tighter access from their local machine into a Kubernetes cluster:

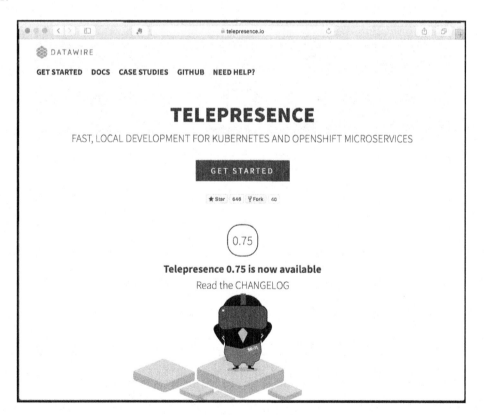

Created by Datawire, which makes additional projects for developers to work with Kubernetes, Telepresence creates a two-way proxy that forwards connections and responses to a process that would be within a pod in Kubernetes to a process running on your local development machine.

Where ksync copies your code and runs it within Kubernetes, Telepresence lets you run the code on your own machine, transparently connecting it as though it were a pod running within Kubernetes.

Interacting with the Kubernetes project

In discussing all these projects, the one where you can get the most information about how to work with Kubernetes is Kubernetes itself. The project hosts a website that includes the formal documentation, a blog, a community calendar, tutorials, and more at `https://kubernetes.io/`:

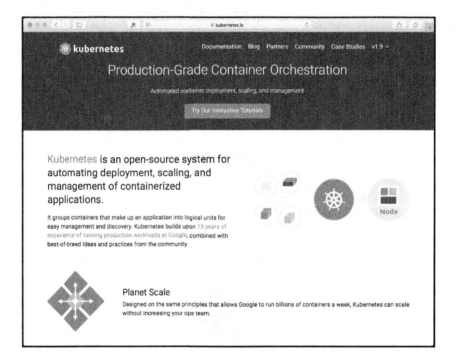

This site makes a great jumping off point to get more information, but certainly isn't the only resource available.

The Kubernetes project is really quite large, so large that it is nearly impossible for any single person to track all of the efforts, evolution, projects, and interests that are going on within the project. To attempt to provide guidance, the Kubernetes project has set itself up with a number of groups to focus on these interests in the form of Special Interest Groups, or SIGs. These groups are the semi-formal subprojects of Kubernetes, and each focuses on some specific subset of Kubernetes. Not surprisingly, many of these SIGs overlap in specifics, and it is not uncommon to find a contributor within Kubernetes being active in a number of SIGs at once.

The complete list of SIGs is available online and is maintained at `https://github.com/kubernetes/community/blob/master/sig-list.md`. Each SIG has specific people called out as leaders, hosts regular meetings, and many of them maintain online notes and even recordings of their online meetings. These SIGs all loosely coordinate to advance Kubernetes, and are in turn coordinated by a Kubernetes steering committee and a number of community managers.

There are also less formal working groups that pop up to focus on specific or short-lived interests that don't have any specific leadership or attendance. All together, the SIGs and working groups can create a tremendous amount of information and depth that is available to look through, and a very open community of people to interact with regarding the project.

The community also manages a calendar of SIG meetings and events, available at `https://kubernetes.io/community/`, and publishes regularly on the Kubernetes blog at `http://blog.kubernetes.io`.

Slack

A common and interactive means of Kubernetes contributors working together is by using online chat channels at Slack. Kubernetes hosts a large number of interactive channels dedicated to SIGs, working groups, and projects within Kubernetes. Anyone may join, and you can sign up for access at `http://slack.k8s.io`.

If you are new to Slack or Kubernetes, then the channels `#kubernetes-users` and `#kubernetes-novices` may be of particular interest. The overall community team also hosts what they call office hours, which is a live stream hosted on YouTube, as well as the Slack channel, `#office-hours`.

YouTube

If you prefer video streams, the Kubernetes community offers a YouTube channel, available at `https://www.youtube.com/c/KubernetesCommunity/`. These include recorded videos from community meetings, as well as sessions from regular Kubernetes conferences. A large number of SIGs also record their regular meetings and post those on YouTube, although they are not consistently coordinated through this channel. If you want to find related content, it is best to track that down through each individual SIG, although you may be able to find what you're looking for under the channel's playlists at `https://www.youtube.com/channel/UCZ2bu0qutTOM0tHYa_jkIwg/playlists`:

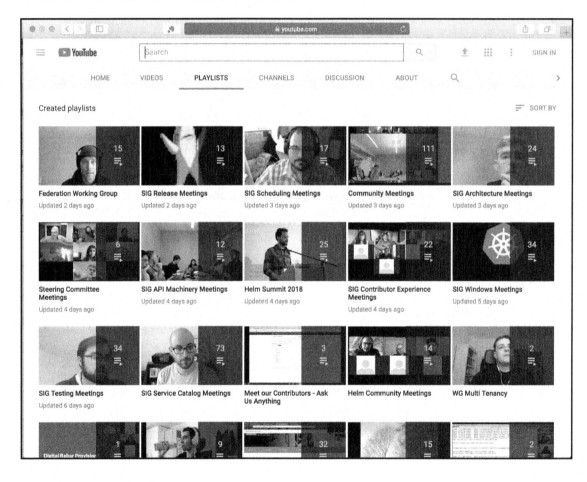

Stack Overflow

Members of the Kubernetes community also watch and offer answers to questions on Stack Overflow. The office hours mentioned earlier encourage folks to post their questions on Stack Overflow and bring those to the office hours for interactive help. You can find Kubernetes-related questions at `https://stackoverflow.com/questions/tagged/kubernetes`. If you search for Kubernetes-related topics on Google, you may also find the results within questions already asked, and answered, on Stack Overflow.

Mailing lists and forums

Kubernetes has a general mailing list/forum, as well as mailing lists for every SIG and frequently for each working group as well. The common forums include:

- `https://groups.google.com/forum/#!forum/kubernetes-users`
- `https://groups.google.com/forum/#!forum/kubernetes-dev`

The list of SIGs at `https://github.com/kubernetes/community/blob/master/sig-list.md` also includes a reference to the individual mailing lists for each SIG.

There is no one path for information on Kubernetes, and the community works very hard to accommodate multiple ways to get information, ask questions, and encourage participation.

Summary

In this chapter, we touched on some of the problems that you may run into when developing and deploying to Kubernetes, and then touched on a number of projects that may be of interest to help you or your team speed up their development process while also taking advantage of Kubernetes. The final portion of this chapter discussed the Kubernetes project itself, how you can interact with it, and where to find more information to leverage this amazing set of tools.

Other Books You May Enjoy

If you enjoyed this book, you may be interested in these other books by Packt:

DevOps with Kubernetes
Hideto Saito, Hui-Chuan Chloe Lee, Cheng-Yang Wu

ISBN: 978-1-78839-664-6

- Learn fundamental and advanced DevOps skills and tools
- Get a comprehensive understanding for container
- Learn how to move your application to container world
- Learn how to manipulate your application by Kubernetes
- Learn how to work with Kubernetes in popular public cloud
- Improve time to market with Kubernetes and Continuous Delivery
- Learn how to monitor, log, and troubleshoot your application with Kubernetes

Mastering Kubernetes
Gigi Sayfan

ISBN: 978-1-78646-100-1

- Architect a robust Kubernetes cluster for long-time operation
- Discover the advantages of running Kubernetes on GCE, AWS, Azure, and bare metal
- See the identity model of Kubernetes and options for cluster federation
- Monitor and troubleshoot Kubernetes clusters and run a highly available Kubernetes
- Create and configure custom Kubernetes resources and use third-party resources in your automation workflows
- Discover the art of running complex stateful applications in your container environment
- Deliver applications as standard packages

Leave a review - let other readers know what you think

Please share your thoughts on this book with others by leaving a review on the site that you bought it from. If you purchased the book from Amazon, please leave us an honest review on this book's Amazon page. This is vital so that other potential readers can see and use your unbiased opinion to make purchasing decisions, we can understand what our customers think about our products, and our authors can see your feedback on the title that they have worked with Packt to create. It will only take a few minutes of your time, but is valuable to other potential customers, our authors, and Packt. Thank you!

Index

CPSIA information can be obtained
at www.ICGtesting.com
Printed in the USA
BVOW11s0813230418
514169BV00023B/1253/P